GW00778057

STORIES OF
PEOPLE & CIVILIZATION

INDIAN

ANCIENT ORIGINS

FLAME TREE PUBLISHING
6 Melbray Mews, Fulham,
London SW6 3NS, United Kingdom
www.flametreepublishing.com

First published and copyright © 2024
Flame Tree Publishing Ltd

24 26 28 27 25
1 3 5 7 9 10 8 6 4 2

ISBN: 978-1-80417-617-7

Cover and pattern art was created by Flame Tree Studio, with elements courtesy of
Shutterstock.com/svekloid/PremiumStock. Additional interior decoration courtesy
of Shutterstock.com/Bariskina.

Judith John (lists of Ancient Kings & Leaders) is a writer and editor specializing in
literature and history. A former secondary school English Language and Literature teacher,
she has subsequently worked as an editor on major educational projects, including *English
A: Literature* for the Pearson International Baccalaureate series. Judith's major research
interests include Romantic and Gothic literature, and Renaissance drama.

The text in this book is compiled and edited, with a new introduction and chapter
introductions. The majority of the text derives from *Ancient India* by Upendra Nath Ball
(The Kamala Book Depot Ltd, 1921). Further portions are from: *Ancient India 2000
B.C.–800 A.D.* by Romesh Chundra Dutt (Longmans, Green, and Co., 1893); *India through
the Ages* by Flora Annie Steel (George Routledge & Sons, Limited, 1911); and *Invasion
of India by Alexander the Great as Described by Arrian, Q. Curtius, Diodoros, Plutarch and
Justin* by J.W. M'Crindle (Archibald Constable and Company, 1896).

A copy of the CIP data for this book is available
from the British Library.

Designed and created in the UK | Printed and bound in China

COLLECTOR'S EDITIONS

STORIES OF
PEOPLE & CIVILIZATION
INDIAN
ANCIENT ORIGINS

With a New Introduction by
ROSHEN DALAL
Further Reading and
Lists of Ancient Kings & Leaders

FLAME TREE PUBLISHING

CONTENTS

CONTENTS

STORIES OF
PEOPLE & CIVILIZATION
INDIAN
ANCIENT ORIGINS

SERIES FOREWORD

Stretching back to the oral traditions of thousands of years ago, tales of heroes and disaster, creation and conquest have been told by many different civilizations, in ways unique to their landscape and language. Their impact sits deep within our own culture even though the detail in the stories themselves are a loose mix of historical record, the latest archaeological evidence, transformed narrative and the unwitting distortions of generations of storytellers.

Today the language of mythology lives around us: our mood is jovial, our countenance is saturnine, we are narcissistic and our modern life is hermetically sealed from others. The nuances of the ancient world form part of our daily routines and help us navigate the information overload of our interconnected lives.

The nature of a myth is that its stories are already known by most of those who hear or read them. Every era brings a new emphasiz, but the fundamentals remain the same: a desire to understand and describe the events and relationships of the world. Many of the great stories are archetypes that help us find our own place, equipping us with tools for self-understanding, both individually and as part of a broader culture.

For Western societies it is Greek mythology that speaks to us most clearly. It greatly influenced the mythological heritage of the ancient Roman civilization and is the lens through which we still see the Celts, the Norse and many of the other great peoples and religions. The Greeks themselves inherited much from their neighbours, the Egyptians, an older culture that became weary with the mantle of civilization.

Of course, what we perceive now as mythology had its own origins in perceptions of the divine and the rituals of the sacred. The earliest civilizations, in the crucible of the Middle East, in the Sumer of the third millennium BCE, are the source to which many of the mythic archetypes can be traced. Over five thousand years ago, as humankind collected together in cities for the first time, developed writing and industrial scale agriculture, started to irrigate the rivers and attempted to control rather than be at the mercy of its environment, humanity began to write down its tentative explanations of natural events, of floods and plagues, of disease.

Early stories tell of gods or god-like animals who are crafty and use their wits to survive, and it is not unreasonable to suggest that these were the first rulers of the gathering peoples of the earth, later elevated to god-like status with the distance of time. Such tales became more political as cities vied with each other for supremacy, creating new gods, new hierarchies for their pantheons. The older gods took on primordial roles and became the preserve of creation and destruction, leaving the new gods to deal with more current, everyday affairs. Empires rose and fell, with Babylon assuming the mantle from Sumeria in the 1800s BCE, in turn to be swept away by the Assyrians of the 1200s BCE; then the Assyrians and the Egyptians were subjugated by the Greeks, the Greeks by the Romans and so on, leading to the spread and assimilation of common themes, ideas and stories throughout the world.

The survival of history is dependent on the telling of good tales, but each one must have the 'feeling' of truth, otherwise it will be ignored. Around the firesides, or embedded in a book or a computer, the myths and legends of the past are still the living materials of retold myth, not restricted to an exploration of historical origins. Now we have devices and global communications that give us unparalleled access to a diversity of traditions. We can find out about Indigenous American, Indian, Chinese and tribal African mythology in a way that was denied to our ancestors, we can find connections, plot the archaeology, religion and the mythologies of the world to build a comprehensive image of the human experience that is both humbling and fascinating.

The books in this series introduce the many cultures of ancient humankind to the modern reader. From the earliest migrations across the globe to settlements along rivers, from the landscapes of mountains to the vast Steppes, from woodlands to deserts, humanity has adapted to its environments, nurturing languages and observations and expressing itself through records, mythmaking stories and living traditions. There is still so much to explore, but this is a great place to start.

Jake Jackson
General Editor

STORIES OF
PEOPLE & CIVILIZATION
INDIAN
ANCIENT ORIGINS

INTRODUCTION
& FURTHER READING

INTRODUCTION TO
INDIAN ANCIENT ORIGINS

India is often seen as a land of mystery, of deep ritual and philosophy, a storehouse of spiritual wisdom and at the same time of scientific achievements. There is progress and change, and yet a continuity with the past.

India's history is linked with the nature of its land: its high snowy mountains, rivers flowing through wide alluvial plains and narrow gorges, and its extensive coastline. Mountains and seas provided natural boundaries for the India of the past, a region that included the three present-day countries of India, Pakistan and Bangladesh. The land was formed gradually over millions of years, as plates on the surface of the earth coalesced and separated. The Tethys Sea, a vast ocean to the north, disappeared as the Asian and European plates clashed; in its place arose the grand Himalayas, the highest mountains in the world. Southern India, separated from the north by the Vindhyan mountains, is a peninsula, formed by ancient gneiss, granite, basalt and other rocks.

The river Sindhu, the Indus in Greek, gave its name to India, as the Greeks used this term to refer to the land to the east of this mighty, rushing river. Even before this the Persians employed the name Hindu for the river and the land east of it, a term later used for its main religion and even for the country as a whole, Hindustan.

FROM THE PAST TO THE PRESENT

From the sixteenth century onwards Europeans entered India, at first for trade, and later for conquest. Of the European powers, which included the Portuguese, Dutch, French and British, the British prevailed, gradually assuming control over most of India. The Portuguese and French retained small territories, on the east and west coasts. In 1947 India consisted of 11 British provinces, along with some additional British areas and 365 Indian states, in which the British also had some influence and control. In August 1947 India gained independence from Britain, but at the same time it was partitioned into two countries – India and Pakistan – divided on the basis of religion, with a Muslim majority in Pakistan and a Hindu majority in India. Partition led to mass migrations, murder and chaos in the northwest, as people found themselves on the wrong sides of the arbitrary, newly created borders and attempted to cross over. Exact figures are not known, but around ten million are thought to have crossed the western borders and about one million people were killed. The administration, police, army, roads, railways, books, furniture and much more, including the National Debt, had to be divided between the two countries. The repercussions still continue today.

Initially Pakistan was in two sections, West and East. In 1971 East Pakistan became the independent nation of Bangladesh. In 1950 India became a Republic with an elected government and a lengthy Constitution that provides equal rights to all citizens. Within India, Hinduism is the main religion, of amounting to 79.8 per cent of the population, according to the 2011 census. Ancient gods and goddesses are still worshipped, yet they are all considered forms of one supreme source of creation. New gods can thus be incorporated, as they are only aspects of the universal divine. Other religions in India are Islam (14.2 per cent), Christianity (2.3 per cent), Sikhism (1.72 per cent), Buddhism (0.7 per cent), Jainism (0.37 per cent); other religions, including Judaism, Bahai, Zoroastrianism and numerous tribal religions (0.24 per cent). In Pakistan and Bangladesh, Islam predominates. According to the 2023 Census of Pakistan, Muslims form 96.47 per cent of the population, Hindus, 2.14 per cent; Christians, 1.27 per cent; Ahmadiyas 0.09 per cent; Sikhs, 0.01 per cent; others, including Zoroastrians, Bahai, Buddhists and atheists, 0.01 per cent. In Bangladesh, according to the 2022 Census, Muslims form 91.04 per cent of the population; Hindus 7.95 per cent; Buddhists, 0.61 per cent; Christians 0.30 per cent, Others, including Sikhs and Bahai, 0.12 per cent. However, the period covered in this book predates Islam and India was one.

NO POLITICAL UNITY

In ancient times, despite it being a convenient term for the land east of the river Indus, there was no political entity known as India. There were always numerous kingdoms, however, enlarged or diminished by conflicts and conquests. There were also different languages, such as Sanskrit, various Prakrits and Pali in the north and Tamil and its variants in the south. The northern and southern languages belonged to Indo-European and Dravidian language groups respectively. Austro-Asiatic languages were also spoken in Central India, as well as Mongolian languages in the northeast and far north. There was also some inflow of Greek and Persian in the northwest. Later, after the tenth century CE, regional languages developed; Persian soon became an important language as the sultans and Mughals made their way to

India, followed by English, from the seventeenth century onwards, with British inroads and conquests.

These three complex and ever-evolving countries of India, Pakistan and Bangladesh have a very ancient past. Ceylon, closely connected with these countries, and mentioned in the extracts below, is now known as Sri Lanka.

PALAEOLITHIC TIMES

Human occupation began early in India, indicated by the finds of stone tools dating to over two million years ago. These tools may have been made and used by *Homo habilis*, who crossed over from Africa to Asia. Summarizing the available evidence, D.K. Bhattacharya (2011) dates this migration to 2.8 to 2.2 million years ago. At least two more migrations from Africa are suggested during the Old Stone Age, dating to 1.5 million to 600,000 years ago, followed by the third migration 60,000 to 50,000 years ago. During these, it was probably *Homo erectus*, followed by Anatomically Modern *Homo sapiens* (AMHS) that came to India. The earliest tools correspond with the Lower or Early Palaeolithic, which forms the first stage of what is characterized as the Old Stone Age. In India the Lower Palaeolithic dates range from around two million years ago to 100,000 BCE. The typical tools are handaxes, cleavers and choppers. The Middle Palaeolithic begins around 100,000 BCE and lasts till approximately 40,000 BCE; it is followed by the Late Palaeolithic, during which tools became smaller and finer. The third migration was after the famous eruption of the Toba volcano which took place near Toba Lake in Sumatra in 74,000 BCE. The effect of this eruption was so widespread that the whole of India was covered in a layer of ash. Yet finds in central India reveal a continuity in stone tools, indicating that earlier human populations survived the devastation caused by the volcano, and mixed with the new entrants.

Though there are numerous finds of stone tools, from the Lower Palaeolithic onwards, finds of human fossils are few. Those that have been discovered show the early presence of *Homo erectus* and archaic *Homo sapiens*.

THE NEOLITHIC AGE

The Late Palaeolithic gradually merged into the Mesolithic and, subsequently, the Neolithic. After 10,000 BCE, with a warmer climate corresponding to the end of the last Ice Age, a new phase began with the advent of farming. The earliest settled site in the subcontinent is that of Mehrgarh in Baluchistan in the northwest, which dates to 7000 BCE. Soon more sites emerged nearby and in other areas of India, including Kashmir and the northern plains. There were Neolithic settlements in peninsula India too. The dates of these varied from 7000 BCE to 3000 BCE, and even later.

AN URBAN CIVILIZATION

In the northwest, a revolution was taking place. Out of the many agrarian settlements an urban civilization arose, its mature phase dating from between 2600 and 1900 BCE. The first cities discovered were in the valley of the Indus river, leading this civilization to be named the Indus Valley Civilization. The two largest cities were Harappa and Mohenjodaro, both located in the Indus Valley. Many more cities were then discovered beyond this region and new names were given to it, including the Sindhu-Sarasvati Civilization or, the preferred nomenclature, Harappan Civilization, after Harappa, the first site to be excavated. Other cities include Rakhigarhi, Kalibangan, Ganweriwala, Lothal and many more.

The cities were usually divided into two parts, the first a raised, walled area that has been called the citadel and the second the main town. The citadel contained large buildings. At Mohenjodaro, for instance, there was a bathing complex, known as the Great Bath, a huge storage room, often referred to as a granary, and a pillared structure resembling an assembly hall. The main town area had planned roads in a grid pattern, along which were houses with one or two storeys. Each house had a bathing area and a drainage system for waste water. The buildings were of baked brick and items of copper, bronze, terracotta and semi-precious stone have also been found, while crops grown included millet, barley, wheat and cotton. The typical pottery is red with black designs.

The population of Mohenjodaro and Harappa is usually estimated at between 39,900 and 40,000 people, but some archaeologists believe it could have been much more. Jane Mcintosh, for instance, in *The Ancient Indus Valley: New perspectives* (2008), feels there could have been as many as 100,000 people at Mohenjodaro. The entire area of the Harappan Civilization covered 1.3 million sq km, larger than any other of ancient times. It maintained trade links with Mesopotamia, crossing through present-day Afghanistan and Iran. Trade connections also extended to Central Asia and the Arabian peninsula. Cemeteries exist near some settlements. Writing has been found on seals, sealings and pot-sherds but, as the script is so far undeciphered, aspects of the civilization remain a mystery. By 1900 BCE the city civilization had declined, perhaps because of ecological changes or over-exploitation of the area. Writing also disappeared. Both cities and writing would re-appear many centuries later.

OTHER SETTLEMENTS

Meanwhile, although there were no cities, there were many Neolithic, Mesolithic and Chalcolithic settlements all over the subcontinent. These included the Kayatha and Savalda cultures in central India, named after their type-sites. Items of copper and semi-precious stones were found at Kayatha, dating from between 2500 and 1800 BCE. Savalda, located in the Tapi river valley, is known for its pottery with geometric designs. In the northern plains, the Neolithic site of Sohgaura covered an area of 60 hectares. Many sites contain evidence of simple mud and reed structures.

THE VEDIC PERIOD

Precisely memorized and recited orally for hundreds of years, the sacred texts known as the Vedas provide a different dimension to India's history. The main texts are the four Vedic Samhitas, followed by groups of texts known as the Brahmanas, Aranyakas and Upanishads. The earliest of the Vedic Samhitas is the *Rig Veda*, also the earliest text known in India. The consensus among most historians is that it dates from between 1900 and 1000 BCE – that is, after the decline of the Harappan Civilization. Other scholars disagree and place it as contemporary with the Harappan Civilization, or even earlier. The *Rig Veda* was composed in an early form of Sanskrit. Was Sanskrit the language of the Harappan Civilization, or did they use some proto-Dravidian language? There are views on both sides, as well as other theories of an Austro-Asiatic language.

The next question, and one that remains a source of controversy in India today, concerns who the Vedic people were. The two main theories are that they were either indigenous, and a continuation of the Harappan Civilization, or migrants who arrived in the region in post-Harappan times. Sanskrit is classified as an Indo-European language, and such a migration is linked with that of other Indo-European speaking people into Asia and Europe, from a central homeland, possibly in the Caspian Steppes or Anatolia. DNA studies on ancient India are just beginning, although in *Early Indians* (2021), Tony Joseph puts forward the view that even the small number of DNA studies available indicate a migration. However, the studies are currently too limited to be conclusive.

Though the *Rig Veda* is primarily a religious text, it has many different aspects. It mentions rivers, mountains and some physical locations, along with numerous clans and tribes. Such references reveal that the Rig Vedic people broadly occupied the region from south Afghanistan to the river Yamuna in the west – that is, almost the same region as that of the Harappan Civilization, though that extended further west into Gujarat and Rajasthan.

There are prayers to deities such as Indra, the god of war, thunder and rain, Surya, the sun god, the Ashvins, twin horsemen who are healers, and many others, as well as philosophical hymns and questions on the nature and origin of the world. The text, along with the other Samhitas, was used in elaborate sacrificial rituals, conducted by up to 16 priests of the brahmana caste. The text also refers to conflicts and battles, to horse-drawn chariots and to cattle as a form of wealth.

R.C. Dutt, in his extract on the Vedic Age, has provided examples of some of the beautiful hymns.

THE LATER VEDIC TEXTS AND THE EPICS

The other Vedic Samhitas include the *Sama Veda*, *Yajur Veda* and *Atharva Veda*. The *Sama Veda* re-arranges some parts of the *Rig Veda*, along with additional verses, and indicates how it is to be sung or chanted during the rituals. The *Yajur Veda*, in its different recensions, provides prayers for the sacrificial rituals. The *Atharva Veda* includes prayers to deities as well as chants for healing.

The Brahmanas contain creation and other stories and myths, along with explanations and elaborations of the sacrificial rituals. The Aranyakas describe different rituals with some philosophical explanations. The Upanishads are purely philosophical texts; their focus is upon Brahman, the eternal, unchanging, ultimate cause of the world. For these texts the location shifts into the Gangetic plains.

The epics of north India, the *Mahabharata* and the *Ramayana*, are among the great Sanskrit literature of the past. Even today they hold a very important place in the Indian psyche, and their stories and characters are often referred to in politics and in daily life. While the *Mahabharata* centres around a mammoth war, the *Ramayana* tells the story of Rama and his beloved wife Sita, her kidnapping by Ravana and her ultimate rescue. Rama is considered to be an ideal king, and also an incarnation of the god Vishnu.

The composition of both of these texts have been dated to after 1000 BCE, though they could refer to earlier times.

URBAN CENTRES ARISE AGAIN

Archaeology continues to provide information about life in the subcontinent. There were numerous different archaeological cultures, in which iron soon began to be used. The earliest use of iron has been pushed back to before 2000 BCE, following recent finds at Mayiladumparai in Tamil Nadu in south India. Early iron-using sites have also been found in the northern plains, for instance at Malhar in Uttar Pradesh, and at sites in Telangana in central India. These date from between 1800 to 1000 BCE.

Megaliths and adjacent habitation sites nearby also yield finds of iron. Megaliths have been found in upland areas in many parts of the subcontinent.

By 600 BCE the practice of agriculture was widespread, accompanied by rearing of cattle, goats and sheep. Thick forests were cleared through burning, and iron axes and sickles must have helped to clear the remaining stubble. Iron hoes and ploughshares are also found at various sites. With this background, urban centres emerged once again. Small states known as Janapadas existed before 600 BCE, but around this time some merged and expanded, incorporating in them the new urban centres. These larger states were known as Mahajanapadas or 'great states'. Sixteen of them are described in Buddhist sources, including Anga, Vanga, Kuru and Panchala. There were other states too, mentioned in Jain and other sources. Archaeology reveals baked brick structures at some cities such as Hastinapura and Indraprastha, as well as terracotta ring wells for water storage, coinage and the beginnings of a new form of writing. A shiny black pottery, known as Northern Black Polished Ware, is also found at northern sites.

LITERATURE, PHILOSOPHY AND RELIGION

Meanwhile there were new developments in philosophy and religion. Between 1000 BCE and 100 CE six systems of philosophy emerged, expressed through numerous texts. That of Vedanta was based on the Vedic texts known as the Upanishads, focusing on understanding and identifying with Brahman. Samkhya explored creation and the world through two principles, Purusha and Prakriti, passive and active. Mimamsa saw the Vedas as a means to enlightenment, while Uttara Mimamsa, a subsequent development, was similar to Vedanta. Nyaya was based on logic. Both Nyaya and Vaisheshika analysed matter, describing it as being composed of atoms. Yoga focused on methods of uniting the individual consciousness with the divine.

Buddhism, Jainism, the Ajivikas and the Charvakas comprised the other trends. Siddhartha, who came to be known as Gautama Buddha, founded the religion of Buddhism, though there are said to have been other Buddhas before him. Born in Lumbini, in present-day Nepal, in 566 BCE, Siddhartha lived and preached in India; he died around 486 BCE, though there are different estimates of his dates. His basic teaching consists of the Four Noble Truths. These stated that life was full of suffering, which was caused by desire. The way out was to live rightly, by following the Eight-fold Path explained by him. Only then could one step out of the cycle of existence and attain nirvana.

The philosophy of Jainism was put forward by Mahavira, the 24th in a line of *Tirthankaras*, meaning 'ford maker', or those who show the way to cross over to nirvana. Both Buddhism and Jainism emphasized individual effort and right living, and did not refer to god. Later, Buddhist and Jain texts were collected and canonized; new forms and sects arose. The concepts of early Buddhism were codified in the Pali Canon, which contains three groups of texts composed in Pali probably finalized by the first century CE. Mahayana and Vajrayana Buddhism have several additional texts. The main Jain texts were compiled between the fourth century BCE and the fifth century CE.

The Ajivikas were another sect prominent at one time, but they died out. Charvakas refer to materialistic sects, many of which existed in ancient India but faded away by medieval times.

In the south a different body of literature composed in Tamil emerged, together referred to as Sangam [also spelt 'cankam'] literature. These works include collections of poems and a Tamil grammar known as Tolkappiyam. Sangam literature does make some references to deities, but is largely a secular body of work.

PERSIANS AND GREEKS

The Persian emperor Darius I, ruled 522–486 BCE, had conquered Gandhara in northwest India in 516–515 BCE, and made it a province of his empire. Later Alexander, the Macedonian world conqueror, defeated the Persian king Darius III and ventured further through Afghanistan into northwest India in 327 BCE. Battles were fought along the way; some local kings were defeated while others were allowed to rule. Without proceeding further into India, Alexander turned back. It is said he had heard of the strength of the army of the Nanda dynasty that ruled in Magadha, in the eastern Gangetic plains. In addition, his soldiers were unhappy and ready to revolt.

A GREAT EMPIRE

One mahajanapada began to dominate the others – Magadha, with its capital at Pataliputra, modern Patna. Magadha was expanded by a series of dynasties, after which the Nandas took over and the mahajanapada grew into what could be called an empire. Then, in

322 BCE, Chandragupta Maurya defeated Dhanananda and established the Mauryan dynasty and empire. Megasthenes, an ambassador of the Greek ruler Seleukos, wrote the *Indika*, part of which is available in the work of later writers. It tells us a lot about life in those times.

Archaeology, inscriptions and other texts reveal still more about the Mauryan empire. Another important work is the *Arthashastra*, a treatise on politics and economy ostensibly composed by Kautilya, also known as Chanakya, the minister of Chandragupta Maurya. However, it depicts the ideal rather than the actual. Thomas Trautmann, in *Kautilya and the Arthashastra* (1971), analysed and revealed the different aspects and layers in the text, indicating it was not composed at one time or by a single person. Others, including Patrick Olivelle, in *King, Governance and Law in Ancient India* (2013), have also pointed this out.

Chandragupta was succeeded by Bindusara; he was followed by his son Ashoka in 269 BCE, who became the most famous Mauryan king. Ashoka is known for his inscriptions or edicts. These were engraved on pillars and rocks from Afghanistan to southern India, in Prakrit languages and Brahmi and Kharoshthi scripts. They recount his ideas, his *dhamma*, or concept of right conduct, and how he wanted people to live, as well as his sorrow at the devastation caused and lives lost by his invasion of the kingdom of Kalinga. Ashoka converted to Buddhism and sent emissaries to spread Buddhism to Sri Lanka and other areas. The empire did not last long after him, and the Mauryas were replaced by the Shungas, then by the Kanvas.

OTHER DYNASTIES

In the Deccan region the Andhras, also known as the Satavahanas, ruled, from the first century BCE or even earlier. Further south were the three dynasties of the Cholas, Cheras and Pandyas, ruling between about 400 BCE and 300 CE.

In the northwest, Indo-Greeks, Indo Parthians and Scythians or Shakas made inroads. The Bactrian Greeks began their rule in northwest India around 200 BCE, the Parthians in the first century CE, and the Scythians in the first century BCE. While the first two remained largely in the northwest, making only a few forays into the plains of northern India, the Shakas began to rule in western India. Rudradaman (130–150 CE) was a major Shaka ruler.

The Kushanas, a branch of the Yuehzi, were the next entrants into India, probably in the second century CE. They ruled over the northern plains, even while local kingdoms co-existed. By this time, in the first few centuries CE, there were urban centres all over India.

Widespread trade links developed, not only within India but also with other countries, including Rome. The coastal site of Arikamedu in south India is among those where Roman amphorae and coins have been found. The *Periplus of the Erythraean Sea*, a Greek text by an unknown author, provides a record of trade in the first century CE.

THE GUPTAS AND CONTEMPORARY DYNASTIES

In northern India the Kushanas were followed by the Gupta dynasty, who ruled with their capital at Pataliputra. Sri Gupta and Ghatotkacha were early Gupta kings, while Chandragupta I, the son of Ghatotkacha, founded an empire. His son Samudragupta was the dynasty's greatest king.

We know about other dynasties from inscriptions that have been discovered. These include Samudragupta's *prashasti*, a eulogistic inscription about him which lists the various kings he conquered or subdued. There are inscriptions of other kings too, as well as numerous coins bearing kings' names. In the Deccan, the Vakatakas were powerful. As the Guptas declined, small independent states emerged. Of these, King Harsha of the Pushyabhuti dynasty established a large empire during his rule from 606 to 647 CE.

Pulakeshin II of the Chalukya dynasty was an important king at the time of Harsha, ruling from 606 to 642 CE. He ruled just south of the Vindhyas up to the river Krishna.

Further south other dynasties and kingdoms emerged. The three southern dynasties of Cholas, Cheras and Pandyas had begun to decline by the third century CE, while the Pallavas began their rule with their capital at Kanchipuram. In the sixth century CE the Kalabhras, a Buddhist group, overthrew the existing dynasties. After a brief period of dominance, the Kalabhras were defeated in turn by the joint armies of the Pandyas, Pallavas and Chalukyas.

Literature, art, architecture, science and mathematics were well-developed in early India, and have been described in the extracts provided. The caste system, with its beginnings in Vedic times, gradually crystallized and spread across India. The four main castes are brahmana, kshatriya, vaishya and shudra, with innumerable subcastes. Outside these are Dalits, earlier termed 'untouchables', and given the name Harijans by Mahatma Gandhi. Although safeguarded in India's constitution, they still struggle for their rights.

AFTER HARSHA

After Harsha many small kingdoms emerged again. Among them were Yashovarman in the Ganga plains, Lalitaditya in Kashmir and, in the south, the Pallavas and Pandyas.

Numerous Rajput dynasties rose in the north. The Palas and Senas ruled in the east, while the Chola dynasty dominated the south from the tenth century CE. These were followed by countless more dynasties, kingdoms and events until we reach the India of today. These include the sultans, followed by the Mughals, the Bahmani and Vijayanagara empires, the European inroads and British rule, then in the twentieth century independence and partition. After independence the three countries of India, Pakistan, and Bangladesh have followed different paths, but those are stories for another time.

HISTORIOGRAPHY AND THE TEXTS IN THIS BOOK

India's complex history can be pieced together through literary sources, archaeology, inscriptions, coins, sculptures and numerous other artefacts, but few connected histories were written until British times. There were early Greek and Roman accounts, descriptions by travellers and biographies and memoirs of kings and rulers. The *Rajatarangini* of Kalhana, dating to the twelfth century CE, sought to provide a history of Kashmir, while Persian accounts described the land and people. The Sanskrit *Puranas*, composed in the early centuries CE and later, provide accounts of dynasties interwoven with accounts of deities and rituals, myths and stories. John Stuart Mill's *History of British India* (1817), one of the earliest to be written by a Briton, portrayed the country in a negative light, but others presented aspects of India's history in a more objective way. The foundation of the Asiatic Society of Bengal in 1784 was a landmark in studies on India. Scholars from Britain and other European countries began to translate, decipher, categorize and compile connected histories within a chronological framework. Indian scholars such as Upendra Nath Ball, an early Indian historian whose work (*Ancient India*, 1921) is featured in this book, took up the challenge too. A small part of the contribution of Romesh Chundra Dutt, another early India scholar, is also presented here (from his *Ancient India 2000 B.C.–800 A.D.*, 1893). The work of Flora Annie Steel (*India Through the Ages*, 1911) finds a place too; though not original, it is important as she compiled a history from sources known at the time.

More than a hundred years have passed since these writers provided their accounts of the past. Even so, a lot of what they wrote is still relevant; their descriptions of early texts and literary sources, as well as the broad chronological framework provided, still have validity. Of course, numerous new discoveries, notably in archaeology, have modified some theories. At the time that they were writing, the extent and nature of the Harappan Civilization was still unknown. Our increasing knowledge of this urban civilization – contemporary with Mesopotamia, yet much larger – has altered earlier views on Indian history.

The Appendix in this book reveals the account of Alexander's voyage to India narrated by a Roman writer, Quintus Rufus Curtius. Though written in the first century CE, it is based on earlier sources and provides a readable and intriguing account.

A Note on Spellings and Dates

In some cases, spellings used in the past (and thus in the extracts in this book) differ from those used today. Examples of current spellings and their older equivalents that you might find in this book are: Fa Hien = Faxian; Hieun Tsang = Xuanzang; Yuch-chih or Yueh-Chih = Yuezhi; Guzerat = Gujerat. Variant spellings too are used in the old texts, for instance, Asoka for Ashoka; Saka for Shaka; Arthasastra for Arthashastra; Kasi for Kashi; Kusa for Kusha;, Sunga for Shunga; Kosala for Koshala; Behar for Bihar; Vaisasika for Vaisheshika. Certain place names have also changed, such as Ganges (now Ganga), Jumna (now Yamuna), Caveri (now Kaveri) and Madras (now Chennai).

Dates often vary in different sources, and the most reliable dates are provided as far as possible in this book.

FURTHER READING

Basham, A.L., *The Wonder that was India* (Calcutta: Fontana and Rupa and Co, 1971)

Bracey, Robert, 'The date of Kanishka since 1960', *Indian Historical Review*, 2017, 44 (1), 1–14

Bhattacharya, D.K., 'Palaeolithic India and Human Dispersal', *Ancient India, New Series*, 1 (2011)

Bryant, Edwin Francis, ed., *The Quest for the Origins of Vedic Culture: The Indo-Aryan Migration Debate* (New Delhi: Oxford University Press, 2001)

Chakrabarti, Dilip K., *Archaeological Geography of the Ganga Plain: The Lower and Middle Ganga* (Delhi: Permanent Black, 2001)

Dalal, Roshen, *The Vedas: An Introduction to Hinduism's Sacred Texts* (Penguin India, 2010)

Dyson, Tim, *A Population History of Modern India* (Oxford University Press, UK, 2018).

Gimbutas, Marija, *The Goddesses and Gods of Old Europe* (University of California Press, 1974)

Habib, Irfan and Vivekanand Jha, *A People's History of India, 5. Mauryan India* (New Delhi: Tulika Books, 2022)

Habib, Irfan, *A People's History of India, 6. Post-Mauryan India* (New Delhi: Tulika Books, 2012)

Heckel, Waldemar, Introduction and Notes, *Quintus Curtius Rufus, The History of Alexander*, trans by John Yardley (Penguin Books, rev. ed., 2001)

Jha, D.N., *Ancient India in Historical Outline*, 4th rev. ed. (New Delhi: Manohar, 2012).

Joseph, Tony, *Early Indians* (Juggernaut, 2021)

Lal, B.B., *The Rig Vedic People* (Aryan Books International, 2015)

Lal, Pranay, *Indica: A Deep Natural History of the Subcontinent* (Penguin Random House India, 2016)

Majumdar, R.C., *Ancient India* (Delhi: Motilal Banarsidass, 10th ed., 2017)

McIntosh, Jane, *The Ancient Indus Valley: New Perspectives* (Bloomsbury Academic, 2008)

Mookerji, R.K., *The Gupta Empire* (Delhi: Motilal Banarsidass, 4th ed., 2017)

Olivelle, Patrick, *King, Governance and Law in Ancient India: Kautilya's Arthashastra* (Oxford University Press, 2013)

Possehl, Gregory, *The Indus Civilisation: A Contemporary Perspective* (Altamira Press, 2002)

Raychaudhuri, Hemchandra, *Political History of Ancient India, From the Accession of Parikshit to the Extinction of the Gupta Dynasty* (4th ed., New Delhi, 2006)

Renfrew, Colin, *Archaeology and Language: The Puzzle of Indo European Origins* (New York: Cambridge University Press, 1987)

Rosenfield, John M, *The Dynastic Arts of the Kushans* (New Delhi, Munshilal Manoharlal, 1993)

Sankhyan, A.R., 2005, 'New Fossils of early Stone Age Man from central Narmada Valley', *Current Science* 88 (5): 704–7

Sastri, K.A. Nilakanta, *A History of South India: From Prehistoric Times to the Fall of Vijayanagar* (Oxford University Press, India, new ed., 1997)

Sharma, R.S., *India's Ancient Past* (Oxford University Press, India, 2006)

Singh, Upender, *A History of Ancient and Early Medieval India* (Dorling Kindersley India, 2009)

Srivastava, B.N., *Harsha and his Times* (Varanasi: Chowkhamba Sanskrit Series Office, 1976)

Steele, R.B., 'Some Features of the Later Histories of Alexander', *Classical Philology* XIII, July 1918, 301

Thapar, Romila, *The Penguin History of Early India* (Penguin India, 2003).

Trautmann, Thomas R., *Kautilya and the Arthasastra: a statistical investigation of the authorship and evolution of the text* (Leiden: Brill, 1971)

World Religion Database (Brill): worldreligiondatabase.org

Roshen Dalal is a writer and researcher living in Dehradun, India. She has an MA and PhD in ancient Indian History from Jawaharlal Nehru University, New Delhi, India. She is the author of fourteen books on Indian and world history, as well as on religion and philosophy, along with one philosophical novel. She writes for both children and adults. Apart from books, she has written numerous articles and book reviews. She is currently engaged in research in historical geography and also in writing a new series of books on Indian history.

THE LAND & THE PREHISTORIC ERA

India, Bharatavarsha, Jambudvipa, Hindustan... these are some of the names for the subcontinent that now includes the three countries of India, Pakistan and Bangladesh. As pointed out in the following extract, the Indian subcontinent has its own natural boundaries of mountains and seas. It was impossible to cross the formidable Himalayas to the north, with entry being only through narrow mountain passes.

The theory of plate tectonics was unknown when U.N. Ball (whose text makes up this chapter) was writing, yet he observes that there were earth movements and ancient oceans where now there is land, and correctly suggests that India was once joined to Africa. In fact, about 180 million years ago, India was part of a landmass named Gondwanaland, including South America, Australia and Africa. The Himalayas arose through the movement of the tectonic plates and are in three broad sections: Inner, comprising the highest ranges; Middle; and Outer, the Siwaliks comprising the Outer or Lower Himalayas. The Himalayas are still rising, and the height of Mt Everest, the highest mountain in the world, is today calculated as 29,031.69 ft, or 8848.86 metres. North of these towering mountains is the Tibetan plateau; the Karakoram and Hindukush ranges lie to the northwest and to the south are the Indo Gangetic plains. Of the great rivers of the northern plains, the Indus and Brahmaputra rivers rise in Tibet and the Ganga (Ganges) and Yamuna (Jumna) in the Western Himalayas.

In this sheltered land, occupation began early – as far back as two million years ago. The vast Palaeolithic period, as explained in the Introduction, saw migrations from Africa into India. Apart from stone tools, which occur in both North and South India, fragments of human fossils of *Homo erectus* or archaic *Homo sapiens* have been discovered in recent times. Early finds of fossils termed *Sivapithecus* and *Ramapithicus* found in the Lower Himalayas, however, are now believed to be orangutan ancestors, not those of humans.

Despite the sparse fossil finds, the evidence from finds of stone tools shows that Palaeolithic people occupied many upland areas of India, from the north to the south. Late Palaeolithic sites, dating from after 40,000 BCE, also have complex rock paintings. The most famous is at Bhimbetka, in central India, where over 500 caves contain rock art depicting people and animals. The lifestyle of humans during the Palaeolithic in India, as elsewhere, consisted of groups of people who subsisted by hunting and gathering food. But there were leisure activities too, including dancing, as depicted in the Bhimbetka paintings. Ostrich eggshells were used to make ornaments and a grave has also been found, its occupant wearing an ostrich-eggshell necklace.

The Palaeolithic merged into the Mesolithic and Neolithic eras, and then a great urban civilization arose. Though Ball mentions Harappa, the nature and extent of this urban Harappan Civilization was unknown when he wrote.

Despite its natural boundaries, many did enter India through its narrow mountain passes. But did the 'Aryan hordes' enter through Almora, as Ball suggests? This seems unlikely. He brings out some theories of Indo-Aryan and Indo-Iranian migration and mentions Zarathushtra, whom he knows by the Greek name Zoroaster, but does not clearly explain the nature of the Avesta – the early Zoroastrian literature that includes a large number of texts and has connections to

Vedic literature. Indo-Iranian languages, among them Vedic Sanskrit and Iranian Avestan, form part of the Indo-European language group. A huge body of literature now exists on the Indo-European speakers and the theory of migration of the so-called Aryans into India.

As for population variants, Risley's division into seven groups is out of date. Instead we refer today to language groups. In addition, gene analysis has provided a valuable new dimension to population studies. Through this it has been discovered that most Indians are a mix of two main groups, Ancestral North Indians (ANI) and Ancestral South Indians (ASI), each of which have various components.

THE PHYSICAL FEATURES

The river Indus has given its name to the vast country lying to its east. The foreign invaders from Persia, Greece and China could not proceed very far from the basin of the mighty river, and they called the country the land of the Indus or India. The Greek historian Herodotus and the historians who came with Alexander used this name, and subsequently the name of the best-known country has been applied to the whole country.

In the Sanskrit epics the country is called Bharatavarsha from an old Aryan tribe of the name of the Bharatas. The older name of the country is Jambudwipa.

The country is cut off by nature from the rest of the world. It is protected by the high mountains on the north-west, north, and north-east; and on other sides it is washed by the broad oceans. In the ancient times the seas were a formidable barrier against the invasions of foreigners. There was no country in the east or west which had a sufficiently strong fleet to undertake the conquest of India; and the

Arabian sea or the Bay of Bengal was not very easy to cross. Crafts from Egypt or Mesopotamia, from China or Java could come with favourable winds along the coast. It was by means of these crafts that trade with foreign countries was carried on, but the idea of conquest could not be conceived.

There were some passes through the mountains which allowed the invasions of foreigners. It is believed that these passes were not impregnable in the remote past. Moreover, geological evidence goes to say that at one time the country to the west of the Aravalli range was under water, and probably India was connected with Africa by land. Volcanic cataclysms and strong upheavals have brought the country to its present shape. These earth movements are still working. The rivers which connected India with Afghanistan and the western countries in the historic period have dried up, and the mountains are raising their heads still higher.

The Gates of India

The beds of the old rivers form the main gateways of India. The most important gorge through which foreign invasions came into India is the Khyber Pass from Kabul down the valley of the Kabul river to Peshawar. Other gates on the north-west are the Gomal Pass between Afghanistan and Dera Ismail Khan, the Kuram through which the river Kuram flows from Afghanistan into the Bannu district, and the Bolan Pass between Shikarpur in Sindh and Kandahar. The fort of Quetta protects the last. If any invader comes from Turkistan via Herat the Bolan Pass will be very convenient for him to follow. There are some Passes across the Himalayas which connect the tableland of the Tibetan region of China with India. But on account of their high altitude they are not of great political importance. In ancient times some immigrations might have come through them, and at the present time they are the only routes for the purpose of trade between India and China. These Passes are divided into three groups, viz., the Shipki group along the Sutlej, the Almora group and the Sikkim group. The Brahmaputra valley allowed large inmigrations in the north-east. This was the route along which the Mongolian tribes came into India, and even now geographers think that it may be recognized as one of the world's highways.

The Seacoast

The coast lines contain a number of harbours on the seacoast both sides. The west coast harbours are better situated and from ancient times trade between Egypt and India passed through these harbours. But commodities from the interior of the country could not be conveniently brought to these places on account of the difficulty of transportation. Baruguża or Broach was the most important port, which was connected with the interior by the Narmada, and the pilgrim route to Prayag, and Mathura. The east coast is shallow, and there was little foreign trade along this coast. But boats used to ply from one port to another, and there was trade connection along this coast from the mouth of the Ganges down to Ceylon. This route is therefore of great importance in the history of ancient India as it indicates the march of culture from one part of the country to another. From Tamralipti to Ceylon it was a voyage of two weeks.

The mainland consists of a number of natural divisions created by rivers and mountains. The Indus valley is watered by the Indus and its tributaries, and Indus valley, extend from Kashmir to the Sea and from the Sulaiman to the Jumna. It was known to the Aryans as the land of the Sapta Sindhu, and it was here that they developed their Vedic culture. This province stands in a peculiar position as all the foreign invasions from the north-west passed through it, and almost all the foreign settlements in India were first planted in the Punjab. To the south-east of this province lies the great Thar or Rajputana desert. It extends up to the Aravalli Range. The States of Jodhpur and Bikanir have grown on the oases of these sandy plains.

At the bend of the Himalayas known as the Siwalik valley Range the two most important rivers of India, the Ganges and the Jumna, have their rise. The Jumna has mixed her waters with the Ganges at Prayag, and the combined stream has fallen into the Bay of Bengal after traversing more than 600 miles. A number of tributaries, such as Ghogra, Rapti, Gandak from the Himalayas have fallen into the Ganges. In the lower portion before falling into the Bay it has been joined by the Brahmaputra from the north-east. The basins of the Ganges and the Brahmaputra are the most fertile parts of India. The lower division forming the delta of the two rivers and their doab are most thickly populated and they have been very prosperous from the ancient times.

The Ganges is the most sacred river of the Hindus. 'No river on the surface of the globe can compare with the Ganges in sanctity. From her source to her outflow in the Bay of Bengal every yard of the river is sacred. To bathe in the Ganges at stated intervals is to wash away sin; to die and be cremated on the riverbank is to attain eternal peace; even to ejaculate the name "Ganga" when afar from her banks is sufficient to atone for the misdeeds of several previous stages of human existence,' says Mr. T. H. Holdich [author and Superintendent of Frontier Surveys in British India]. The total length of the Ganges is about 1,550 miles. A large number of the great cities in northern India have grown on the banks of the Jumna and the Ganges. Delhi, Mathura, and Agra stand the Jumna; while Kanauj, Benares, and Pataliputra stand on the Ganges. Prayag stands at the confluence of the Ganges and the Jumna. These rivers are navigable almost up to the foot of the mountains, and troops and trade could easily be carried by boats on them.

The homogeneity of culture in northern India is greatly due to these rivers. The history of the provinces watered by them is interconnected. The lower division of Bengal east of the Bhagirathi lies at a great distance from the north-west frontier. The invaders became exhausted after coming to the middle country and we therefore do not find much disturbance in the life of Bengal. In the Mahomedan period the Muslim governors under the early Delhi sultans conquered the province, and they enjoyed autonomy and became independent on account of the distance.

Delhi occupies a unique position. It stands on the Jumna, and below it lies the great desert. The invaders from the north-west must therefore pass through Delhi. It is the key to the Aryavarta or Madhyadesa. The master of Delhi could protect the frontiers as well as he could command the vast plains to the east. So the master of Delhi could be the master of India. It is on account of its strategic position that Delhi was selected as the capital of northern India by the Pathan rulers.

Mathura was a seat of the Saka satraps and before that of Hindu kings. Agra was the royal residence of the Mughal emperors, Kanauj was the capital of the Hindu kings in ancient times. The most important king of Kanauj being Harshavardhan. Pataliputra was the capital of the Mauryas, the Kanvas, and of the Guptas. In recent times Calcutta, the early capital of British India, stands on the Ganges.

The country lying between the Jumna, the Aravalli Range, and the Satpura hills presents certain special features. It is mainly hilly. The Vindhya hills runs through these tracts. The Chambal and its tributaries water the land between the Aravalli and the Vindhyas. The Rajput states lie in this region. The mountains made the forts impregnable, and the Rajput clans could defend themselves against foreign invasions without much difficulty. The region south of the Vindhyas down to the Narmada and the Satpura is almost of the same nature. The Vindhyas, the Satpura, the rivers Narmada and the Tapti, and the Dandak forest towards the mouth of these rivers were great barriers against invasions from the north into the south. But the hills are not very high. There are good roads in some places, and the rivers are fordable. They have therefore not been able to resist invasions of strong men from the north. In later times too the people of the south spread their powers up to the Sutlej.

The Peninsula proper from the Satpura southwards is known as the Deccan. A chain of mountains, called the Western Ghats, has run along the western coast. The Konkan is the strip of land between the Ghats and the Sea. There is also a similar chain along the least coast, but it is not so high. The plateau between the two Ghats is watered by the rivers Godavari, Krishna, and Caveri. It is very fertile and was very prosperous in ancient times. The wealth of the south is proverbial. Its large quantity of gold and, jewels attracted the Mahomedan rulers of the North. The natural barriers, however, stood in the way of the consolidation of the country.

The Himalayas

The Himalayas stand as a separate unit. The chain of mountains between the bends of the Indus and the Brahmaputra is called by the geographers the Himalayas. It separates India from China. Mount Everest is the highest peak of the world, measuring 29,002 ft. Kinchin Jungha beats all others in the grandeur of beauty. There is no mountain chain in the world so grand and sublime as the Siwalik Range. During winter the tops of the Himalayas remain covered over with ice, and with the coming of the summer when it is melted, the rivers become full [...]. Towards the south lie the kingdoms of Kashmir, Nepal, Sikkim, and Bhutan. Buddha was born in the Nepal Terai and he died there [...].

It is believed that a horde of Aryans entered by the Sutlej valley or by the valleys of the Almora group and proceeded along the foot of the mountains to the Madhyadesa. This theory is in agreement with the Puranic legends, which hold Kailas as the abode of the gods. The Himalayas therefore is considered very sacred by the Hindus.

The Border Lands

To the north of India stands the great tableland called the Pamirs. It is popularly known as the roof of the world, as such a broad and high tableland is not found anywhere else in the world. Here 'the drainage areas of the three great river systems of the Indus, the Oxus, and the Tarim meet, the representatives as it were of the still greater ethnic areas of India, Iran and Turkestan'. Beyond the Pamirs lie the great Central Asian plains which were at a time very prosperous. The region between the Aral, the Caspian, and the Pamirs is supposed to be the cradle of the Aryan civilization.

To the east of the Pamirs lie the tableland of Tibet, the region of the mysterious Lamas, and the rest of China's Celestial Empire. The Hindukush is practically a continuation of the great mountain range round about the Pamirs. It was called by the Greeks Olympus, and some of the most important events of the Indian history are connected with this region. It formed a part of ancient India, and since 1648 it has been permanently separated from India as a political unit. The Aryans from Central Asia dwelt for a long time in this tract and this was the parting place of the Iranians and the Indo-Aryans. The Greeks settled here for about three centuries. In later times most of the Mahomedan invasions into India came from the hilly countries of the Hindukush. The sturdy races of the mountainous regions on the north-west found it an easy affair to conquer and exploit the peaceful people in the plains of India. [...]

Political Importance of Geography

India thus presents all the features of a vast continent. It extends from the tropics to the temperate zone, and from the Sulaiman to the borders of Burma it is about 1,750 miles. The coastline measures 3,400 miles. On account of its vastness of extent and the difficulty of communication from one part to another it was not possible to maintain its political unity. At times powerful monarchs subjugated the territories on all sides but as soon as they died their empires fell into pieces. On account of the broad natural divisions there arose a number of states sometimes much larger than many of the modern states of Europe. One of the problems of these states was the maintenance of their integrity [...].

The existence of these small states was an advantage in a way, because no foreign conqueror could become master of the country by defeating one or two rulers. Darius, Alexander, the Sakas, the Hunas, none of these could conquer the whole of the vast territory, nor even the Mahomedans in the later times.

Unity

In spite of the broad political divisions we find the growth of one civilization throughout India. Aryan culture has spread from the north to the south, and from the west to the east. Rivers of the north as well as of the south are sacred to the Hindus. Rameswaram is as much a place of sanctity as Hardwar. The people throughout the country hold in reverence the same scriptures. The caste system in its four broad divisions is in existence throughout. The foreign invaders were merged in the vast population of the country. Even the Pathans and the Mughals were gradually assimilating Hindu culture.

The difference in culture of the foreign invaders has given rise to a number of complicated problems of great political importance. If the old conditions had existed, and if the culture of the conquerors had been less virile than that of the people then most probably they could have been assimilated, and India would have been the land of one nation with a common culture, common ideal, and common hope. In spite of the disturbing factors in modern times the civilization of India displays not only an originality but also a continuity which has scarcely a parallel elsewhere in the globe. India has assimilated foreign culture and what it has received it has presented to the world in its own way. It is on account of this characteristic that the Indian civilization has not been swept away by foreign culture. It may be very safely said that India owes this mainly to her physical conditions.

SOURCES OF HISTORY

Materials for a Connected History

'The date for the reconstruction of the early history of all nations are necessarily meagre,' says V.A. Smith [Irish Indologist, historian], 'largely consisting of bare lists of names supplemented by vague and often contradictory traditions which pass invisibly into popular mythology. The historian of ancient India is fairly well provided with a supply of such lists, traditions, and mythology; which, of course, require to be treated on the strict critical principles applied by modern students to early histories of both western and eastern nations. The application of those principles in the case of India is not more difficult than it is in Babylonia, Egypt, Greece, or Rome.'

Modern research has brought to light vast materials for a connected history of ancient India. In 1784 Sir William Jones founded the Asiatic Society of Bengal. Since then a number of scholars devoted themselves to the study of the ancient literature of India, and of her coins, inscriptions, and archaeological remains. Their labours have borne immense fruits, and we have now a fair idea of the progress of civilizations in India from the advent of the Aryans. The Indian literatures have been carefully studied. The inscriptions have been deciphered and examined, the archaeological remains have been thoroughly surveyed, and the accounts of the foreign writers have been analysed. It cannot, however, be said that the work is finished and that no more research is necessary. The field is vast and there is yet a great deal to be done in all the various lines of research connected with the past of India.

The sources of the early history be of India may divided into three broad classes, viz., (1) Literary, (2) Archaeological, and (3) Epigraphic.

Literary Sources

The literary sources are numerous, but there is scarcely any book in ancient Indian literature which can be said to be strictly historical. In Kautilya's Arthasastra Itihasa forms a subject of study by a Prince.

Purana, Itivritta (history), Akhyaika (tales), Udaharana (illustrative stories), Dharmasastra, and Arthasastra are (known by the name) Itihasa. History in this sense is a comprehensive thing. But one does not find in it a correct narrative of events in the time order. The Vamsavalis or the dynastic lists in the Puranas are of historical value, and they have been considered to contain much genuine and valuable historical tradition. But the information available is meagre and the details discrepant. They have to be corroborated by other more reliable evidence. The Bhavisya Purana gives a list of kings from the Kurukshetra war to the Andhras (260–61 CE). Other Puranas such as Matsya, Vayu, and Brahmanda borrowed the version of the Bhavisya. The Vayu comes up to the Gupta period (325–30 CE). The Puranic accounts begin with the commencement of the Kali Age.

We have to find other sources for information before the Puranic Age. The two great epics, the *Mahabharata* and the *Ramayana*, do not claim to be history. But it has been held by scholars that parts of the *Mahabharata* were composed about 1000 BCE and the book received its final shape in about 500 CE. The episodes described in the *Mahabharata* are probably based upon some historical events. The story of the *Ramayana* is one of such episodes. The *Mahabharata* deals with the life of the Aryans in the Kuru-Panchala land and the Gangetic valley, and the *Ramayana* describes the march of Aryan civilization from northern India into the south down to Ceylon. These two books a valuable source of information, regarding the polity of the Aryans.

The Vedas and other Vedic literature give us some idea about the social conditions of the early Aryan settlers in India before the epic period. They contain a description of the country in which they lived, and the gods they worshipped. They are the earliest literary records of man's manners and customs. The late Mr. [Keshav Gangadhar] Tilak [Indian nationalist, teacher, and an independence activist] would put the Vedic accounts at about 4500 BCE. The European scholars consider 1200 BCE as the latest date of the composition of the Vedas.

If we accept Mr. Tilak's view then we have records of the social, political, moral, and intellectual life of the Indians from 4500 BCE. In any case 3000 BCE will not be far from the truth.

The Buddhist and the Jaina literatures are of greater importance than the Sanskrit literature as in some cases the dates of their composition can be approximately calculated. The birth stories of the Buddhas contained in the Jatakas throw a flood of light on the condition of India in the sixth and fifth centuries before Christ. Later Buddhistic chronicles such as Dipavamsa and Mahavamsa contain much historical information.

In the domain of pure historical literature we have scarcely any. Bana's *Harsha Charita* is an historical romance containing an account of Harshavardhana of Kanauj (606–48 CE). The book is valuable as it provides some important data for literary and political chronology. The *Vikramankadeva Charita* of Bilhana is another historical romance dealing with the life of the Chalukya king Vikramaditya VI of Kalyani (1076–1126 CE). Neither in the book of Bana nor in that of Bilhana there is any mention of date, for which we have to depend upon other sources.

The only Sanskrit work claiming a directly historical character is the *Rajatarangini*, a chronicle of the kings of Kashmir, written by Kalhana in 1148 CE. But the narrative of the book is legendary till the author approaches his own times.

Other literary works, such as poems and dramas, give indirect help in constructing a history of ancient India. A good deal of information has been obtained from a comparative study of the languages, especially in the field of mythology and religion. The history of a word is the history of the development of cultures and civilizations. Comparative Philology has discovered relations between the civilizations of India, Persia, and Europe.

Besides the indigenous literature of India, the foreign accounts are a valuable source of information. These foreign accounts have cleared many an obscure passage. The dates of these works are known, and with their help the Indian chronology has been properly arranged. The writings of the Greek writers Herodotus, Ktesias, Megasthenes, and the historians who came with Alexander are of surpassing interest. Herodotus wrote in the fifth century before the birth of Christ. He gives an account of the relations between India and Persia. The fragments of Megasthenes contribute detailed information about the administration of Chandragupta [also spelled Chandra Gupta] Maurya. The Chinese historian Ssu-ma-ch'-ien wrote a history in about 100 BCE. His book is especially valuable for its accurate chronology regarding the early annals of India. The writings of the Greeks and the Romans in the early centuries of the Christian era supply also materials for a history of ancient India.

But the Chinese travellers Fa-Hien and Hiuen Tsang have left records which have been of great help in reconstructing the history of India. Fa-Hien visited India between 399 and 414 CE and Hiuen Tsang between 629 and 645 CE. Fa-Hien gives valuable information regarding the times of Chandragupta II, and Hiuen Tsang that of Harshavardhana. Their accounts are especially full with reference to the places connected with the life of Buddha.

Of all other foreign visitors Alberuni stands out prominently. His book is an authentic narrative of Hindu manners, science, and literature down to the invasion of the Mahomedans. It was completed in 1030 CE.

Archaeology

We have not written records for all the stages in the history of man. The gaps have been filled up by archaeological research.

'Knowledge of the condition of mankind in the dim ages of the past which lie beyond the ken of history or tradition is attainable only by scientific interpretation of the scanty material relics of human workmanship – the tools, weapons, tombs, and pottery which survive from those remote times,' says V.A. Smith. The successive stages of civilization can be distinguished by noting the degrees of progress in the art of using metals. Thus the prehistoric period has been divided into the Old Stone Age, the New Stone Age, the Bronze Age, and the Iron Age by a study of the implements used.

The students of archaeology have not only examined the relics of the old implements, they have also carefully studied the arts and architecture of the people. These old relics have been very useful in tracing the growth of human civilization where literary evidence is lacking. Man's handiworks have stood forth as the dumb memorial of his life and activities. The old buildings of Takshasila, Giribraja and Pataliputra, the Stupas at Piprahwa, Bharhut and Sanchi the monolithic columns at Lauriya-Nandangarh, Rummindei and Sarnath, the paintings in the Ajanta caves, the temples of Mathura, the sculpture found in the north-west frontiers and many other remains of this kind have supplied many a missing link. Some of the complex problems of chronology have been solved with the help of the archeological finds.

The most important illustration is the chronology of the Kushan period arranged with the help of the finds at Takshasila. The style of architecture and sculpture and the materials used in them are witnesses of the influence of the different civilizations upon each other. The earliest Indian building discovered is the *stupa* at Piprahwa on the Nepal frontier. It is assigned to 450 BCE. The stone walls of Giribraja are the oldest extant stone buildings in India. They are the remains of about 600 BCE. But the remains of the New Stone Age are not very rare. They go back as far as 2000 BCE. Some remains of the still remote Old Stone Age have been discovered in the Narmada and the Godavari valleys. The gaps between the Old Stone Aga and between the New Stone Age and the historic period have not been sufficiently surveyed, and the story of the origin of Indian civilization is still shrouded in darkness.

Epigraphy

The most important source of early Indian history is the inscriptions on stone, rocks, seals, metals, and coins. These inscriptions were not intelligible to the people three generations ago, as they were in unknown characters.

The bilingual coins struck by the Greek princes provided a clue to the decipherment of the old alphabets. These alphabets are of two kinds, viz., Brahmi and Kharoshthi. Brahmi has been shown to be the parent of all the modern alphabets of India. Probably it is derived from Phoenician writing brought into India through Mesopotamia by merchants. Kharoshthi is a variety of Aramaic script and was in use in Western Asia in 500 BCE. It disappeared from India in 800 CE. Sir M. Aureil Stein [British archaeologist] discovered some Kharoshthi manuscripts in Khotan. A large number of the inscriptions have been found in the different parts of India. A patient examination of these inscriptions have enriched our knowledge of the ancient political history of India. They have helped in finding dates and in identifying names. Such inscriptions are long enough to give us an idea of the social and political condition of the people.

The edicts of Asoka were engraved upon rocks and pillars. They are scattered from the Yusufzai territory to the borders of Mysore, from Guzerat to Orissa. These edicts were the injunctions issued by Asoka. No other monarch followed the example of Asoka. So his edicts stand as a class by themselves. Most of the inscriptions are commemorative, dedicatory, or donative. They have been engraved on stone slabs, or copper plates, or seals of various types. The history of the Gupta period has been written with the help of inscriptions. The inscriptions found in southern India are of comparatively later times. For the period before the Christian era more documents are found in northern India than in the South. The oldest document is the inscription on the Piprahwa vase assigned to about 450 BCE.

Indian Chronology

The dates mentioned in the inscriptions are not of the same era. Different monarchs started different eras. It is therefore difficult to say from the year in an inscription to which era it refers. In solving the chronological problems references in contemporary literature of foreign countries have been greatly useful.

The identification of Chandragupta with Sandrakotos of the Greek writers was the first point attained in fixing thy time order. The reference to Antiochos Theos and other Greek princes in an edict of Asoka still further determined the chronology of the Maurya kings. Dr. Fleet succeeded in pointing out the starting year of the Gupta period as 319–20. M. Sylvain Levi [French orientalist and Indologist] discovered that Meghvarna of Ceylon was a contemporary of Samudragupta and thus the chronology of the Guptas has been finally settled. The recent discoveries at Taxila have solved the chronological problems of the Kushan period. So we have now an almost accurate chronological table starting with the time of the Buddha.

EARLY EPOCHS OF CIVILIZATION

'**H**uman races of earlier times,' writes B.G. Tilak, 'have left ample evidence of their existence the surface of this globe.' Innumerable implements have been unearthed, and they have been utilized by the archaeologists in reading the history of man in his primitive life. After a careful study of these remains they have divided human civilization into different stages according to the metals used.

First, is the Paleolithic or Old Stone Age, when man used chipped stone implements, rude in form. Remains of extinct animals are associated with this period. Second, Neolithic or New Stone Age, when man had made some progress in the use of his implements. They are generally of ground or polished stone. Man has begun to use pottery, and the fauna connected with the implements are still to be found. The dead received a burial and the tombs were frequently of massive stones. There is a great gulf between the Paleolithic and the Neolithic Ages. But the Neolithic Age passes imperceptibly into the Bronze Age when man has learnt the use of metals. This is the third stage in the evolution of culture. The final stage is that of Iron. In some cases the transition from one stage to another is abrupt. In India the traces of a Bronze Age are not so conspicuous. Implements of pure copper have been found in some parts. Here people passed directly from polished stone to iron.

Paleolithic Men

The chipped stone instruments discovered in the Paleolithic neighbourhood of Madras and the Narmada and Godavari valleys are the remains of the oldest inhabitants of India. The skulls and bones of these men have not been found. They made no pottery and built no tombs. They might have used sticks, stones, and bones in getting their food by hunting wild animals or in plucking fruits. Most probably did not know the use of fire. The animals of that time are extinct.

Neolithic Men

Implements of the Neolithic period are found throughout India except in Bengal. Remains of the polished implement factories have been found in southern India. The enamelled pottery found at Harappa takes us to the period of the Sumerian civilization. The people at this stage used pottery, at first handmade, and then turned on the wheel. Men kept domestic animals, cultivated land, and made sufficient progress in civilization. They buried their dead and constructed tombs. Cremation was a later practice. Tombs of this period are not found in plenty. Cockburn found two graves in Mirzapur, U. P., in which skeletons lay north and south on a thick stone slab, and the grave was also enclosed in a stone circle. At Pallavaram, near Madras, earthen mounds covering terra cotta coffins have been discovered. Many prehistoric cemeteries have been found in the Tinnevelly district, the most ancient seat of pearl and conch shell fishery. Some people suppose that these graves are of the foreign settlers who came for trade. The Neolithic men learnt the use of gold before copper or iron.

Copper Age

In Europe men used an alloy of copper and tin for their implements in the post-Neolithic period. But there was no Bronze Age. People used iron immediately after polished stone as in the south or copper as in northern India. Four hundred and twenty-four copper implements and 102 thin silver plates were discovered in 1870 at Gungeria, a village in the Balaghat district of the United Provinces. Copper is also mentioned in the *Atharva Veda*. Roughly speaking these copper and silver implements came into use in about 2000 BCE.

Iron Age

When iron was introduced cannot be definitely said. It was in common use in Egypt in the seventh century BCE. It was in use in Babylonia from very ancient times. 'The Iron Age in India,' says V.A. Smith, 'may well go back to 1500 or even 2000 BCE.'

The Primitive Indian

The ethnography of modern India is not a sufficient guide to the discovery of the earliest inhabitants of India.

We have already seen that the surface of the country has undergone considerable changes. The peninsula from the Aravalli southwards bears evidence of a very remote antiquity. It has been permanent land for millions of years. The Gangetic and the Indus valleys are of comparatively later growth. So the earliest inhabitants of India must have lived in the Deccan.

The remains of the Paleolithic man have not as yet been discovered north of the Narmada. Certain tribes are now found in the Aravallis and the Salt Range who may be the descendants of the aborigines of India. Some scholars once held the view that the negroes of Africa were the kinsmen of the aborigines of India, and the Andamanese were a group of that family. The theory has not been corroborated and no serious scholar supports it. The primitive Indian was in the stage of Paleolithic civilization.

The Dravidians

Sir Herbert Risley [British ethnographer and colonial administrator] has divided the peoples of India into seven main types on the basis of their physical features. Of these types the Dravidians are probably the oldest. They are distinguished from the rest of the population of India by their low stature, black skin, and long forearm.

The Dravidians occupy the oldest geological formation in India. Whether they were the earliest inhabitants of India is a matter of controversy. But there is no evidence of the existence of any other people except some tribes in the Central Indian hills who may claim priority over the Dravidians. The Paniyans of Malabar and the Santals of Chota Nagpur belong to this family. The original type has been modified by an admixture with the Aryans, Scythians, and Mongolians, especially in the upper strata. Dravida or Tamil is the oldest language of India.

The relations between the North and the South of India were not so close on account of the physical barriers. When the Aryans settled in the north the civilization of southern India was not at all affected by them. The Dravidian civilization may therefore be called the pure unadulterated civilization of ancient India. But unfortunately the materials for a history of ancient Dravidian culture are scanty [...]. It is believed the Dravidians lived in the whole of India before the coming of the Aryans. They were reduced to the position of the Sudras in northern India, but they maintained their integrity in the South for a considerable period. Even now the civilization of southern India is a continuation of the old Dravidian civilization with a veneer of Aryan culture. The arts, architecture, and literature of southern India are distinctively Dravidian.

The Mongolians

Immigrations of foreign people have come into India either by the north-east or the north-west. The Mongolians of China entered India by the Brahmaputra valley or across the Himalayas. The Kanets of Kulu, the Lepchas of Darjeeling and Sikkim, the Limbus, Murmis and Gurungs of Nepal, the Bodos of Assam, and the Burmese belong to the Mongolian family. There has been also an admixture of the Mongolian blood with that of the Dravidian in the people of Bengal and Orissa. The Mongolian immigration has been slow and imperceptible [...].

The Tantric form of worship in Bengal is considered a result of Mongolian influence. The Mongolians have not done much in changing the political life of the country.

The Aryans

The most important immigrants came by the north-west passes. Of them the Aryans are the oldest. According to the European scholars these Aryans lived in Central Asia. When their country dried up they spread in different directions. Some of them went to Europe and others came southward to the banks of the Oxus and the Hindu Kush region. In course of time they came into India in successive hordes, and some groups settled in Persia. The immigration into India continued for a considerable length of time. The process might have commenced 4,000 years before the birth of Christ.

In the beginning they settled in the north-west frontier and the Punjab. They came with their families and maintained unsullied their Aryan blood and culture. A second wave of the Aryan invaders came by Gilgit and Chitral and established themselves in the plains of the Ganges and the Jumna. Most probably they could not bring their families, and therefore formed alliances with the Dravidians. A mixed type of people arose out of this union of the Aryans and the Dravidians. The Aryans of the Punjab looked down upon the people of the eastern parts and used contemptuous epithets whenever they referred to these people. A third wave came down the Indus and entered into Central India by Kathiawar and Guzerat. It is also believed that the Aryan settlers in Babylonia came to India by the coastline and entered into India by the ports. The Aryan invaders by whatever route they might have come have changed the history of India. The original inhabitants accepted their language, customs, and religion. The whole of India has gradually become Aryanized and whatever we know of India is really the history of the spread of Aryan civilization in the country.

Modern research, with the help of comparative anatomy, comparative philology, and comparative mythology, has succeeded in collecting much valuable information regarding the Aryans before they entered India. The word 'Arya' is derived from a root which means ploughing; and it is inferred from this that the people who first learnt the art of cultivation adopted this title as a mark of distinction, and subsequently the name might have been applied to the entire race. Later on, Arya came to mean 'honourable' or 'noble'.

It is generally believed that the Aryans lived in Central Asia before they separated. The tract of land, watered by the Amu Dariya and the Murghab, and bounded by the Caspian Sea on the west, the Hindu Kush on the south, the Kailas range on the east, and the Kizelkum and other sandy deserts on the north, was the original home. The Mahratta scholar Tilak holds that the 'Vedic and the Avestic evidence clearly establish the existence of a primeval Polar home.' [...] The Aryans might have come from their Arctic home to the Central Asian plateau, but the matter requires careful examination.

By a study of the words in the languages of the peoples spread over the globe from India to Ireland the scholars have drawn up a picture of Aryan life before they separated. They were then divided into three classes, one lived by hunting, the second by tending flocks of cattle, and the third by agriculture. This indicates a settled state of society far in advance of primitive life. 'The life of the hunter was hard, rude, and more or less violent; that of the shepherd inactive, slothful and nomadic; and that of the agriculturist stable, normal and regular,' says M. Flotard. 'The hunter and the shepherd were under the necessity of moving about in quest of game or fresh pasture, easily moveable dwellings or tents were best suited to their requirements; the agriculturist remained attached to his field, built solid and fixed houses, and cultivated in his mind a profound sentiment of respect for religion and morality. The family and the tribe were the most dear to the nomads; but the nation, the people, the country and the city claimed the greatest consideration from the agriculturists.'

People knew the art of weaving. They manufactured cloth out of wool. Furs, skins, and woollen fabrics were used for clothing. They could manufacture pottery and arms. Of the metals they knew the use of gold, copper, and iron. Their food differed according to their mode of living. The hunters lived up in meat, the shepherds and the agriculturists on the produce of their fields supplemented by milk and occasionally by meat. The hunters and the shepherds used to take fermented drinks. The Soma was their principal beverage.

The ancient Aryans could compose poetry and metrical compositions of various kinds were current among them. The hymns of the *Rig Veda*, and the gathas [songs or poems] in the Zend Avesta are but evidence of the development of the poetic genius of the Aryans. Although there is a strong similarity in the languages of the Indo-European family their alphabets are distinctly of different types. This has led to the conclusion that the Aryans did not know the art of writing, otherwise some similarity in the alphabets could have been traced.

There is incontestable proof of the Aryans having cultivated the laws of morality and civil government. The law of marriage was strict. Marriage among blood relations was forbidden. They fully recognized the rights of property and inheritance. There were fixed rules for the punishment of theft, robbery, and fraud. 'A strong sense of right and wrong, of virtue and vice,' says [historian] Rajendra Lal Mitra, 'was a prevailing characteristic of their moral life; and abundant evidence is at hand to show that they had an honest, truthful, and law-abiding career guided by elders, chiefs, and kings to whom they paid great respect, and whose orders they carried out with diligence.'

They had a settled form of government, for the maintenance of which taxes and contributions were realized. The form of government was monarchic with a king at the head. The family life was patriarchal.

The earliest Aryans probably had no idea of God. As they made some progress they might have believed in cruel and vindictive gods and spirits whom they dreaded or tried to cheat by cunning. Gradually they created a host of divinities presiding over the different elements and natural phenomena such as earth, water, air, sky, etc. But this is possible when the religious sentiment has been awakened. Men must have been impressed with a sense of the divine or felt a yearning for a knowledge of the supernatural. In such a spirit the sun, the fire, the stars, the elements, all appear as the visible emblems of the unknown Great Cause. Ultimately man is led to the Great Cause itself. The belief in one Supreme God was searched by the Aryans, but it did not attain the fixity and uncompromising firmness of the Vedantic Theism.

The conception of one Supreme God was not contradictory to the conception of many subordinate divinities. Even Zoroaster, an ardent reformer of the ancient faith, admitted these divinities as angels or spirits, good or bad. Muhammad also recognized the existence of celestial hierarchy of angels and archangels to carry out the behests of the Supreme Divinity. That the Aryans had the conception of one Supreme God proves the high order of their civilization. They did not always call the Supreme Being by the same name nor did they always assign the same attributes to him. They all, however, beheld in fire and in light a manifestation of the Divinity. The Iranians considered fire as the only means of divine manifestation. The Sun was held in profound veneration as the emblem of the Invisible God. The Hindus and the Parsis still worship the Sun; the former made so much progress in the knowledge of the universe that they denied that the Sun ever rose or set.

Worship of God was celebrated by hymns and prayers accompanied by offerings of the products of the flocks and the fruits of the earth. There was no temple nor monument. 'The universe was the only temple worthy of the grandeur of the Supreme Being, the vault of heaven was the only shelter for the ceremonies celebrated in his honour by the chief of the family who was the high priest, the foremost chanter, and the first prophet of the divinity.'

There was also a strong belief among the Aryans that there were certain malevolent spirits always at war with God. Plague and storms and inundations were caused by them.

Migration of the Aryans

It is very difficult to say when and why the Aryans left the original home. The cause probably was partly economic and partly religious. They could not go to the east as it was thickly populated by the Turanians. So they pushed on the three other sides where they did not meet with much opposition. The first Aryan colonists in the north are known as Mesagetae. In the west the European races, known as the Slavonic, the Lithuanian, and the Teutonic are of Aryan origin…. Four different streams went westward through Persia, viz., the Celts, the Thracian, the Armenian, and the Hellenico Italian. The last and the most important movement, so far as India is concerned, was towards the south. They came to Afghanistan and settled in the country round about the Hindu Kush.

The settlement in Afghanistan was not altogether peaceful. The shepherds and the agriculturists followed different modes of living. The shepherds were violent and adventurous, but the agriculturists were peace loving and steady in their habits. The attributes of the gods of these people differed according to their way of living. The god of the shepherds was wrathful and warlike, while the god of the agriculturists was peaceful and mild. The difference of ideals led to quarrels. The shepherds drove the agriculturists out of Afghanistan. The defeated party came to India. The victors spread their branches in Persia. In Zend Avesta Ahuras, that is Asuras, are all that is good and virtuous, and the Deos or Devas are the demons. The reverse is the case in the Vedas. This shows the antagonism between the two peoples [...].

THE VEDIC AGE

The Vedic age in this section refers to the period when the *Rig Veda* was composed. This is the earliest of four Vedic samhitas, and Romesh Chunder Dutt (whose text makes up this chapter) describes the other samhitas and associated texts in the next section, the Epic Age. Though the date of the *Rig Veda* is uncertain, its composition was surely before 1000 BCE. During this period the term 'Hindu', used by Dutt in the passages below, was not actually in use; it would thus be more accurate to refer to them as the 'Vedic people' and to the deities as Vedic gods. Writing in 1893, R.C. Dutt was unaware of the Harappan Civilization. Recent research has ruled out any conquest or invasion, though many historians still believe that a migration into India took place.

The most widely accepted theory is that the Vedic people entered India after 2000 BCE, when the Harappan Civilization was in decline. If this is correct, however, they did not come into conflict with aborigines or barbarians, but with a highly advanced, literate people who had lived in an urban civilization, albeit one now declining. As Dutt points out, the *Rig Veda* does refer to conflicts. Who were the people involved? Early historians saw conflicts between two main groups of *aryas*, against the *dasa* and *dasyus*, the former being the fair-skinned invaders and the latter the dark-skinned original inhabitants. Recent historical interpretations are more nuanced, however, and reject these theories. In *India's Ancient Past* (2006), R.S. Sharma suggests that '*arya*', used just 36 times in the *Rig Veda*, generally denotes a cultural group who spoke an Indo-Aryan language. He sees the *dasas* as an earlier *arya* group, and the *dasyus* as the original inhabitants. It also must be kept in mind that several scholars believe that there was no migration at all; the Vedic people were indigenous, or else reached the subcontinent at a very early period. Conflicts were therefore between various groups of clans and tribes, not between outsiders and insiders. In addition, as Upinder Singh summarizes in *A History of Ancient and Early Medieval India* (2008), the archaeological and skeletal record reveals no migration between 2000 and 1000 BCE.

R.C. Dutt's account is important for historiography, and for an understanding of how historians viewed the Vedic texts, when the great cities of the Harappan Civilization were yet to be excavated. Indeed these theories, put forward so long ago, of an *arya–dasa/dasyu* divide, of invasion or migration from outside, are still prevalent among many historians and are only now being challenged. Examples of the beautiful Rig Vedic hymns are provided, though today there are many variants of the earlier translations.

There are intriguing similarities between not only Greek and Vedic gods, but also between Norse and Celtic deities, which all point to the cultural similarities that link Indo-European speakers.

WARS WITH THE ABORIGINES

The history of [...] the Vedic Age is the history of the conquest of the Punjab from the aborigines. And although we have no connected account left to us of the main incidents of this war of centuries, yet the *Rig Veda* – the collection of hymns composed in this early age – is full of stirring passages and martial songs, which enable us to realize the war-like ardour of the Hindu colonists and conquerors of the Punjab.

They cleared the primeval forests, beat back or exterminated the dark-skinned children of the soil, widened the limits of cultivation and of civilization, and spread Hindu dominion and Hindu religion from generation to generation, and from century to century. The story of the extermination of barbarians by civilized races is much the same in ancient and in modern times; and the banks of the Indus and its tributaries were cleared of their aborigines 1,800 years before Christ, much in the same way in which the banks of the great Mississippi have been cleared, 1,800 years after Christ, of the many brave and war-like Indian tribes, who lived, and ruled, and hunted in the primeval woods of America. The white man came [...] with a greed of conquest; he cleared trackless and impenetrable forests, built fair villages and towns on the sites of fastnesses and swamps, and turned a dark and unexplored continent into haunts of civilized men, and the seat of [European] forms of religion, society, and government. The dark man had no place in this new world; he perished, struggling bravely but vainly in his last fastness, or he left the land and fled to wilder and remoter regions, as yet untrod by the white conquerors.

Indra, the rain-giving sky, is also the martial deity of the conquering Hindus, and in the hymns addressed to this deity we find numerous invocations for help against the dark aborigines called the *Dasyu* or the *Dasa*, who fought with all the obstinacy and skill of barbarians. A few such passages will give us a true and realistic idea of this obstinately contested war of centuries.

'Indra, invoked by many, and accompanied by his fleet companions, has destroyed by his thunderbolt the Dasyus and Simyus who dwelt on earth, and distributed the fields to his white worshippers. The thunderer makes the sun shine, and the rain descend.'
Rig Veda, I 100, 18.

'*Indra with his thunderbolt, and full of vigour, has destroyed the towns of the Dasyus and wandered freely. O holder of the thunderbolt! be thou cognizant of our hymns, and cast thy weapon against the Dasyu, and increase the vigour and the fame of the A'rya.*'
Rig Veda, I. 103, 3.

'*Indira protects his A'rya worshipper in wars. He who protects him on countless occasions protects him in all wars. He subdues for the benefit of (Aryan) men, the races who do not perform sacrifices. He flays the enemy of his dark skin, kills him, and reduces him to ashes. He burns those who are harmful and cruel.*'
Rig Veda, I. 130, 8.

'*O Destroyer of foes! Collect together the heads of these marauding troops, and crush them with thy wide foot! They foot is wide.*

'*O Indra! destroy the power of these marauding troops. Throw them into the vile pit, the vast and vile pit!*

'*O Indra! thou hast destroyed three times fifty such troops! People extol thus thy deed; but it is nothing to thy prowess!*'
Rig Veda, I. 133, 2-4.

'*O Indra! Rishis still extol thy ancient deed of prowess. Thou hast destroyed many marauders to put an end to the war; thou hast stormed the towns of enemies who worship no gods; thou hast bent the weapons of enemies who worship no gods.*'
Rig Veda, I. 174, 7, 8.

It will be seen from hymns like these that the natural feeling of hostility between the A'rya or Aryan conquerors and the *Dasyu* aborigines was further embittered by difference in religion and religious rites. The Aryan believed in the 'bright gods' of Nature, in the sky, the sun, the fire, and the storms; he sacrificed to them daily, and wherever he conquered, he carried with him his worship of Nature's deities and his cherished sacrificial rites. The dark-skinned *Dasyu* of the Punjab believed in no such gods, and performed no sacrifices, and this impiety and irreligion brought death and destruction on him, according to the belief of the sacrificing Hindu. Again and again the Hindu appealed to his martial deity, and confidently invoked his aid against men who were without faith and without rites.

Here and there we come across the names of wily barbarians, who continued the unequal combat with obstinacy, concealed themselves in fastnesses or in swamps, and harassed and plundered the Hindu settlers when they could.

'Kuyava gets scent of the wealth of others and plunders it. He lives in water and pollutes it. His wives bathe in the stream; may they be drowned in the depths of the Sifa River.

'Ayu lives in water in a secret fastness. He flourishes amidst the rise of waters. The rivers Anjasí, Kulisí, and Vírapatní protect him with their waters.'
Rig Veda, I. 104, 3, 4.

'The fleet Krishna lived on the banks of the Ansumatí river with ten thousand troops. Indra of his own wisdom became cognizant of this loud-yelling chief. He destroyed the marauding host for the benefit of (Aryan) men.

'Indra said, "I have seen the fleet Krishna. He is lurking in the hidden region near the Ansumatí, like the sun in a cloud. O Maruts! I desire you to engage in the fight and destroy him."

'The fleet Krishna then appeared shining on the banks of the Ansumatí. Indra took Brihaspati as his ally, and destroyed the fleet and godless army.'
Rig Veda, VIII. 96, 13–15.

How clearly these brief but realistic passages describe the running fight which was kept up by the retreating barbarians with the invincible conquerors. Renowned black warriors with their families and tribes concealed themselves in pathless woods, and in swamps and morasses made impregnable by the rise of rivers. From these unexplored wilds, they obtained information of the property and wealth and cattle of the white men living in fair villages; suddenly they proclaimed their presence by their uncouth yells, and in a moment the work of destruction was done, and the fleet plunderers disappeared as suddenly as they came. The colonists would not tamely bear such attacks; and often a raid by the aborigines was followed by a more determined and destructive expedition by the white settlers. Forests were explored and cleared; swamps and rivers were crossed; strong fastnesses were taken; and the offending chief and his 'fleet and godless army' were at last hunted down and exterminated. It was by such reprisals that new forests were explored and brought under cultivation, river after river was crossed, settlement after settlement arose on the sites of swamps and woods, and the great Aryan nation marched east ward until they fairly colonized the whole of the Punjab.

We know that the Spaniards owed their successes in America to a great extent to their horses, animals previously unknown to the American Indians, and regarded by them with a strange terror. It would seem that the war horses of the Hindus inspired the black aborigines of India with equal terror. The following passage from a hymn to *Dadhikra*, or the deified war horse, will be read with interest:

'*As people shout and raise a cry after a thief who has purloined a garment, even so the enemies yell and shout at the sight of Dadhikra! As birds make a noise at the sight of the hungry hawk in his descent, even so the enemies yell and shout at the sight of Dadhikra, careering in quest of plunder, of food and cattle.'*

'*Enemies fear Dadhikra, who is radiant and destructive as a thunderbolt. When he beats back a thousand men, he becomes excited and uncontrollable in his strength.'*
Rig Veda, IV. 38, 5, 8.

Equally terrible to the aboriginal warriors was the war drum of the Hindus, of which we find an account in hymn VI. 47. 'The drum sounds loud to proclaim to all men (the hour of battle). Our leaders have mounted their steeds and have formed in order. O Indra! let our warriors who fight in chariots win victory.'

In another remarkable hymn many of the weapons of war then used by the Hindus have been described, and the composition therefore has a historical value.

1. '*When the battle is nigh, and the warrior marches in his armour, he appears like the cloud! Warrior, let not thy person be pierced; be victorious; let thy armour protect thee.*

2. '*We will win the cattle with the bow; we will win with the bow; we will conquer the fierce and proud enemy with the bow! May the bow foil the designs of the enemy! We will spread our conquests on all sides with the bow.*

3. '*The string of the bow when pulled approaches the ear of the archer. It whispers words of consolation to him, and it clasps the arrow with a sound, as a loving wife clasps her husband.*

5. '*The quiver is like the parent of many arrows, the arrows are like its children. It hangs, sounding, on the back of the warrior, it furnishes arrows in battle and conquers the enemy.*

6. '*The expert charioteer stands on his chariot and drives his horses wheresoever he will. The reins restrain the horses from behind. Sing of their glory!*

7. *'The horses raise the dust with their hoofs, and career over the fields with their chariots with loud neighings. They do not retreat but trample the marauding enemies under their hoofs.'*
Rig Veda, VI. 75.

Well might the uncivilized children of the soil retreat before these invincible conquerors who fought from their chariots, whose arrows were pointed with deer-horn or iron, and who were protected by their armour. We know from other passages that Hindu warriors also used helmets and shoulder plates or shields, javelins, and battle axes, and sharp-edged swords. Against troops so armed and led in order, the barbarians could offer little effective opposition. Occasionally there was war between hostile Hindu tribes; and a battle between two opposing Hindu armies, fighting with their chariots and horses, their armour, javelins, and arrows, was not unlike those battles repeated day after day between the Greeks and the Trojans, of which we have such vivid accounts left to us in the pages of Homer.

For it should be remembered that the Hindu tribes, although constantly engaged in war with the aborigines, had nevertheless their petty jealousies and quarrels among themselves, which not unoften broke out into internecine wars. All the Hindu tribes of the Punjab were brave fighting nations; their kings were warriors and leaders of men; and jealousies and hostilities among rival tribes and rival chiefs were inevitable. Such wars became more frequent after the aborigines had been entirely subdued or expelled, and there was no common enemy to conquer. Tribe often rose against tribe, and state against state; and in one historically remarkable hymn we are told that no less than ten kings combined against the great king Sudas – the greatest hero of the *Rig Veda* – and Sudas was victorious over them all. The white-robed Tritsus or Vasishthas, who were the priests of

Sudas's court, were proud of the ever-memorable day of victory, and have celebrated it in verse which we must quote in full.

1. 'O Leaders, Indra and Varuna! your worshippers, relying on your help, and seeking to win cattle, have marched eastwards with their weapons. Crush, Indra and Varuna, your enemies, whether Dasas or A'ryas, and defend Sudas with your protection.

2. 'Where men raise their banners and meet in battle, where nothing seems to favour us, where the men look up to the sky and tremble, then, O Indra and Varuna! help us and speak to us.

3. 'O Indra and Varuna! the ends of the earth seem to be lost, and the noise ascends to the skies. The troops of the enemy are approaching. O Indra and Varuna! whoever listen to our prayers, come near us with your protection.

4. 'O Indra and Varuna! you pierced the yet-unassailed Bheda and saved Sudas. You listened to the prayers of the Tritsus in the hour of battle. Their priestly vocation bore fruit.

5. 'O Indra and Varuna! the weapons of the enemy assail me in all directions; the foes assail me among marauding men. You are the owners of both kinds of wealth. Save us in the day of battle.

6. 'Both parties invoked Indra and Varuna for wealth at the time of war. But in this battle you protected Sudas with the Tritsus who were attacked by ten kings.

7. 'O Indra and Varuna! the ten kings who did not perform sacrifices were unable, though combined, to beat Sudas.

8. 'You gave vigour, Indra and Varuna, to Sudas, when surrounded by ten chiefs; when the white-robed Tritsus, wearing braided hair, worshipped you with oblations and hymns.

9. 'Indra destroys the enemy in battle; Varuna protects our pious rites. We invoke you with our praises. Bestow on us felicity, O Indra and Varuna.

10. 'May Indra, Varuna, Mitra and Aryaman, grant us wealth and a spacious home. May the lustre of Aditi be harmless to us; we recite the praise of the divine Savitri.'
Rig Veda, VII. 83.

MANNERS AND CIVILIZATION

Wherever the conquerors came, they cleared forests and introduced agriculture, which was the main industry of the ancient, as it is of modern Hindus. The very name, A'rya, by which the conquerors called themselves, is derived from a root which indicates tilling, and there is a beautiful short hymn on ploughing, which may be quoted as the oldest pastoral in the Aryan world.

1. 'We will till this field with the Lord of the Field; may he nourish our horses; may he bless us thereby.

2. 'O Lord of the Field! bestow on us sweet and pure and butter-like and delicious and copious rain, even as cows give us milk. May the Lords of Water bless us.

3. 'May the crops be sweet unto us; may the skies and the rains and the firmament be full of sweetness; may the Lord of the Field be gracious to us. We will follow him unharmed by foes.

4. 'Let the oxen work merrily; let the men work merrily; let the plough move on merrily. Fasten the traces merrily; ply the goad merrily.

5. 'O Suna and Síra! accept this hymn. Moisten this earth with the rain you have created in the sky.

6. 'O fortunate Síta (Furrow)! proceed onwards, we pray unto thee. Do thou bestow on us wealth and an abundant crop.

7. 'May Indra accept this Síta; may Púshan lead her onwards. May she be filled with water and yield us corn year after year.

8. 'Let the ploughshares turn up the sod merrily; let the men follow the oxen merrily; let the god of rains moisten the earth with sweet rains. O Suna and Síra! bestow on us happiness.'

Rig Veda, IV. 57.

This ancient agricultural song is marked by that simplicity and joyousness in active pursuits which mark all the most ancient effusions of the Hindus.

But cultivation on the Punjab on an extended scale was impossible, except by means of sinking wells and digging irrigation channels, and it is not remarkable that we find allusions to such contrivances in the songs of the *Rig Veda*. Pastureland too was extensive; chiefs and leaders of men owned large herds of cattle, and warriors and poets prayed to the gods for increase of cattle and of wealth. Society was yet in its infancy, and was not yet marked by a hard and fast division into ranks; and we find in the *Rig Veda*, as in the pages of Homer, that the same chiefs who owned broad acres and pastured large herds of cattle in times of peace, distinguished themselves as leaders of men in times of war, and returned home after victories to worship their gods at their own firesides with copious libations, and with cakes or the flesh of victims. The earliest records and traditions of all Aryan nations point to this simple stage of civilization, when communities lived by agriculture and by pasture, when division into classes was little known, when all able-bodied men were warriors, and when great chiefs and leaders returned with their people to the plough after the war was over. Such is the picture of early Hindu life which the *Rig Veda* presents to us.

Barley and wheat were the principal produce of the field, and rice was as yet unknown. Animal food was however also largely indulged in, the bull and the ram were frequently sacrificed, and even the flesh of the horse was relished by the earlier Hindus, although in later times the sacrifice of the horse was reserved for imperial festivities only. The juice of the soma plant was a favourite drink, and was copiously used at sacrifices, and the poets of the *Rig Veda* go into ecstasies over the virtues and powers of this exhilarating beverage. In the end Soma was worshipped as a deity, as we shall see in the following chapter.

The simpler arts of civilized life were practised by the Punjab Hindus. Carpentry and weaving were well known, and considerable progress was made in the working of metals, of gold and silver and of iron. The weapons of war and various gold ornaments of which we find frequent mention show the progress made in these arts.

Of armour and helmets, javelins, swords, and arrows we have already made mention. Three thousand warriors covered with mail are spoken of in one remarkable verse (VI. 27, 6). In other places we are told of necklaces and bracelets and anklets, of golden plates for the breast, and of golden crowns for the head (V. 53 and 54, &c.). All these allusions show that a considerable advance was made by the Punjab Hindus in the working of metals.

Architecture too had made some advance, and there are allusions to 'mansions with a thousand pillars'. But we find no distinct mention of sculpture; and the religion of the early Hindus, which was not idolatrous, did not foster that art.

The rules of social life were simple and patriarchal. The father of the family was its head, his sons and grandsons with their wives often lived under the same roof, and owned their lands and herds in common. The sacred fire was lighted in the house of every pious householder, the women of the family prepared the soma wine and other sacrificial requisites, and the benignant gods of the sky, firmament, and earth were invoked in simple hymns to be present at the sacrifices, and to bestow health and progeny and wealth on the sacrificers. Wives joined their husbands at these domestic sacrifices, and some beautiful hymns are still preserved to us which are said to have been composed by female worshippers.

There were no unhealthy restrictions upon Hindu women in those days, no rules to keep them secluded or debarred from their legitimate place in society. A girl generally selected her own husband, but her parents' wishes were for the most part respected. We have frequent allusions to careful and industrious wives who superintended the arrangements of the house, and, like the dawn, roused everyone in the morning and sent him to his work. Girls who remained unmarried obtained a share in the paternal property. Widows could re-marry after the death of their husbands.

The ceremony of marriage was an appropriate one, and the promises which the bride and the bridegroom made were suitable to the occasion. We will quote a few verses from a remarkable hymn on this subject:

(*Address to the bride and bridegroom.*) '*Do ye remain here together; do not be separated. Enjoy food of various kinds; remain in your own home, and enjoy happiness in company of your children and grandchildren.*'

(*The bride and bridegroom say.*) '*May Prajapati bestow on us children; may Aryaman keep us united till old age.*'

(*Address to the bride.*) '*Enter, O bride! with auspicious signs the home of thy husband. Do good to our male servants and to our female servants, and to our cattle.*

'*Be thy eyes free from anger; minister to the happiness of thy husband; do good to our cattle. May thy mind be cheerful, may thy beauty be bright. Be the mother of heroic sons, and be devoted to the gods. Do good to our male servants and to our female servants, and to our cattle.*

'*O Indra! make this lady fortunate and the mother of worthy sons. Let ten sons be born of her, so that there may be eleven men with the husband.*'

(Address to the bride.) 'May thou have influence over thy father-in-law and thy mother-in-law, and be as a queen over thy sister-in-law and brother-in-law.'

(The bride and bridegroom say.) 'May all the gods unite our hearts; may Matarisvan and Dhatri and the goddess of speech unite us together.' **Rig Veda, X. 85, 42 to 47.**

These few verses give us a clear insight into the patriarchal family system of the olden days. The bride was a newcomer into her husband's family, and she was received with appropriate injunctions. The male servants, the female servants, and the very cattle were of the family, and the bride was asked to be kind and considerate and good to them all. Free from anger, and with a cheerful mind, she must not only minister to her husband's happiness, but be devoted to the gods worshipped in the family, and be kind to all its dependants. She must extend her gentle influence over her husband's father and mother, she must keep under due control his brothers and sisters, and be the queen of the household. And thus she must remain, united to her husband until old age, the virtual mistress of a large and patriarchal family, and respected and honoured as Hindu women were honoured in ancient times.

Polygamy was allowed in ancient India as it was allowed among all ancient nations; but it was probably confined to kings and great chiefs only. The ordinary people were content with one wife. Sons inherited the property of their father, and in the absence of sons, the daughter's son or some other boy might be adopted.

Burial was probably the first form of funeral ceremony among ancient Hindus; but this was soon followed by cremation, and the ashes were then buried in the earth. A few verses from the funeral service will interest, and will show that the hopes of a future world cheered the last moments of a Hindu's life in ancient times, as they do at the present day.

'O thou deceased! proceed to the same place where our forefathers
have gone, by the same path which they followed. The two kings Yama
and Varuna are pleased with the offerings; go and meet them.

'Proceed to that happy heaven and mix with our forefathers. Meet
Yama, and reap the fruits of thy virtuous deeds. Leave sin behind, enter
thy home.

'O ye shades! leave this place, go away, move away. For the
forefathers have prepared a place for the deceased. That place is beautiful
with day, with sparkling waters and light. Yama assigns this place for
the dead.'

Rig Veda, X. 14, 7 to 9.

It is remarkable that there is no mention of a hell and its tortures
in the *Rig Veda.*

RELIGION

The religion of the Hindus in the first or Vedic epoch was the
worship of Nature leading up to Nature's God.

The hardy and enterprising conquerors of the Punjab were
a warlike race with a capacity for active enjoyments, and an
appreciation of all that was lovely and joyous in nature. They
looked up to the beauteous and bright sky, and worshipped it
under the name of *Dyu*, equivalent to the Greek *Zeus* and the first
syllable of the Latin *Jupiter*. They also called the sky of day the
name of *Mitra*, corresponding to the Zend *Mithra*; and they called
the sky of night *Varuna*, corresponding to the Greek *Ouranos*.
These common names under which the sky god was worshipped
by the different Aryan nations of the ancient times prove that the

sky was worshipped under these names by the primitive Aryans in their original home.

But while the Hindu Aryans of the Punjab continued to worship the ancient sky god under the ancient names of Dyu, Mitra, and Varuna, they paid special homage to the *sky that rains*, which they called *Indra*. For in India the rise of rivers and the luxuriance of crops depend on the rain-giving sky; and in course of time Indra became the most prominent deity in the Hindu pantheon. He was conceived as a warlike deity, battling with the clouds, called Vritra, to obtain copious torrents of rain for man, and fighting with the demons of darkness, called Panis, to restore to the world the light of the morning. The Maruts or storm gods were supposed to help Indra in his contest with the reluctant clouds, for in India the first showers of the rainy season are often attended with storms and thunder. And the deity, at once so beneficent and so warlike, was naturally a favourite with the martial and conquering Hindus; and as we have seen before, they constantly invoked him to lead them against the retreating barbarians, and to bestow on the conquerors new lands and wealth, cattle and progeny.

It will help us to enter into the spirit of the warlike and simple Hindu worshippers of the olden times if we read some verses describing the battles of Indra with the cloud.

1. *'We sing the heroic deeds which were done by Indra the thunderer. He destroyed Ahi (clouds), and caused rains to descend, and opened out the paths for the mountain streams to roll.*

2. *'Indra slew Ahi resting on the mountains; Tvashtri had made the far-reaching thunderbolt for him. Water in torrents flowed towards the sea, as cows run eagerly towards their calves.'*

3. 'Impetuous as a bull, Indra quaffed the soma juice; he drank the soma libations offered in the three sacrifices. He then took the thunderbolt, and thereby slew the eldest of the Ahis.

4. 'When you killed the eldest of the Ahis, you destroyed the contrivances of the artful contrivers. You cleared the sun and the morning and the sky, and left no enemies behind.

5. 'Indra with his all-destructive thunderbolt slew the darkling Vritra (clouds) and lopped his limbs. Ahi now lies touching the earth like the trunk of a tree felled by the axe.

8. 'Glad waters are bounding over the prostrate body as rivers flow over fallen banks. Vritra when alive had withheld the waters by his power, Ahi now lies prostrate under the waters.'

Rig Veda, I. 32.

Let us contrast with this the following verses addressed to Varuna the sky god of righteousness, and we shall perceive how the ancient Hindus worshipped the sky in its different aspects under different names, now as the Lord of tempests and of rain, now as the Lord of mercy.

3. 'O Varuna! with an anxious heart I ask thee about my sins. I have gone to learned men to make the inquiry; the sages have all said to me, "Varuna is displeased with thee".

4. 'O Varuna! for what deed of mine dost thou wish to destroy thy friend, thy worshipper? O thou of irresistible power, declare it to me, so that I may quickly bend in adoration and come to thee.

5. 'O Varuna! deliver us from the sins of our fathers. Deliver us from the sins committed in our person. O royal Varuna! deliver Vasishtha like a calf from its tether, like a thief who has feasted on a stolen animal.

6. 'O *Varuna! all this sin is not wilfully committed by us. Error or wine, anger or dice, or even thoughtlessness has begotten sin. Even an elder brother leads his younger astray. Sin is begotten even in our dreams.*

7. '*Freed from sins, I will serve as a slave the god Varuna, who fulfils our wishes and supports us. We are ignorant; may the A'rya god bestow on us knowledge. May the wise deity accept our prayer and bestow on us wealth.*'

Rig Veda, VII. 86.

Next to the sky, the sun was the most prominent object of the worship of the ancient Hindus. *Aditi* was the limitless light of sky, and her sons, the *A'dityas*, were the suns of the different months of the year. *Súrya*, answering to the Greek Helios, the Latin Sol, and the Teuton Tyr, was, however, the most popular name by which the sun was worshipped. *Savitri* is another name of the same deity, and the sacred hymn, the Gayatrí, which is still repeated every morning by pious Brahmans all over India, as the first act of their daily devotions, is a verse addressed to their deity. It runs thus in translation:

'*We meditate on the desirable light of the divine Savitri who influences our pious rites.*'

Rig Veda, III. 62, 10.

Viewed in other aspects the sun had other names. Pasture was still extensively followed by the Punjab Hindus as a means of living, and the simple shepherds looked on the sun as their guide and protector in all their migrations, and called him *Púshan*.

1. '*O Púshan! help us to finish our journey, and remove all dangers. O son of the cloud! do thou march before us.*

2. 'O *Púshan!* do thou remove from our path him who would lead us astray, who strikes and plunders and does wrong.

3. 'Do thou drive away that wily robber who intercepts journeys.

7. 'Lead us so that enemies who intercept may not harm us; lead us by easy and pleasant paths. O *Púshan!* devise means for our safety on this journey.

8. 'Lead us to pleasant tracks covered with green grass; may there not be excessive heat by the way. O *Púshan!* devise means for our safety on this journey.'

Rig Veda, I. 42.

One more name of the sun it is necessary to mention. Vishnu, which in later Hindu mythology has become a name of the Supreme Preserver of all beings, was a name of the sun in the Vedic age. The rising sun, the sun at zenith, and the setting sun were considered the three steps of Vishnu striding across limitless space.

Fire or *Agni* was an object of worship. No sacrifice to the gods could be performed without libations or offerings to the fire, and Agni was therefore considered to be the priest among the gods. But Agni is not only the terrestrial fire in the *Rig Veda*; he is also the fire of the lightning and the sun, and his abode was in heaven. The early sages Bhrigus discovered him there, and Atharvan and Angiras, the first sacrificers, installed him in this world as the protector of men.

Vayu, or the wind, is sometimes invoked in the *Rig Veda*. The *Maruts*, or storm-gods, are oftener invoked, as we have seen before, and are considered the helpers of Indra in obtaining rain for the benefit of man. *Rudra*, the loud-sounding father of the Maruts, is the Thunder, and in later Hindu mythology this name has been appropriately chosen for the Supreme Destroyer of all living beings.

83

We have said that Agni, or fire, received special homage because he was necessary for all sacrifice. The libation of soma juice was similarly regarded sacred, and *Soma* was worshipped as a deity. Similarly, the prayer which accompanied the libations or offerings was also regarded as a deity, and was called *Brahmanaspati*. In later Hindu mythology, Brahman is selected as the name of the Supreme Creator of all living beings.

We have now enumerated the most important gods of the Vedic pantheon, but it is necessary to add a word about the twin gods of the *Rig Veda*, Morning and Evening. Light and Darkness naturally suggested to the early Aryans the idea of twin gods. The sky (Vivasvat) is the father, and the Dawn (Saranyu) is the mother of the twin *Asvins*, and the legend goes on to say that Saranyu ran away from Vivasvat before she gave birth to the twins. We have the same legend in Greek mythology; and Erinnys (answering philologically to Saranyu) ran away from her lover, and gave birth to Areion and Despoina. The original idea is that the ruddy nymph (Dawn and Gloaming) disappears, and gives birth to Light and to Darkness.

But whatever the original conception may have been, the Asvins have lost their primitive character in the *Rig Veda*, and have simply become physician gods, healers of the sick and the wounded, tending mortals with kindness. Similarly the twins, *Yama* and his sister *Yamí* (children of the same parents, Sky and Dawn, and originally implying Light and Darkness), have also acquired a different character in the *Rig Veda*. Of Yamí we hear little, but Yama is the ruler of the future world, the beneficent king of the departed. Clothed in a glorious body, the virtuous live in the future life by the side of Yama, in the realms of light and sparkling waters. Two short extracts from hymns to Yama and to Soma respectively, will illustrate the idea of future life and future felicity which the Hindus of the Vedic age entertained.

1. 'Worship Yama, the son of Vivasvat, with offerings. All men go to him. He takes men of virtuous deeds to the realm of happiness. He clears the way for many.

2. 'Yama first discovered the path for us. That path will not be destroyed again. All living beings will, according to their acts, follow by the path by which our forefathers have gone.'
Rig Veda, X. 14.

7. 'Flowing Soma! take me to that immortal and imperishable abode where light dwells eternal, and which is in heaven. Flow, Soma! for Indra.

8. 'Take me where Yama is king, where are the gates of heaven, and where mighty rivers flow. Take me there and make me immortal. Flow, Soma! for Indra.

9. 'Take me where is the third heaven, where is the third realm of light above the sky, and where one can wander at his will. Take me there, and make me immortal. Flow, Soma! for Indra.

10. 'Take me where every desire is satiated, where Pradhma has his abode, where there is food and contentment. Take me there and make me immortal. Flow, Soma! for Indra.

11. 'Take me where there are pleasures and joys and delights, and where every desire of the anxious heart is satiated. Take me there, and make me immortal. Flow, Soma! for Indra.'
Rig Veda, XI. 113.

The deities named above are the most important gods of the *Rig Veda*. Of goddesses there are only two who have any marked character or individuality, viz., Ushas or Dawn and Sarasvati the river goddess.

There is no lovelier conception in the *Rig Veda* than that of the Dawn, and there are no fresher or more beauteous passages in the lyrical poetry of the ancient world than some of the hymns dedicated to Ushas. She is described as the far extending, many tinted, brilliant Dawn, whose abode is unknown. She harnesses her chariots from afar and comes in radiance and glory. She is the young, the white-robed daughter of the sky, the queen of all earthly treasures. She is like the careful mistress of the house who rouses everyone from his slumbers and sends him to his work. And yet she is radiant as a bride decorated by her mother for the auspicious ceremony, and displaying her charms to the view. Such are the fond epithets and beautiful similes with which the Hindu Aryans greeted the fresh and lovely mornings of a tropical sky.

It is remarkable that the Hellenic Aryans of the time of Homer regarded the lovely Eos with much the same feeling of poetic fondness. But the mystery is explained when we learn that Eos is the same name as Ushas, and that the other Greek names of the Dawn correspond philologically to Hindu names of the same deity, and there can be little doubt, therefore, that the Hindu and the Hellenic Aryans alike derived their conceptions and their names of the Dawn goddess from the primitive Aryans.

This remark does not apply in the case of Sarasvatí, who is purely a Hindu goddess. Sarasvatí is the name of a river in the Punjab, deemed to be holy because of the religious rites which were performed on its banks and the sacred hymns uttered there. By a natural development of ideas she came to be considered the goddess of those hymns or the goddess of speech, in which character she is worshipped in India to the present day.

From the foregoing account the reader will perceive that there was an essential difference between the Hindu gods of the Vedic age and the Greek gods of the Homeric age. The Hindu conceptions go nearer to the original Nature worship of the primitive Aryans, even as the Sanskrit language is nearer and closer than the Greek to the original Aryan tongue. Among the Greeks of the Homeric age, the gods and goddesses have already attained a marked individuality; their history, their character, their deeds, engage our attention; their connection with the powers and manifestations of Nature almost escapes us. The Hindu gods of the Vedic age, on the contrary, are obviously still Nature's powers and manifestations; they have scarcely any other character or history. We can more clearly identify Dyu with the sky than Zeus, and Ahana and Dahana are more obviously and manifestly the Dawn than Athena and Daphne. The Hindu conceptions are more ancient, more archaic, more true to their original sources. The Greek conceptions are more developed, and have passed farther from the domain of Nature worship to that of polytheism.

It is probably owing to this difference that the Hindus attained to a conception of the one supreme God sooner than the Greeks. It was an easy step from the worship of natural powers to the conception of Nature's God; but it was not easy for the Greeks, who had already invested their gods with distinct characters and histories, to set them aside and rise to the conception of one God. The Greeks of the Homeric age failed, therefore, to rise to the worship of the Supreme Deity, which the Hindus succeeded in doing even in the Vedic Age.

In some of the latest hymns of the *Rig Veda* we find that the worshipper correctly interpreted the names of the different gods as only different names of the same great Power, the Father of all, the Creator of all.

1. *'The all-wise Father saw clearly, and after due reflection created the sky and the earth in their watery form, and touching each other. When their boundaries were stretched afar, then the sky and the earth became separated.*

2. *'The Creator of all is great; he creates and supports all; he is above all, and sees all; he is beyond the seat of the seven Rishis. So the wise men say, and the wise men obtain fulfilment of their desires.*

3. 'He who has given life, he who is the Creator, he who knows all the places in this universe, – he is one, although he bears the names of many gods. Other beings wish to know him.'
Rig Veda, X. 82.

This is the earliest indication of Hindu monotheism, that monotheism which has continued to be the true religion of the Hindus for over three thousand years, in spite of the legends and allegories and 'the names of many gods' with which the popular mind has been fed from age to age.

One more extract, a sublime hymn to the same supreme God, will enable us to understand this the earliest phase of Hindu monotheism.

1. 'In the beginning the Golden Child existed. He was the Lord of all from his birth. He placed this earth and sky in their proper places. Whom shall we worship with offerings?

2. 'Him who has given life and strength, whose will is obeyed by all gods, whose shadow is immortality, and whose slave is Death. Whom shall we worship with offerings?

3. 'Him who by his power is the sole King of all the living beings that see and move; him who is the Lord of all bipeds and quadrupeds. Whom shall we worship with offerings?

4. 'Him by whose power these shadowy mountains have been made, and whose creations are this earth and its oceans; him whose arms are these quarters of space. Whom we worship with offerings?

5. 'Him who has fixed in their places this sky and this earth; him who has established the heavens and the highest heaven; him who has measured the firmament. Whom shall we worship with offerings?

6. 'Him by whom the sounding sky and earth have been fixed and expanded; him whom the resplendent sky and earth own as Almighty; him

*by whose support the sun rises and gains lustre. Whom shall we worship
with offerings?'*
Rig Veda, X. 121.

It will thus be seen that the religion of the sturdy conquerors
of the Punjab was a progressive religion, leading from Nature up
to Nature's God. We see the entire journey of the human mind in
the *Rig Veda* – a work unique in the world for this reason – from
the simple, child-like admiration of the ruddy dawn or the breaking
storm, to the sublime effort to grasp the mysteries of creation and its
great Creator.

While a few of the advanced spirits of the age rose to this height,
the nation still continued to invoke their beloved gods, and poured
libations and offered cakes to them with their prayers. There were
no temples and no hereditary priests. Each pious householder, each
patriarch of his family, lighted the sacrificial fire in his own home,
poured the soma juice in libations, and prayed to the gods for health
and crops, for cattle and progeny.

Great kings and chiefs, however, performed their religious
sacrifices with ostentatious prodigality, and families of priests were
supported by such chiefs and presided at all royal observances. In
course of time such families, who followed the same vocation from
generation to generation, became known for their skill in composing
or reciting hymns and performing rites. Different collections of
hymns were preserved in such families, handed down from father to
son, and preserved by memory alone, and it is to this pious custom
that the Aryan world owes the preservation of the earliest of Aryan
compositions now extant, i.e., the hymns of the *Rig Veda*.

But although certain families followed the vocation of priests from
father to son, and were therefore rewarded by princes and respected

by the people, there was no hereditary distinction yet between the priest and the people, and the caste system of India was unknown in the Vedic Age. The only insuperable distinction which existed in that age was between the conquerors and the conquered, the Hindus and the Aborigines, the *A'ryans* and the *Dasyus*, as they are styled in the *Rig Veda*. Among the Aryan Hindus themselves no such distinction was yet known, and the patriarchs and leaders of the Punjab Hindus composed their hymns, fought their battles, and ploughed their fields before the castes of the Brahmans, Kshatriyas, and Vaisyas were formed.

THE EPIC AGE

The Epic Age sees the emergence of new states in the Gangetic plains. They cannot strictly be called 'Hindu states', as the term Hindu was not used for religion at this time.

The two great epics, the *Mahabharata* and *Ramayana*, represent this age. The period to which they refer is uncertain, but it is certainly later than that of the *Rig Veda*. The basic story of the *Mahabharata*, a lengthy epic with 100,000 verses, is the story of a conflict between cousins, the 100 Kauravas and the five Pandavas, ending in a mammoth war in which kings from far and near took part. The war led to devastation on all sides. There are numerous sub-stories within the epic and the famous and most sacred text, the *Bhagavad Gita*, also forms part of it.

The date of the great war described in the *Mahabharata* is given by Dutt (whose text makes up this chapter) as the thirteenth-century BCE, but historians have provided widely divergent dates, ranging from 3100 to 1000 BCE. One also has to keep in mind that this is an epic, not a historical text. A war, if it took place at all, may have been different from the conflict described. The core regions of these texts are not the Indus valleys of the northwest. While the *Mahabharata* war takes place in the upper Gangetic plains, around the city of Delhi, the events of the *Ramayana*, the other great epic, occur further east, in the regions of present eastern Uttar Pradesh, extending into Bihar.

The Later Vedic texts, composed after the *Rig Veda*, also describe this period. These include three later Vedic *samhitas*, the *Yajur Veda*, *Sama Veda* and *Atharva Veda*, along with associated texts of the Brahmanas, Aranyakas and Upanishads. In these texts we learn about the new states being formed, among them Kuru, Panchala, Kashi and Koshala. These were known in Buddhist texts as *Mahajanapadas*, or 'great states'.

Archaeology presents a compelling picture of this region, but most of the archaeological discoveries were made long after the time in which Dutt wrote. The earliest occupation in the Gangetic plains is represented by Neolithic cultures, followed by Late Harappan sites, Ochre Colour Pottery sites and Copper Hoard sites. These three were roughly contemporary, dating from around 2000 to 1200 BCE. They were followed by a culture represented by Black and Red Ware, and after that by Painted Grey Ware. Although there was migration from the west, therefore, people were already living in the region. Attempts have been made by historians and archaeologists such as B.B. Lal to equate the archaeological cultures with people and kingdoms mentioned in the Later Vedic texts and the epics, but the validity of this remains uncertain. Dutt refers to the Kurus and Panchalas, and to the Kauravas and Pandavas, but his equation of the Pandavas with the Panchalas is unlikely. Contrary to his view, polyandry was known in ancient India, and in fact still exists in certain regions, for instance the Jaunsar Bawar region of the mountainous state of present-day Uttarakhand. However, it was never common or widespread. Dutt also describes other kingdoms in the region and reflects on aspects of life and religion. We cannot presume, as he does, that there was one language, culture and religion in this area. Even Rig Vedic Sanskrit shows evidence of borrowing from other languages, while the various archaeological cultures suggest that different groups lived in the region.

As larger settled states emerged, new developments in religion took place. These are revealed in the Later Vedic texts and in the Upanishads, which contain a profound philosophy.

HINDU KINGDOMS ON THE GANGES

Kurus and Panchalas

When the Hindus had conquered and settled in the wide extent of country from the Indus to the Sutlej and the Sarasvati, they were not long in sending out colonies farther east, towards the Ganges. The stream of emigrants and colonists increased from age to age, until the banks of the Ganges were studded with fair villages and towns surpassing in wealth and civilization those of the motherland, Punjab. In the *Rig Veda* the home of the Hindus is the Punjab, and the allusions to the distant shores of the Ganges are rare. In the literature of the next succeeding epoch, which we may call the Epic Age, the shores of the Ganges are the home of most renowned and civilized Hindu kingdoms; the mother country of the Punjab is already thrown into the shade.

Among the colonists who emigrated from the Punjab to the banks of the Ganges, the Kurus and the Panchalas were not the least distinguished. The Kurus were originally known under the name of Bharatas, and had figured in the wars of Sudas, of which we have spoken. Numbers of them left their home and migrated eastwards, until, in the fourteenth century before Christ, they had founded a flourishing kingdom on the upper course of the Ganges. The nation was still known as the Bharatas, or under the newer name of Kurus, from the name of their kings, and they built their capital at Hastinapura, on the Ganges.

The Panchalas also came from the Punjab. The Punjab Hindus, or some tribes among them, are called in the *Rig Veda*, Pancha Jana or Pancha Krishti, i.e., the 'five tribes', or the 'five agricultural races', and it is probable that the descendants of these races colonized the shores of the Ganges under the name of the Panchalas or 'five tribes'. They settled immediately to the south of the Bharatas or Kurus, and had founded a powerful kingdom there by the fourteenth century before Christ, and called their capital Kampilya.

Other nations from the Punjab also came and settled on the course of the Upper Ganges and the Jumna, among whom the Yadavas, the Matsyas, and the Surasenas were the most important. They are known to us from the share which they took in the great war, of which we will speak farther on.

The Kurus and the Panchalas lived in peace and friendly rivalry for a long time, and developed a civilization surpassing that of their sturdy and rough ancestors in the Punjab. Kings had polished courts, and delighted in assembling the wise and the learned of the age, who held controversies on morals, religion, and philosophy. Priests rejoiced in the performance of elaborate sacrifices, lasting for days, or weeks, or years, for the edification of monarchs; and were rewarded according to their learning and their merits. Learned men received pupils for education, and all Aryan Hindus made over their children at an early age to the charge of such teachers or *Gurus*.

Every boy lived with his Guru for years together, served him in a menial capacity, begged alms for his support, tended his flocks, swept his house, and acquired from him from day to day, and from year to year, the sacred knowledge of the Vedas and of other branches of learning which were the cherished heritage of the ancient Hindus. After caving the Guru, and rewarding him handsomely, some young men prosecuted their studies further in *Parishads*, answering to modern universities, where a number of teachers bestowed instruction in different subjects; and after the completion of their education they returned to their homes, married, and settled down as householders.

The sacrificial fire was lighted on the occasion of the marriage, and every pious Hindu kept up the fire in his house, and offered to it libations and offerings as required by his religion. The hymns of the Veda were still uttered at the sacrifices, and the same religion, the same customs and rites, the same common language, prevailed among the different Hindu communities which flourished on the Ganges and the Jumna over three thousand years ago.

Indeed, as we study the state of the Hindu races of this epoch, each race forming a separate community and a kingdom of its own, and all races rejoicing in the same language, the same religion, and the same common civilization and manners, we are strongly reminded of the Greek cities which flourished side by side before the Peloponnesian war. Rivalries, and even hostilities, were as common among the Hindu races as among the Greek cities, while communications of a more friendly nature kept up their mutual relations. The schools of learning of the different races vied with each other, and the Parishads of the Kurus and the Panchalas attracted large numbers of students from other nations.

In the midst of all this friendly rivalry, the Hindu tribes never relaxed their preparations for war. Princes of the royal houses and of the military classes were early trained in arms as in arts, and were familiar with the bow and the arrow, the sword, the javelin, and the *chakra* or quoit. Jealousies among the different races broke out not unoften into open hostilities; and, as if to complete the parallel between the Indian states and the Greek cities, there was a great and sanguinary war in the thirteenth century before Christ, answering to the Peloponnesian war of Greece, in which all the known Hindu tribes of northern India joined, and which ended in great carnage and slaughter.

This war forms the subject of the great Hindu epic known as the *Mahabharata*; and, as might be expected, the real causes and events of the struggle are lost in fables and myths. The war was waged between the great races, the Kurus or Bharatas and the Panchalas, and the name of the epic signifies 'the Great Bharata'.

Neither the Kurus nor the Panchalas, however, are the heroes of the epic as it has come down to us. The Pancha Pandava, or the five sons of Pandu, are the heroes, and their common wife, the daughter of the king of the Panchalas, is the heroine. The origin of this fable of the five Pandavas and of their common wife, which now forms the central story of the Hindu epic, has given rise to much discussion, into which it is needless to enter. It is certain that this central story is a myth.

The most probable supposition is that the Pandavas were a distinct race, who helped or led the Panchalas in the war; that the race is metaphorically represented in the epic as five brothers, and that their alliance with the Panchalas is metaphorically represented as their marrying a maiden of the Panchala house. Polyandry was unknown to the Hindus of ancient India, as it is to the Hindus of the present day.

It has also been supposed that at an age subsequent to the time of the war, and when kings of the Pandava race wielded supreme power, the epic was first compiled from ballads, legends, or recollections relating to the great contest. Naturally, therefore, the supposed forefathers of the ruling race were represented as the heroes of the strife; and although belonging to a distinct race, they were represented as cousins of the Kuru princes, so that later generations might not look upon them as usurpers.

From what has been stated above, it is apparent that we shall seek in vain in the epic for the real incidents of the war. But, nevertheless, it throws much light on the age of which we are now speaking, and no history of India, therefore, is complete without some account, however brief, of the war, even as disguised in the existing epic.

A king of the Kurus left two sons, of whom Dhritarashtra, the elder, was blind, and Pandu, the younger, ascended the throne of Hastinapura. Pandu died, leaving five sons, the heroes of the epic, and jealousies and quarrels soon arose between them and the 100 sons of their uncle, Dhritarashtra.

The five sons of Pandu were trained in arms by their preceptor, Drona. The eldest, Yudhishthira, never became much of a warrior, but was versed in the religious lore of the age, and is the most righteous character in the epic. Bhima, the second, was known for his great size and giant strength, and is the Hercules of the poem. Arjuna, the third, is the real hero of the epic, and excelled all in the skill of arms. Nakula, the fourth, learned to tame wild horses, and Sahadeva, the fifth, became proficient in astronomy. These brothers incurred the jealousy and hatred of their cousins from their youth up.

At last the day came for a public exhibition of the skill which the princes had acquired in the use of arms. A spacious area was enclosed. Nobles and ladies sat around to watch the tournament. The blind Dhritarashtra was led to his seat, and foremost among the ladies were his queen and the widow of Pandu, and the population of Kuru-land flocked around to see and admire the skill of their beloved princes.

There were fights with swords and clubs, and skill in archery was tried by severe tests. Arjuna distinguished himself above all the rest, and, amidst the ringing cheers of the assembled multitude, concluded his wonderful feats by doing obeisance to the venerable preceptor, Drona.

The dark cloud of jealousy lowered on the brow of the sons of Dhritarashtra, and when the time came for the election of a king, they rebelled against Pandu's eldest son ascending his father's throne. The just and aged Dhritarashtra had to yield; his sons obtained the royal power, and the five Pandavas were sent into exile.

Heralds now went through the different Hindu states, announcing that the daughter of the king of the Panchalas would select a husband by the ancient *Swayamvara* rite; in other words, she would herself choose her lord from among the most skilful warriors of the time. A heavy bow of great size was to be wielded, and an arrow was to be sent through a whirling *chakra* or quoit into the eye of a golden fish set high on a pole. The happy warrior who did this would win the princess.

Princes and warriors flocked to Kampilya, the capital of the Panchalas. The princess appeared with her brother among the assembled nobles, with the garland which she was to bestow on the victor of the day. Many tried to wield the bow, but in vain. An unknown warrior then stepped forward, drew the bow, and shot the arrow into the eye of the golden fish. Murmurs of discontent arose, like the sound of troubled waters, from the ranks of the warriors at the success of this unknown archer; but the latter threw off his disguise, and proclaimed himself the proud, the exiled Arjuna.

Then follows the strange myth that the five brothers went to their mother and said that a great prize had been won. Their mother, not knowing what the prize was, told her sons to share it among them; and as a mother's mandate cannot be disregarded, the five Pandavas wedded the princess as their common wife. The

Pandavas were now allied with the Panchalas, and their claim to their father's throne could no longer be gainsaid. A division was therefore made of the kingdom to prevent a war. The division was, however, unequal. Hastina pura and the best portion of Kuru-land fell to the share of the sons of Dhritarashtra. Forest lands on the Jumna were given to the Pandavas, where they cleared the woods, and built their new capital of Indraprastha, on the site of modern Delhi.

From this new capital the Pandavas spread their conquests far and wide, and Yudhishthira invited the princes of all neighbouring countries, including his kinsmen of Hastinapura, to attend the great coronation ceremony. A quarrel arose in the assembly between Sisupala, king of the Chedis, and Krishna of the Yadava race, and the latter killed Sisupala on the spot. Thenceforward Krishna remained a staunch ally of the Pandavas; and in the epic in its present form he is represented as a deity who had assumed human form in order to help the Pandavas to their rights.

But the newly crowned king was not long to enjoy his kingdom. With all his righteousness, Yudhishthira had a weakness for gambling, and the eldest son of Dhritarashtra challenged him to a game. His kingdom, wealth, himself and his brothers, and even his wife, were staked by Yudhishthira and lost, and behold now the five brothers and their wife the slaves of their rivals! That proud princess was dragged by the hair to the assembly and insulted, and bloodshed was imminent, when the old Dhritarashtra was led into the room and stopped the tumult. It was decided that the Pandavas had lost their kingdom, but should not be slaves. They agreed to go into exile for twelve years, after which they should remain concealed for a year. If the sons of Dhritarashtra failed to discover them within this last year, they would get their kingdom back.

Thus the Pandavas went again into exile, and, after twelve years of wandering, took service in disguise in the thirteenth year under the king of Virata. Their wife also took service in the same court as the queen's handmaid. A difficulty arose. The queen's brother became enamoured of the handmaid and insulted her. Bhima interfered and killed the lover in secret.

Cattle-lifting was not uncommon among the princes of those days, and the princes of Hastinapura carried away some cattle from Virata. Arjuna, then in the service of Virata, could not stand this; he put on his armour and recovered the cattle, but was discovered. The point whether the year of secret exile had quite expired was never settled, and thus the poet leaves undecided the question of the justice of the war which followed.

The Pandavas now made themselves known and claimed back their kingdom. The claim was refused, and both parties prepared for a war, the like of which had not been witnessed in India. All the Hindu nations joined one side or the other, and a great battle was fought in the plains of Kurukshetra, north of Delhi, which lasted for eighteen days. The story of this battle, with its endless episodes, need not detain us. All the great Kuru warriors and princes were killed, and Yudhishthira waded through blood to the ancient throne of Kuru land.

Such is the main outline of the plot of the *Mahabharata*, and the story throws much light on the manners of the Hindus of the Epic Age. We find how young princes were early trained in arms, how they rejoiced in tilts and tournaments in their own fashion, how ladies came out in public and witnessed the prowess of their sons, brothers, or husbands. Girls were married at a proper age, and youthful princesses, famed for their beauty, often selected their lords from the assembled warriors; and jealousies among kings and nations broke out into sanguinary wars, but the bitterness of feuds was restrained by strict laws of chivalry.

We also learn from the epic that the Gangetic Hindus were more civilized than their sturdy forefathers of the Punjab. Kings ruled over larger countries, manners were more polished, the sphere of knowledge was more extended. Religious rites were also more elaborate, social rules were more highly developed, and the science of war itself was more fully organized. But nevertheless, the stubborn valour and determination of Vedic warriors break through the more polished manners of the Epic Age, and the proud colonist races who founded the great and civilized kingdoms on the banks of the Ganges had not yet lost the vigour of national life which had animated their ruder forefathers in the Punjab.

Kosalas, Videhas, And Kasís

While the Kurus and the Panchalas, and other less known races, remained in lands adjoining the upper course of the Ganges, other Aryan tribes penetrated farther eastwards, and settled lower down the same river. The Kosalas were among the most distinguished of these colonists. Their ancestors are said to have fought in the wars of Sudas in the Punjab, and they now marched eastwards with their priests, the Tritsus or Vasishthas, and founded a powerful and extensive kingdom, stretching from the Ganges as far east as the Gandak river; and they brought with them the same religion and institutions, the language, learning, and arts, which were the common heritage of all Aryan Hindus. Ayodhya or Oudh was their capital town.

A still more celebrated tribe, the Videhas, marched farther eastwards, crossed the Gandak river, and settled in the country now known as Tirhut, to the north of the Ganges. Their earliest traditions narrate that their ancestor, Madhava Videha, came from the banks of the Sarasvati in the Punjab, with his priest Gautama, and, after travelling through various lands and crossing many rivers, came to the country of Tirhut. The hero then inquired, 'Where am I to abide?' 'To the east of this (Gandak river) be thy abode,' replied the god Agni, and the Videha thereupon settled in Tirhut. The country was marshy and uncultivated at that time, but the industrious colonists drained swamps, burnt down forests, extended the limits of cultivation, and founded their capital of Mithila.

A third distinguished nation, the Kasís, also came from the west and settled on the banks of the Ganges, and founded their far-famed capital, still known as Kasi or Benares, the holiest city in India.

It may be easily imagined that these colonist nations did not neglect the religion and the religious rites of their forefathers. Indeed, colonists in all parts of the world cherish the institutions of their motherland with an almost superstitious regard, and the Hindu colonists in the Gangetic valley accordingly came to attach a far greater importance to the forms and rites of Hindu worship than their ancestors had done in the Punjab. It was these rites that distinguished them from the outer barbarians, and that connected them with the earliest days of their glorious conquests in India. Coming to new lands, and surrounded by new and uncivilized aboriginal races, they adhered closely and steadfastly to those forms and institutions which marked them as Aryans, and which they cherished as their sacred inheritance. And as the distance of their new settlements from the Punjab increased with every fresh conquest, and as centuries divided them from the days of their early civilization and religion, they clung to the forms of that religion and civilization with an increasing veneration and regard, until the *forms* and *rites* concealed the substance and became their new *religion*.

It is necessary to clearly comprehend these facts in the history of the early Hindus in order to understand the change which now came over their manners. The same deities that were worshipped in the Punjab were worshipped by the Gangetic Hindus, and the same prayers of the Veda were uttered. But the simple forms of sacrifice now became more elaborate and cumbrous; every little rite was invested with a hidden meaning, every necessary act connected with worship came to be regarded as sacred, and the spirit of the religion of the Vedas was lost in the performance of elaborate sacrifices which took days and months and years. Kings now ruled over larger and richer and more populous kingdoms than the warrior chiefs of the Punjab, and had therefore both the power and the inclination for more ostentatious forms of sacrifice. Priests, too, now formed themselves into a separate class or caste, and had an interest therefore in making the performance of sacrifices difficult, and even impracticable, for others. And the people of the Lower Gangetic regions, living in a genial but enervating climate, lost something of the sturdiness of their forefathers, and became more submissive and luxurious, more addicted to ostentatious display and elaborate forms. Thus a great change came almost imperceptibly over the spirit of Hindu religion. In the Vedic Age men worshipped with gratitude and wonder the great and beneficent manifestations and powers of nature, offered prayers and food and libations to the fire, to express their devotion and their friendliness to the gods. In the Epic Age men's eyes were gradually withdrawn from the objects of worship, and the mere forms and ceremonials of the sacrifice, the performance of every petty rite in the proper way and at the proper time, and the utterance of every word with the proper accent, engrossed the attention of priests and people, and took the place of religion itself.

The hymns of the Vedas were classified and arranged for the purpose for which they were now required. The entire body of the hymns was known as the *Rig Veda*. By an ancient custom some of these hymns were chanted in some forms of sacrifice, and a collection of these select hymns, set to music, was called the *Sama Veda*. Again, special sacrificial formulas were required for the use of the officiating priests, and these formulas were separately collected and known as the *Yajur Veda*. These were the three Vedas recognized by the Gangetic Hindus, but a later composition known as the *Atharva Veda* was after wards recognized as the fourth Veda. The Vedas were thus separately compiled early in the Epic Age, before the Kuru-Panchala war.

But the religious literature of this age does not consist of the Vedas alone. As has often occurred in other countries and in other ages, dogmatic explanations and commentaries soon came to acquire a greater importance than the texts themselves. Each Veda has a number of such commentaries, and these commentaries, or Brahmanas, as they are called, form the most voluminous portion of the literature of this age. They are generally uninteresting and vapid.

But a healthy reaction was at hand. It would seem that earnest and thoughtful kings in this period felt some impatience at this display of priestly erudition and pedantry, and, while still conforming to the rites laid down by the priests, started healthier speculations as to the destination of the human soul and the nature of the Universal Being. Nothing in the history of ancient India is more curious than this ancient rivalry between kings and priests at this remote age; and nothing is more fresh and life-giving than the earnest speculations which arose from this rivalry, and which are known as the Upanishads.

The kings of the Videhas and the Kasís took a leading part in starting these pious inquiries. Janaka, king of the Videhas, was the most saintly character of the age, and was deeply versed in its pious learning. His court was crowded by the learned and the wise. His great priest, Yajnavalkya, compiled a new edition of the *Yajur Veda*, which is known as the *White Yajur Veda*, and also an elaborate commentary or Brahmana of this Veda. But Yajnavalkya was not the only honoured priest in Janaka's court. All learned men from the different Gangetic kingdoms sought the bounty of the king of the Videhas, and none sought it in vain. Even Ajatasatru, the king of the Kasís, himself a celebrated patron of learning, exclaimed in despair, 'Verily, all people run away, saying, Janaka is our patron.'

The names of Janaka and Ajatasatru are preserved in the Upanishads for the part they took in starting earnest speculations and pious inquiries. The Upanishads will form the subject of a future chapter, but it is necessary to quote one or two short legends here to show how these learned and saintly kings explained to the self-sufficient priests of the time the true scope and object of religion.

Janaka of Videha, we are told, once met three priests, one of whom was his court priest, Yajnavalkya. A discussion ensued, and the three priests were humiliated and sad, until Yajnavalkya followed the king in his car and learnt the truth from him.

Similarly, once upon a time a boastful priest, Balaki, challenged Ajatasatru, king of the Kasís, to a discussion. In the course of the dispute, however, the priest was defeated and remained silent and sad. Ajatasatru then said, 'Thus far do you know, O Balaki!'

'Thus far only,' replied Balaki.

'O Balaki!' then explained the royal sage, 'he who is the maker of all those, he of whom all this is the work, he (God) alone should be known.'

Similarly, a Brahman or priest, Svetaketu, came to an assembly of the Panchalas, and there had a discussion with Jaivali, a Kshatriya or king. The Brahman was defeated, and came sad and sorrowful to the Kshatriya to learn the truth. The king explained the truth, and said, 'This knowledge did not go to any Brahman before you, and therefore this teaching belonged in all the worlds to the Kshatriya (royal) class alone.'

Such are some of the legends which have been handed down to us, indicating faintly but unmistakably the rivalry which raged between the priestly and military classes just when these classes were forming into separate castes, and they also disclose to us the share which the royal caste took in originating or promoting the inquiries which are preserved to us in the Upanishads, and which have formed the basis of Hindu monotheism to the present day. Janaka was one of these earnest inquirers, and as such his name is entitled to respect.

But the mass of the Hindus of the present day remember Janaka and the Videhas, and the Kosalas also, because their names have been woven into one of their national epics. The *Ramayana* is as popular and as widely read by millions of Hindus to the present day as is the *Mahabharata*; and thus the memory of the ancient civilization which the early Hindus developed in the Gangetic states is still cherished in the recollections of their modern descendants. It is difficult to say which portions of the story of the *Ramayana* are based on facts, but as it reflects the manners and customs of the time, it should be told, however briefly, in a historical work.

Dasaratha, king of the Kosalas, had three queens honoured above others, of whom Kausalya bore him his eldest son, Rama; Kaikeyí was the mother of Bharata, and Sumitra gave birth to Lakshmana and Satrughna. The young princes, according to the customs of the times, were versed in arms and also in the learning of the age, and Rama, the eldest born, was as pious and truthful as he was distinguished in feats of arms. Dasaratha in his old age had decided on making Rama the Yuvaraja or reigning prince; but the beauteous Kaikeyí insisted that her son should be Yuvaraja, and the feeble old king yielded to the determined will of his wife.

Before this, Rama had won the daughter of Janaka, king of the Videhas, at a great assembly. Kings and warriors had gathered there to wield a heavy bow, which was the feat required to win the princess's hand, but Rama alone could lift it, and he bent it till it broke in twain. And now, when the town of Ayodhya was ringing at the prospect of the installation of Rama and his newly married consort, it was decided in Kaikeyi's chambers that her son Bharata must be Yuvaraja, and further that Rama must go into exile for fourteen years.

The duteous Rama submitted to his father's wishes. His faithful half-brother, Lakshmana, accompanied him, and the gentle Síta would not part from her lord. Amidst the tears and lamentations of the people of Ayodhya, Rama and Síta and Lakshmana departed from the city.

The old King Dasaratha did not long survive the banishment of his brave and beloved boy. A pathetic story is told that in his youth he had once gone out to hunt, and had accidentally shot a boy, and thus caused the death of an old and broken-hearted father. The curse of the deceased now had effect on Dasaratha with terrible severity, and the king of the Kosalas died in sorrow for his banished son.

Bharata now came to Rama in the wilderness, and implored him to return to Ayodhya as king. But the truthful Rama felt that the promise he had made to his father was not dissolved by his death, and he proceeded on his journey in the wilderness, directing Bharata to return and reign as king.

For thirteen years the banished prince wandered with his wife and his devoted brother in Dandaka forest and towards the sources of the Godavari River. The whole of southern India was then inhabited by non-Aryan aborigines. The poet has introduced them as monkeys and bears, and the non-Aryans of Ceylon are described as monsters.

Ravana, the monster-king of Ceylon, heard of the beauty of Síta, now dwelling in the wilderness, and in the absence of Rama took her away from their hut and carried her off to Ceylon. Rama obtained a clue of her after long search; he made alliances with the barbarian tribes of southern India, and prepared to cross over to Ceylon and win back his wife.

A natural causeway runs nearly across the strait between India and Ceylon. The poet imagines that this causeway was constructed by Rama's army with huge boulders and rocks carried from the continent.

The army crossed over, and the town of Lanka was besieged. Chief after chief was sent out by Ravana to break through the besiegers and disperse their forces, but they all fell in the war. At last Ravana himself came out, and was killed by Rama. Síta was recovered, and she proved her untainted virtue by throwing herself into a lighted pyre and coming out uninjured.

The fourteenth year of exile being now passed, Rama and Síta returned to Ayodhya and ascended the throne; but the suspicions of the people fell on Síta, who could not, they thought, have returned untainted, and Rama bowed to the suspicions of the people and sent poor suffering Síta, with her unborn offspring, into exile.

Valmíki, a saint, and the reputed author of this epic, received her in his hermitage, and there her twin sons, Lava and Kusa, were born. Years passed by, the twins became manly and warlike boys, proficient in arms, and Valmiki composed the poem of the *Ramayana*, and taught the boys to repeat it.

Then Rama decided to celebrate the famous horse sacrifice, as a token of his supreme sovereignty. A horse was sent out whom none might restrain without incurring the hostility of the great king of Ayodhya. The animal came as far as Valmíki's hermitage, and the spirited and playful boys caught it and detained it. Rama's guards in vain tried to recover the animal from the youthful warriors. At last Rama himself came and saw the princely boys, but did not know who they were. He heard his own deeds chanted by them, and it was in a passion of grief and repentance that he at last knew them and embraced them as his own sons.

But there was no joy in store for Síta. The people's suspicions could not be removed, and the earth, which had given poor Síta birth, yawned and received its long-suffering child. Síta in the *Rig Veda* is the field furrow, worshipped as an agricultural deity; and the reader will see how this first conception of Síta still asserts itself in the *Ramayana*, in which she is described as born of the earth, and received back into the earth. But this allegory is lost to the Hindus of the present times; to them she is an all-suffering, devoted, saint-like wife. To this day Hindus hesitate to call their children by the name of Síta; for if her gentleness, her virtue, her uncomplaining faith, and her unconquerable love to her lord were more than human, her sufferings and sorrows too were more than what usually fall to the lot of woman. There is not a Hindu woman in the length and breadth of India to whom the story of suffering Síta is not known, and to whom her character is not a model and a pattern; and Rama too is a model to men for his faithfulness, his obedience, and his piety. The *Mahabharata* is a heroic epic, the *Ramayana* is a didactic epic; and these two grand poems have been for the millions of India a means of moral education, the efficacy of which is not inferior to that of the Bible among Christian nations.

MANNERS AND CIVILIZATION

We have in the last two chapters described the state of the Hindu nations of the Gangetic valley, their flourishing and prosperous kingdoms, their schools of learning, their elaborate religious rites and observances, and their settled and civilized life, contrasting with the ruder and less settled life of their ancestors of the Punjab. The was with the aborigines were at an end; no foreign nations invaded India or influenced Hindu manners, no extraneous influences disturbed the even development of Hindu civilization. The great confederation of Hindu races, from the banks of the Jumna to those of the Gandak, lived by themselves; the outside world did not exist for them. The lofty Himalayas divided them from the nations of the north. Impenetrable forests and the Vindhya mountains separated them from the south. To the east, Bengal was yet undiscovered, uncivilized, and marshy; and their own sturdy kinsmen of the Punjab kept out all foreign invaders from the west. Within these limits the Hindu races lived in the Epic Age in a state of complete isolation from the world, such as has perhaps never been paralleled in ancient or modern times. The Kurus and the Panchalas, the Kosalas and the Videhas, and the other Gangetic tribes, lived in a world of their own, ignorant of any civilized religion or rites but their own, ignorant of any civilized language or learning save their own, identifying Hindus with mankind, and Hindu manners with civilized social law. It will be easily imagined that under the influence of an isolation so absolute and complete, the manners, laws, and social rules of the Hindus acquired a rigidity and fixedness unexampled among other nations of the world, ancient and modern.

In the Vedic Age, the Hindus were constantly engaged in wars with the aborigines; and long after they were subdued, the distinction between the conquerors and the conquered endured. The Aryan Hindus never mixed socially with the despised Dasyus even after the later had been subdued, and had adopted the settled and civilized life of the conquerors; and thus was generated the first social distinction between men dwelling side by side in villages and towns, and living by cultivation and the same arts of peace.

This distinction between Aryans and Dasyus naturally suggested and led to other distinctions among the Aryas themselves in the Epic Age. As religious rites became more elaborate in the Epic Age, and as great kings in the Gangetic states prided themselves on the performance of vast sacrifices with endless rites and observances, it is easy to understand that priests, who alone could undertake such rites, rose in the estimation of the people, until they were regarded as aloof from the people, as a distinct and separate community – as a *caste*. They devoted their lifetime to learning these rites; they alone were able to perform them in all their details; and inference in the popular mind was that they alone were worthy of the holy task. And when hereditary priests were thus separated from the people by their fancied sanctity and real knowledge of elaborate ritual, it was considered scarcely correct, on their part, to form mésalliances with the people outside their holy rank. They still condescended to choose brides from among the people, but maidens of priestly houses never gave their hands to men outside their circle; and this custom gradually became fixed and rigid, until the priests formed a separate caste – the Brahmans of India.

Similar causes led to the rise of the royal caste. In the Vedic Age the greatest kings, like Sudas, were but renowned warriors and leaders of hosts, owned cultivated lands and herds of cattle like other people, and were of the people. The Epic Age kings ruled over more extensive kingdoms, lived in august and pompous courts, and were looked up to with veneration by the thousands of submissive and peaceful men who formed the body of the people. As kings thus became more august and more addicted to the forms of royalty, as the people became more submissive and enervated and loyal, it was not considered correct for maidens of the royal and military classes to marry men from the ranks, although warriors might still choose brides from the people. And thus the warriors of the Epic Age formed themselves into a separate caste – the Kshatriyas of India.

The mass of the Aryan people still retained their ancient name of Visa or Vaisya, and formed a separate caste – the Vaisyas of India; while the conquered aborigines, although they had now adopted the civilized life and the language of their conquerors, were still kept at arm's length, and formed the lowest caste – the Súdras of India.

Similar distinctions have from time to time crept in among other nations, but have nowhere acquired the in flexible rigidity of the caste system of India. In Europe, for instance, the priests, the barons, and the humble people formed in the Middle Ages widely distinct communities, answering to some extent to the Brahmans, the Kshatriyas, and the Vaisyas of antiquity. But the priests of medieval Europe did not marry, and were recruited from the ablest and cleverest of the people. The knights, too, were glad to welcome into their ranks the bravest warriors from any grade of society. And the sturdy people themselves fought for their liberties and their chartered rights on battlefields and in council halls, and gradually rose in power, in influence, and in wealth, until the marked distinctions of the Middle Ages were obliterated. The influences of modern civilization, which have united not only different classes of people, but distinct races and tribes into nations in Europe, have not been felt in India until within the last 100 years; and thus the ancient distinctions of caste, considerably modified and multiplied, still exist in modern India, a mystery and a marvel to all foreigners.

While the Aryan Hindus were thus divided into three separate castes in the Epic Age, they still enjoyed, however, the common privileges of Aryans, namely, the acquisition of religious learning and the practice of religious rites. We have elsewhere stated that Hindu boys left their parents at an early age, and lived with their Gurus or teachers for years to acquire a knowledge of the Vedas and the sciences as then known. Clever young men then went to Parishads and other seats of learning, and often a boy of one race, Kuru or Panchala, travelled to renowned schools of learning in the land of the Videhas or of the Kasís to acquire all that the age could teach. There was indeed a friendly rivalry among the cultured races of the Gangetic states in this respect; and even when they were at war with each other, their seats of learning, their religious hermitages, and their renowned sages and teachers were always respected. The descendants of the ancient Vasishthas and Viswamitras and Gautamas of the Vedic Age kept up the reputation of their families for learning and religious lore, and renowned sages of these families were invited to all royal courts, and rewarded by all cultured kings. Janaka of Videha yielded to none in his respect for learning, and an account which is preserved to us in the *Brihadaranyaka Upanishad* of a great assemblage at his court will illustrate the manners of the times.

'*Janaka Videha performed a sacrifice at which many presents were offered to the priests. Brahmans of the Kurus and the Panchalas had come thither, and Janaka wished to know which of the Brahmans was the best read. So he enclosed a thousand cows, and ten padas of gold were fastened to each pair of horns.*

'And Janaka spoke to them:

"Ye venerable Brahmans, he who among ye is the wisest, let him drive away these cows." Then those Brahmans durst not, but Yajnavalkya said to his pupil, "Drive them away, my dear." He replied, "O glory of Saman!" and drove them away.'

The assembled Brahmans became angry at this presumption, and plied the proud Yajnavalkya with abstruse questions, but Yajnavalkya was a match for them all. There was one in that great assembly – and this is a remarkable fact, which illustrates the manners of the ancient Hindus – who was not deficient in the learning of the times although she was a lady. She rose in the open assembly and said:

'O Yajnavalkya, as the son of a warrior from the Kasís or Videhas might string his loosened bow, take two pointed foe-piercing arrows in his hand, and rise to battle, I have risen to fight thee with two questions. Answer me these questions.' The questions were put and answered, and the lady was silent, and the assembly acknowledged the superior learning of Yajnavalkya.

Passages like this throw much light on the manners of the ancient Hindus and the position of their women in society. There was as yet no unhealthy restraint on their movements, and they had a share in the learning of the times. They took a part in sacrifices and religious duties, they attended great assemblies, and they had their legitimate influence in society. Impartial students of ancient history will admit that women held a more honoured place among the ancient Hindus than among the ancient Greeks and Romans.

Young men, when they completed their education, were allowed to marry and to settle down as householders. Husband and wife then lighted the domestic sacrificial fire and offered daily oblations, and the fire was ever kept lighted in the houses of all pious Hindus. Besides daily oblations, numerous religious rites were prescribed, either at different seasons of the year, or at the time of certain domestic occurrences, and some account of these rites will be given in a subsequent chapter. It is enough to state here that while kings and wealthy men delighted in elaborate sacrifices, all pious Hindus, be they rich or poor, performed their little rites at their domestic firesides. No idol was worshipped, and no temple was known; the descendants of the Vedic Hindus still went through their religious ceremonies in their own homes, and offered oblations and prayers according to ancient rule.

Hospitality to strangers is prescribed as a religious obligation, while the essence of a Hindu's duties is inculcated in such passages as these:

'Speak the truth. Do thy duty. Do not neglect the study of the Veda. After having brought to thy teacher the proper reward, marry and beget children. Do not swerve from truth. Do not swerve from duty. Do not neglect what is useful. Do not neglect greatness. Do not neglect the teaching of the Veda.

'Do not neglect the sacrifices due to the gods and the fathers. Let thy mother be to thee like unto a god. Let thy father be to thee like unto a god. Blameless acts should be regarded, not others. Good works performed by us should be regarded by thee.'
Taittiriyaka Upanishad

The wealth of rich men consisted in gold and silver and jewels, in cars, horses, cows, mules, and slaves, in houses and fertile lands, and herds of cattle. The use of gold and silver, of tin, lead, and iron was well known. Elephants had been domesticated, and we are often told of rich presents of elephants and cars and slave-girls with graceful ornaments on their necks. Rice, wheat, barley, and other kinds of grain were the food of the people, and various preparations of milk were relished. The flesh of the cow was an article of food, and some wine was consumed at sacrifices.

We have said before that Hindu women in these ancient times had their legitimate influence on society. Child marriage, which is now practised in India, was unknown then, and the stories of the epics which we have narrated will show that royal princesses were married after they had attained womanhood. The marriage of widows, which is now prohibited among Hindus, was allowed in ancient times, and the rites which a widow had to perform before she entered into the married state again are distinctly laid down. Marriage among blood relations to the third or fourth generation was prohibited.

The study of the Vedas was considered the most important duty and the most cherished heritage of all Hindus. The Vedas were supposed to embody all the learning which it was given to man to acquire; and it is curious to note that as the infant sciences came into existence in India, they were considered as supplementary to the Vedas, and as helps to the performance of Vedic rites. Indeed, it is not an exaggeration to state that the sphere of knowledge was enlarged, and the sciences were discovered in India in the pursuit of religious rites and observances. A thoughtful writer and student of Hindu literature rightly remarks:

'The want of some rule by which to fix the right time for the sacrifices gave the first impulse to astronomical observations; urged by this want, the priest remained watching night after night the advance of the moon through the circle of the Nakshatras, and day after day the alternate progress of the sun towards the north and the south. The laws of phonetics were investigated because the wrath of the gods followed the wrong pronunciation of a single letter of the sacrificial formulas; grammar and etymology had the task of securing the right understanding of the holy texts. The connection of philosophy and theology – so close that it was

impossible to decide where the one ends and the other begins – is too well known to require any comment.'

These were the sciences which were cultivated in the schools of learning of the Gangetic states; and it is an important fact in the history of the Hindus that all these sciences sprang from the practice of their religious rites. The writer whom we have quoted above lays down the principle which all Indian historians recognize, that whatever science 'is closely connected with ancient Indian religion must be considered as having sprung up among the Indians themselves.'

An elementary knowledge of astronomy was acquired by the Hindus in the Vedic Age, but it was in the Epic Age that this science received much development. The year was divided into twelve lunar months, and a thirteenth month was added every fifth year to adjust the lunar year with the solar year. The twenty-eight Nakshatras or constellations through which the moon passed in her monthly journey were observed and named. The progress of the sun to the north and to the south of the equator was noted, and the position of the solstitial points was also marked. An observation of the position of the solstitial points was made when the compilation of the Vedas was completed, and some mathematicians have calculated from this that the event took place in 1181 BCE.

The study of other sciences was prosecuted in the Epic Age. Grammar, etymology, phonetics, and prosody were cultivated with great care, as they regulated the proper utterance of prayers, as the position of the heavenly bodies fixed the auspicious moments for sacrifices. Attention was also paid to ethics and ratiocination. Arithmetic is pre-eminently a Hindu science, and was developed as early as the Epic Age, while minute rules for the construction of altars of different shapes and sizes, led to the discovery of geometrical principles.

The administration of law was still rude, and, as among other ancient nations, trial by the ordeal of fire was recognized. To discover the truth was the end and object of law, and law was described as truth. 'If a man declares what is true, they say he declares the law; and if he declares the law, they say he declares what is true. Both are the same.' (*Brihadaranyaka Upanishad*)

RELIGION

The gradual change which crept over the spirit of the religion of the Hindus in the Epic Age has already been indicated. The increase in wealth and civilization, and the comparatively settled and easy life of the people, gave birth to a taste for great and pompous sacrifices; and a hereditary priestly caste naturally attached great importance to the forms and ceremonials which accompanied these rites. And in the performance of these elaborate sacrifices the attention of the worshipper was to a great extent diverted from the deities, who were the true objects of devotion, to the minutiae of rites, the erection of altars, the fixing of the proper astronomical moments for lighting the fire, the correct pronunciation of prayers, and to the various requisite acts accompanying a sacrifice.

The literature of a nation is but the reflection of the national mind; and when the nation turned its religion into forms and ceremonials, religious literature became to some extent inane and lifeless. We miss in the voluminous Brahmanas of this age the fervency and earnestness of the Vedic hymns. We find, on the other hand, grotesque reasons given for every minute rite, dogmatic explanations of texts, penances for every breach of form and rule, and elaborate directions for every act and movement of the worshipper. The works show a degree of credulity and submission on the part of the people, and of absolute power on the part of the priests, which remind us of the Middle Ages in Europe.

We willingly leave this subject and turn to the legends contained in the Brahmanas, some of which are interesting. That which is the best known in Europe is one resembling the account of the deluge in the Old Testament. Manu, the mythical progenitor of man, was washing his hands when a fish came unto him and said, 'Rear me; I will save thee.' Manu reared the fish, and it told him, 'In such and such a year the flood will come. Thou shalt then attend to me by preparing a ship.' The flood came, and Manu entered into the ship, which he had built in time, and the fish swam up to him and carried the ship beyond the northern mountain. The ship was fastened to a tree, and when the flood subsided Manu descended. 'The flood swept away all the creatures, and Manu alone remained here.' (*Satapatha Brahmana*)

In some of the legends of the Brahmanas we notice how poetical similes used in the *Rig Veda* were transformed into mythological tales. The simile of the sun pursuing the Dawn-goddess lent itself easily to a tale of Prajapati seducing his daughter, and thus creating and peopling this universe. Hindu commentators saw the origin of this myth, and the learned Kumarila, who lived some five centuries after Christ, thus explains it:

'*Prajapati, the Lord of Creation, is the name of the sun, and he is called so because he protects all creatures. His daughter Ushas is the dawn; and when it is said that he was in love with her, this only means that at sunrise the sun runs after the dawn.*'

Various other accounts of the creation are given in the different Brahmanas. We are told in the *Taittiriyaka Brahmana* that in the beginning nothing was except water, and a lotus leaf stood out of it. Prajapati dived in the shape of a boar and brought up some earth, and spread it out, and fastened it down by pebbles. That was the earth.

In the *Satapatha Brahmana* we are told that the gods and the Asuras (enemies of gods) both sprang from Prajapati, and the earth trembled like a lotus leaf when the gods and Asuras contended for mastery. And elsewhere in the same Brahmana we are told, 'Verily in the beginning Prajapati existed alone.' He created living beings, and birds and reptiles and snakes, but they all passed away for want of food. He then made the breasts (of mammals) teem with milk, and so the living creatures survived.

These examples will suffice. We have seen that the Hindus of the Vedic Age were led from the worship of Nature up to Nature's God, and were able to conceive the great idea that in the beginning nothing existed except the Deity, and that the whole universe was his handiwork. The more speculative Hindus of the Epic Age reproduced the same idea, and their various guesses as to the way in which God created the universe are among the earliest conjectures of man into the mysteries of creation. But nobler and more earnest efforts were made in this Epic Age to know the unknown God, and these strivings of the Hindu mind are imbedded in the works called the Upanishads, of which we have spoken before, and which are among the most remarkable works in the literature of the world.

The idea of a Universal Soul, of an All-pervading Breath, is the keystone of the philosophy and thought of the Upanishads. This idea is somewhat different from monotheism, as it has been generally understood by other nations. The monotheism of other nations recognizes a God and Creator as distinct from the created beings, but the monotheism of the Upanishads, which has been the monotheism of the Hindus ever since, recognizes God as the Universal Being; – all things have emanated from him, are a part of him, and will resolve themselves into him.

This is the truth which the poor fatherless boy Satyakama learnt from the great book of Nature. He was a poor child of a poor servant girl, and did not know who his father was. When he came to a Guru to learn according to the custom of the times, and the Guru asked after his family, the truthful boy replied, 'I do not know, sir, of what family I am. I asked my mother, and she answered, "In my youth, when I had to move about much as a servant, I conceived thee. I do not know of what family thou art."' The Guru was pleased with the truth-loving boy, and kept him in his house.

And the boy, according to the custom of the times, served his teacher menially, and went out to tend his cattle; and in course of time he learnt the great truth which Nature, and even the brute creation, teach those whose minds are open to instruction. He learnt the truth from the herd which he tended, from the fire that he lighted, from the flamingo and diver-bird that flew around him when in the evening he had penned his cows and laid wood on the evening fire. His teacher was struck, and asked, 'Friend, you shine like one who knows God; who then has taught you?' 'Not men,' was the young student's reply. And the truth which he had learnt was that the four quarters, and the earth, the sky, the heavens beyond, and the ocean, and the sun, the moon, the lightning and the fire, and the organs and minds of living beings – yea, the whole universe, was God. (*Chhandogya Upanishad*)

This is the truth which the learned priest Yajnavalkya explained to his beloved wife Maitreyí when she refused all wealth which her husband offered to her, and thirsted for that which would make her immortal; and the priest, gratified by the noble wish of his spouse, then explained to her that the Universal Soul dwells in the husband and in the wife and in the sons, in Brahmans and in Kshatriyas, and in all living beings, in the gods above and in the creatures below – yea, in all the universe. (*Brihadaranyaka Upanishad*)

This is the truth which is inculcated in numerous passages in the Upanishads in language simple and fervent and solemn, the like of which has never been composed by Hindus of later times.

'The Intelligent, whose body is spirit, whose form is bright, whose thoughts are true, whose nature is like ether (omnipresent and invisible), from whom all works, all desires, all sweet odours and tastes proceed; – He who embraces all this, who never speaks and is never surprised,

'He is my soul within the heart, smaller than a corn of rice, smaller than a corn of barley, smaller than a mustard seed or kernel of a canary seed. He also is my soul within my heart, greater than the earth, greater than the sky, greater than the heavens beyond, greater than all these worlds.

'He from whom all works, all desires, all sweet odours and tastes proceed, who embraces all this, who never speaks and is never surprised, He – my soul within my heart – is God. When I shall have departed from hence, I shall mingle with him.'

Chhandogya Upanishad

This is the truth which is explained in 100 beautiful similes. The Universal Soul is like the honey, in which drops collected by bees from distant trees mingle; it is like the ocean, in which rivers coming from distant regions are lost; it is like the saline water, in which particles of salt can no longer be discerned.

'At whose wish does the mind, sent forth, proceed on its errand?' asks the pupil. *'At whose command does the first breath go forth?*

At whose wish do we utter this speech? What god directs the eye or the ear?' The teacher replies: 'It is the ear of the ear, the mind of the mind, the speech of the speech, the breath of the breath, the eye of the eye....That which is not ex pressed by speech, but by which speech is expressed, ... that which does not think by mind, but by which mind is thought, ...that which does not see by the eye, but by which one sees, ...that which does not hear by the ear, but which by the hearing is heard, that which does not breathe by breath, but by which breath is breathed, – that alone is God – not that which people here adore.'
Kena Upanishad

It is easy to see in the above passage an effort made by the sages and thinking men in the ancient age to shake themselves from the trammels of meaningless ceremonials and the fanciful gods whom 'people here adore', and to soar to a higher region of thought, to comprehend the incomprehensible, the breath of the breath and the mind of the mind. It was a manly and fervent effort made by the Hindus three thousand years ago to know the unknown God; and the daring but pious thinkers thus describe the Deity whom they tried to conceive:

'He, the Soul, encircled all bright, incorporeal, scathe less, without muscles, pure, untouched by evil, a seer, wise, omnipresent and self-existent, – He disposed all things rightly for eternal years.'
I'sa Upanishad

Such were the earliest efforts made by the Hindus to discern the attributes and nature of the unknown Deity. They are among the earliest efforts of man to comprehend his maker, and we find them in the imperishable works of the Hindus, the Upanishads.

Another new and startling idea is also first met with in these works. Other nations have believed in the resurrection of the soul; the Hindus believed in the past as well as in the future existence of the soul; and this idea of the transmigration of souls is first taught and explained in the Upanishads.

The idea is that the same soul passes through various bodies according to its acts, before it can be freed from all its imperfections and mingle in the Deity. 'According to his deeds and according to his knowledge, he is born again as a worm, or as an insect, or as a fish, or as a bird, or as a lion, or as a boar, or as a serpent, or as a tiger, or as a man, or as something else in different places.' And after passing through various worlds, the purified soul approaches God. (*Kaushitaki Upanishad*)

This doctrine of transmigration of souls, which was first taught in India, and which other ancient nations borrowed from the Hindus, is explained in many beautiful similes. The progress of the soul through different bodies is like the progress of the caterpillar moving from blade to blade, or like the changes in the gold which the goldsmith turns into newer and more beautiful forms. And when at last the soul is thus purified of all its imperfections, it finally casts off the body and mingles with God. 'As the slough of the snake lies on an anthill, dead and cast away, thus lies the body; but the disembodied immortal spirit is God, it is Light.' (*Brihadaranyaka Upanishad*)

The creation of the world also puzzled the sages of the Upanishads. We are told in the *Chhandogya* that the self-existent grew into an egg, and the egg burst itself into two halves, the heaven and the earth. And elsewhere in the same work we are told that the self-existent first sent forth fire, and the fire sent forth water, and the water sent forth the earth.

The *Aitareya A'ranyaka* discusses the first material from which the universe was created; and, as in the *Rig Veda* and in the Jewish account of the creation, water is said to be the first material cause.

And in the *Brihadaranyaka Upanishad* we are told that the self-existent Soul formed himself into the male and the female, and the creation proceeded therefrom.

The mysteries of death were no less strange to the early sages than the mysteries of creation, and a beautiful legend is told of a sage, Nachiketas, who asked Death to reveal his mysteries. But Death was unwilling to reveal his secrets, and said,

'Choose sons and grandsons who shall live a hundred years, herds of cattle, elephants, horses, gold. Choose the wide abode of the earth, and live thyself as many harvests as thou desirest.

'If you can think of any boon equal to that, choose wealth and long life. Be king, Nachiketas, on the whole earth. I make thee the enjoyer of all desires.

'Whatever desires are difficult to attain among mortals, ask for them, anything to thy wish. These fair maidens with chariots and musical instruments, such are indeed not to be obtained by men, – be waited on by them whom I give thee, but do not ask me about dying.'

But Nachiketas said, 'These things last till tomorrow, O Death! for they wear out the vigour of all the senses. Even, the whole of life is short. Keep thou thy horses, keep dance and song for thyself.'

Pressed by the pious inquirer, Death at last revealed his great secret, which is the cardinal idea of Hindu monotheism.

'The wise who by meditation of his own soul recognizes the soul ... as God, – he indeed leaves joy and sorrow far behind.

'A mortal who has heard this and accepted this, – who has separated it from all qualities, and has reached the subtle Being, rejoices because he has

cause for rejoicing. The house of God is open, I believe, O Nachiketas.'
Katha Upanishad

Such were the efforts of the Hindus of the Epic Age to learn the mysteries of the Deity and of the soul, of creation and of death. And though in these ancient ideas we find much that is fanciful, and though they are clothed in quaint similes and legends, yet it is impossible not to be struck with the freshness, the earnestness, and the vigour of thought which mark these yearnings after the truth. A great German philosopher, Schopenhauer, has recorded his high admiration for the Upanishads in striking words which have been often quoted. 'From every sentence, deep, original, and sublime thoughts arise, and the whole is pervaded by a high and holy and earnest spirit. Indian air surrounds us and original thoughts of kindred spirits.... It has been the solace of my life; it will be the solace of my death.'

THE MARVELLOUS MILLENNIUM

The 1,000 years from 1000 BCE were a time rich in philosophical and spiritual innovations. Several systems of philosophy developed in India at this time, of which Vedanta is based on the fourth category of Vedic texts, the Upanishads. To Flora Annie Steel (whose text features in this chapter), writing in 1911, all other philosophies that emerged at this time, including that of Samkhya, are far inferior – though Samkhya has in fact a very complex philosophy on the nature and process of the origin of life. The Upanishads dwell on Brahman, referred to by Steel as the universal soul. Brahman is indeed that, but is also far more: the unchanging, eternal, origin and cause of all that is.

She goes on to describe Buddhism, though her statistics regarding the numbers of Buddhists are not quite correct. According to the World Religion Database, in 1900, there were 558 million Christians and 127 million Buddhists in the world. Figures Steel provides for Buddhists in earlier centuries are also far more than actually existed, nor was half of India ever converted to Buddhism. She also takes a brief look at the Yoga, Nyaya, Vaisheshika and Mimamsa philosophies. In a succinct way, Steel explains the essence of these, as well as developments in mathematics and social laws. However, it would be a vast exaggeration to say that every Hindu learnt the Dharma Sutras, or that every Hindu was educated. Education was confined to male upper castes, usually to brahmanas.

As for political aspects, Steel brings in the accounts of Megasthenes, the Greek ambassador at the court of Chandragupta Maurya (r. 322–297 BCE), which provide an interesting picture of the period.

Some of those speaking Indo-Aryan languages did migrate west and south, but the concept of conquest over aborigines is no longer valid. Nor was the term *rakshas* used for all who were alien to them, but only for a specific group.

Going on to Steel's accounts of the Shishunaga and other kings, many more studies of this period now exist. With less information available at the time, she surmises they were Scythians and came from the northeast, neither of which is correct. Bimbisara, a king to whom she refers, is not considered today to be of the Shishunaga dynasty, but of a different, Haryanka dynasty. It is the *Puranas* that place him with the Shishunagas, but Buddhist sources are now considered more authentic. Legendary dynasties before the Haryanka were the Pradyota and Brihadratha. Ajatashatru succeeded Bimbisara, after which, because of several subsequent cases of patricide, Shishunaga, one of the ministers, was elected king. The Shishunaga dynasty ruled for 70 years, followed by Mahapadma Nanda and the Nanda dynasty. Even today there are different accounts of the duration and dates of the Nanda dynasty. Recent research, recorded by Irfan Habib and Vivekanand Jha in *Mauryan India* (2004), suggests that they ruled only for 22 years, from 344–322 BCE, and not 159 years as earlier theorized.

Steel's account reflects the knowledge of the time in which she wrote. Her brief descriptions of philosophy, and extracts from texts, are valuable.

Ball (whose text also features in this chapter) also presents a picture of these times, and his account of the Shishunaga dynasty is similar to that of Steel. Jainism also emerged in the sixth century BCE, with a very rational but complex philosophy that cannot be briefly explained; Buddhism too continued to flourish. Once again we come across the Mahajanapadas, such as Magadha and Koshala, and the rise of the Nanda dynasty. Under Darius I northwest India became a province of Persia in the sixth century BCE; this was followed by the invasion of Alexander in the 4th century BCE. At this time India was still divided into a number of small kingdoms.

1000 BCE TO 1 CE
(Flora Annie Steel)

A millennium indeed! A thousand years of Time which [...] must be treated, as a whole, as perhaps the most wonderful period in the history of the world. For, just as in the fifteenth and sixteenth centuries humanity appears to have set its mind on art, and such names as Shakespeare, Dante, Rafael, Leonardo da Vinci, Palestrina, Cervantes, and 100 others are to be found jostling each other in history, so, during these 1,000 years, the mind of man throughout the whole world appears to have been set on solving the great secret of Life and Death.

The answer was given in many ways by the Greek and Roman philosophers, by Confucius in China, by Christ in Judea, by Buddha and the great systems of Indian philosophy in Hindustan; and yet the question is still being asked with the old intensity, the old keen desire for answer!

Its Literature

Now, since these thousand years have, in India, left behind them a very remarkable literature which, even in these latter days, is the root of all life and thought in that vast peninsula, it is as well to attempt a slight sketch of the time, as a whole, before embarking on actual history; though to do the latter we shall, after treating of the religious age, have to hark back to the year 620 BCE.

At the commencement, then, of this 1,000 years, the Aryans were still pushing their way westwards and southwards from the alluvial plains of northern India.

It seems likely that the tide of their conquest followed that of the retreating sea. However that may be, certain it is that they found before them dark, almost impenetrable, swampy forests, swarming with enemies of all kinds. Who or what these were we have at first small record. Doubtless the human foes belonged to the aboriginal tribes which are still to be found clinging to the far mountain uplands and inaccessible fastnesses which the Aryans did not care to annex. But in the literature of which mention has been made, all and sundry are disdainfully dismissed with the epithet '*Rakshas*', or evil demons.

The Upanishads

Behind this shrinking verge of devildom, however, we know that 'the children of light' were settling down; towns were springing up, waste land was being cleared and cultivated, schools were being established, and many principalities rising into power. But of all this we have as yet no record at all, until about one-half of the millennium was over. On the other hand, we have exhaustive literary evidence of what the minds of men were busying themselves about, first in the Upanishads, and then in the myriad Sutras or Aphorisms, on every subject, apparently, under the sun, which are still extant.

Regarding the former – of which the German philosopher, Schopenhauer, wrote: 'They have been the solace of my life; they will be the solace of my death' – though some of these treatises or essays belong, undoubtedly, to the dying years of the Epic Age, they fall far more naturally into place during the opening years of this, the succeeding one. Their bold hypotheses covering all things were the first reaction against the soul-stifling formalisms of the Brahmanas; these, again, being due to the development of the dignity of the priestly class, which followed naturally on the excessive militarism so noticeable in the *Mahabharata*. Of a truth, its stalwart warriors, forever engaged in deadly combat and stirring adventures, could as heads of households have had little time for the due performance of domestic ceremonials after the customs of their fathers. Hence the rapid growth of the professional priesthood.

The fatal facility, however, with which speculative thought, after throwing off the shackles of canon and dogma, finds fresh slavery for itself in scientific formalism, is shown by the succeeding Sutra literature, in which every department of thought and action is crystallized and codified into cut-and-dried form.

Kapila's Philosophy, Vedanta Teaching

A reaction from this, again, is to be found in the succeeding philosophy of Kapila and his disciples, which must have been promulgated a century or so before the birth of Gautama Buddha. Frankly agnostic, many of the conclusions of this Sankhya system are to be found in the works of the latest German philosophers. Like theirs it is cold, and appeals not to the masses, but to speculative scholars. Still, it is strange that the very first recorded system of philosophy in the world, the very first attempt to solve the Great Question by the light of reason alone, should differ scarcely at all from the last. The human brain fails now, as it failed then; for Kapila's doctrine never really overset those of the Upanishads, though the system of philosophy founded upon these last (and therefore called the Vedanta) was not to come for many years. But what, indeed, can or could overset the doctrine laid down in these same Upanishads, of a Universal Soul, a Universal Self, which is – to use the very words of the text:

'Myself within the heart smaller than a corn of rice, smaller than a mustard seed, smaller than the kernel of a canary seed: myself within the heart greater than the earth, greater than the sky, greater than heaven. Lo! He who beholds all beings in this Self, and Self in all beings, he never turns away from it. When to a man who understands, the Self has become all things, what sorrow, what trouble can there be to him who has once beheld that unity? He, the Self, encircles all, bright, incorporeal, scatheless, pure, untouched by evil; a seer, wise, omnipresent, self-existent, he disposed all things rightly for eternal years. He therefore who knows this, after having become quiet, subdued, satisfied, patient and collected, sees Self in Self, sees all in Self. Evil does not overcome him, he overcomes all evil. Free from evil, free from stain, free from doubt, he becomes True Brahman. The wise who, meditating on this Self, recognizes the Ancient who dwells forever in the abyss, as God – he indeed leaves joy and sorrow far behind; having reached the subtle Being, he rejoices because he has obtained the cause of rejoicing.'

Such words as these live forever, a veritable Light in the Darkness of many philosophies.

Gautama Buddha

Yet even the Vedanta teaching failed to satisfy the masses; its atmosphere was too rarefied for them. So about the middle of the millennium a new Teacher arose. Gautama Buddha was born about the year 560 BCE at Kapilavastu, and the followers of the religion of which he was the founder number at this present day nearly one-third of the whole human race.

A magnificent work truly, look at it how we may! Yet it becomes the more astounding when we enquire into the religion itself; for it holds out no bait to humanity. It neither gives the immediate and certain grip on a spiritual and therefore eternal life which the Vedanta promises, neither does it proclaim the personal individual immortality for which the Christian is taught to look.

Yet it holds its place firmly as first favourite with humanity. There are some 500 million Buddhists, as against some 300 million Christians; while about the tenth century of our era fully one-half the world's inhabitants followed the teaching of Gautama.

Why is this? Wherein lies the charm? Possibly in its pessimism, in the declaration that all is, must be, suffering.

'Hear! O Bhikkhus! the Noble Truth of Suffering. Birth is suffering, decay is suffering, illness is suffering, Death is suffering.

'Hear! O Bhikkhus! the Noble Truth of the cause of suffering. Thirst for pleasure, thirst for life, thirst for prosperity, thirst that leads to new birth.

'Hear! O Bhikkhus! the Noble Truth of the cessation of Suffering. It is the destruction of desire, the extinction of thirst.

'Hear! O Bhikkhus! the Noble Truth of the Pathway which leads to the cessation of suffering. Right Belief, Right Aspirations, Right Speech, Right Conduct, Right Means of Livelihood, Right Exertion, Right-mindedness, Right Meditation.'

In these few words lies the whole teaching of Buddhism. To king and beggar alike, the world is evil; there is but one road to freedom, and that must be trodden alike by all. In that road none is before or after others.

Now to the poor, to the oppressed, there is balm in this thought. Lazarus does not yearn for Abraham's bosom! Before all lies forgetfulness, peace, personal annihilation.

This, then, was the teaching which Gautama Buddha, the son of a king, gave as a gift to his world; and his world, wearied yet once more with formalism, with the ever-growing terrorism of caste and creed, welcomed it with open arms. The progress of the Buddhistic faith was fairly astounding, and half India was converted in the twinkling of an eye. Of the life led by the founder himself much has been written. Many of the incidents bear a strange resemblance to those in the life of Christ. [...]

Buddha, it will be observed, answered no questions. He left the insoluble alone. He simply preached that holiness meant peace and love, that peace and love meant pure earthly happiness.

So, even while they accepted the morality of Buddhism, and acquiesced in its negation, the keener speculative minds were still busy trying to find some key to fit the Great Lock.

Yoga, and Other Philosophies

The Yoga system of philosophy followed on the Sankhya, the Nyaya and the Vaisasika on the Yoga; finally, the two Mimamsa or Vedanta philosophies. Of these the Yoga is merely a repetition, with some alteration, of the Sankhya; the Nyaya – which is to the Hindu what the Aristotelian system was to the Greek, and which is still the school of logic – finds its complement in the scientific and atomic theories of the Vaisasika. This last, which is the first effort made in India to enquire into the laws of physics, is curiously provocative of thought. A Rip-van-Winklish feeling creeps into the mind as the eyes read that all material substances are aggregates of atoms, that the ultimate atom must be simple, that the mote visible in the sunbeam, though the smallest perceptible object, must yet be a substance, therefore a thing composed of things smaller than itself.

Once again the question arises, 'How much further have we gone towards solution?'

Of the Vedanta system enough has already been said. It is pure Monism, matter being but a manifestation of the Supreme Energy, the Supreme Soul, the Supreme Self which comprises all things, holds all things, is all things.

So much for the speculative thought of this remarkable age. But when we turn to other subjects, we find the same truly marvellous acumen displayed in almost every field of enquiry.

Panini, whom Max Muller called the greatest grammarian the world has ever seen, lived in the middle of this millennium, and by resolving Sanskrit to its simple roots, paved the way for the Science of Languages. It is strange, indeed, to think of him in the dawn of days discovering what was to be rediscovered more than 2,000 years afterwards, and adopting half the philological formulas of the present century.

So with geometry, a science which certainly developed from the strict rules concerning the erection of altars, as the science of phonetics grew from the study necessary to ensure absolutely accurate intonations of the sacred text. Of the former science much is to be found in the Sulva Sutras; amongst other things, the celebrated theorem that the square of the hypothenuse is equal to the square of the two other sides of a rectangular triangle. This proposition is ascribed by the Greeks to Pythagoras, but it was known in India long before his time, and it is supposed that he learnt it while on his travels, which included Hindustan.

Geometry, however, was not destined to take hold of the Indian mind. The cognate science of numbers speedily took its place, and the acute Asiatic intellect soon evolved Algebra out of the arithmetic which they had rendered of practical use by the adoption of the decimal system of notation.

For all these many discoveries the world is indebted to this marvellous millennium.

Regarding the social life of this time the Dharma Sutras give us endless laws – which are the originals of later and codified laws – concerning almost every subject under the sun. As every Hindu student (and every Hindu had to be student for a definite number of years) had to learn these Sutras by heart, it may safely be predicted that they faithfully reflect the general conduct of affairs. They are extraordinarily minute in particular, and from them it may be gathered that life had become much more artificial. Amongst the king's duties is that of 'guarding household weights and measures from falsification'. It may also be noticed that 'the taxes payable by those who support themselves by personal labour differ materially from those paid by mere possessors of property'. Any injury, also, to a cultivator's land or to an artisan's trade was punished with great severity, and violence in defence of them was held justifiable. A legal rate of interest was settled, and the laws of inheritance were laid down minutely, as also were those of marriage. Indeed, as Mr R. C. Dutt puts it:

'Everything that was confused during the Epic period was brought to order – everything that was discursive was condemned; opinions were arranged and codified into bodies of laws, and the whole social system of the Hindus underwent a similar rigid treatment.'

Briefly, it was at once an age of keen speculation and rapid crystallization almost unequalled in the history of any nation. Nor have we to found this estimate of it solely by inference from the literature which it has left behind it. We have other evidence on which to draw. True, the earliest foreign notice of India is that of Hekataios of Miletus, who wrote about 520 BCE, but he seems only to have been aware of its existence. The next is that of some inscriptions of the Persian king, Darius, which may be dated about 486 BCE, while Ktesias of Knidos, who collected travellers' tales about the East, wrote a little later. But Alexander's Indian campaign, which began in the year 327 BCE, brought many Western eyes to wonder at what they saw, and from this time Greece practically gives us the chronology of Hindustan.

Megasthenes' Accounts

Of what these Western eyes saw we gain glimpses in the few fragments of the works of Megasthenes which have withstood the destruction of time. Living, as he did, in the fourth century BCE as Ambassador at the court of Paliputra, he gives us a picture of the times well worth reading, with a few extracts from which this chapter may well conclude.

'The inhabitants, having abundant means of subsistence, exceed, in consequence, the ordinary stature, and are distinguished by their proud bearing. They are also found to be well skilled in the arts, as might be expected of men who inhale a pure air and drink the very finest water... they almost always gather in two harvests annually; and even should one of the sowings prove more or less abortive, they are always sure of the other crop. It is accordingly affirmed that famine has never visited India, and that there has never been any general scarcity in the supply of nourishing food.... But, further, there are usages observed by the Indians which contribute to prevent the occurrence of famine among them; for *whereas amongst other nations it is usual, in the contests of war, to ravage the soil, and thus to reduce it to an uncultivated waste, among the Indians, on the contrary, by whom husbandmen are regarded as a class that is sacred and inviolable, the tillers of the soil, even when battle is raging in their neighbourhood, are undisturbed by any sense of danger, since the combatants allow them to remain quite unmolested. Neither do they ravage a land with fire nor cut down its trees.... The Indians do not raise monuments to the dead, but consider the virtues which men have displayed in life and the songs in which their praises are celebrated, sufficient to preserve their memory.... All the Indians are free, and not one of them is a slave. The Indians do not even use aliens as slaves, and much less one of their own countrymen.... They live frugally and observe very good order. Theft is of very rare occurrence. The simplicity of their laws and their contracts is proved by the fact that they seldom appeal to law. They have no suits about pledges or deposits, nor do they require either seals or witnesses, but make their deposits and confide in each other. They neither put out money at usury or know how to borrow.... Truth and virtue they hold alike in esteem.... In contrast to the general simplicity of their style, they love finery and ornaments. Their robes are worked in gold, adorned with precious stones, and they wear flowered garments of the finest muslin. Attendants walking behind hold umbrellas over them; for they have a high regard for beauty, and avail themselves of every device to improve their looks....*

'Of the great officers of state, some have charge of the market, others of the city, others of the soldiers, while some superintend the canals and measure the land, some collect the taxes, and some construct roads and set up pillars to show the by-roads and the distances....

'Those who have charge of the city are divided into six bodies of five each. The first body looks after industrial art. The second *attends to the entertainments of strangers, taking care of them, well or ill, and, in the event of their dying, burying them and forwarding their property to their relatives. The third enquires of births and deaths, so that these among both high and low may not escape the cognisance of Government. The fourth deals with trade and commerce, and has charge of weights and measures. The fifth supervises the sale of manufactured articles which are sold by public notice, and the sixth collects the tithe on such articles. There is, beside the city magistrates, a third body, which directs military affairs. One division of this has charge of the infantry, another of the cavalry, a third of the war chariots, a fourth of the elephants; while one division is appointed to co-operate with the admiral of the fleet and another with the superintendent of the bullock trains used for transporting the munitions of war.'*

So much for the East before it was gripped by the West. With a full-blown War Office, and a statistical registration of births and deaths, it appears to have gone far on the course of our civilization.

Concerning the 'Brahmanes', as the old writers term the Brahmans, Megasthenes says of them that they live in groves, and

'spend their time in listening to sermons, discourses, and in imparting knowledge to such as will listen to them. The hearer is not allowed to speak, or even to cough, and much less to spit, and if he offends in any of these ways, he is cast out from their society that very day, as being a man who is wanting in self-restraint. Death is with them a very frequent subject of discourse. They regard this life as, so to speak, the time when the child within the womb matures, and death as the birth into a new and happy life. They go about naked, saying that God has given the body as sufficient covering for the soul.'

One may still hear this teaching given in the mango groves, or in the shade of a banyan tree, throughout this India of the twentieth century.

And it still satisfies the hearers.

THE SESUNAGA (AND OTHER) KINGS, 620–327 BCE
(Flora Annie Steel)

We stand now on the threshold of actual history. Before us lie 2,500 years; and behind us? Who can say? From the far distance come the reverberating thunders of the *Mahabharata*, still filling the ear with stories of myth and miracle. But the days of these are over. Henceforward, we are to listen to nothing save facts, to believe nothing to which our ordinary everyday experience cannot give its assent.

Who, then, were these Sesunaga [today usually spelled Sisunaga or Shishunaga] kings of whom we read in the lists of dead dynasties given in the Puranas – those curious histories of the whole cosmogony of this world and the next, some of which can now be fairly proved to have existed in the very first centuries of our era, and with them an accredited claim to hoar antiquity?

How came these kings by their name Ses, or Shesh-naga? A name which indubitably points to their connection with the sacred snake, or 'nag'.

Scythians

Were they of Scythic origin? Nothing more likely. Certain it is that Scythic hordes invaded India from the north-east, both during and after the age of the Epics. It is conjectured, also, that they met in conflict with the Aryan invaders from the north-west on the wide, Gangetic plains, possibly close to the junction of the Sone River with the Ganges.

Here, at any rate, lay the ancient kingdom of Magadha, the kingdom of these Sesunaga kings.

There were ten of these kings, and of the first four, we, as yet, know nothing. But almost every year sees fresh inscriptions deciphered, new coins discovered, and therefore it is not unlikely that someday these mere dry-as-dust names, Sesunaga, Sakavarna, Kshema-dharman, and Kshattru-jas, may live again as personalities. At present we must be content with imagining them in their palace at Raja-griha, or 'The kings abode surrounded by mountains'.

It has a curiously distinguished, dignified sound, this description. One can imagine these Sesunaga princes, their Scythian faces, flat, oblique-eyed, yet aquiline, showing keen under the golden-hooded snake standing Uraeus-like over their low foreheads, riding up the steep, wide steps leading to their high-perched palaces, on their milk-white steeds; these latter, no doubt, be-bowed with blue ribbons and bedyed with pink feet and tail, after the fashion of processional horses in India even nowadays. Riding up proudly, kings, indeed, of their world, holders of untold wealth in priceless gems and gold – gold, unminted, almost valueless, jewels recklessly strung, like pebbles on a string.

This legend, indeed, of countless uncounted gold, of fair women, and almost weird, rough luxury, lingers still around the very name of Snake King, and holds its own in the folklore of India.

In these days the kingdom of Magadha – so far as we can judge, a Scythic principality – was just entering the lists against that still more ancient Aryan kingdom of Kosala, of which we read in the *Ramayana*. But there were other principalities in the settled country which lay between the extreme north-west of the Punjab and Ujjain, or Malwa. Sixteen such states are enumerated in various literary – chiefly religious – works, which were probably compiled in the fifth century BCE; but these, again, are mere dry-as-dust names.

First Breath of Reality

The first breath of real life comes with Bimbi-sara, the fifth Sesunaga king. He, we know, conquered and annexed the principality of Anga and built the city of New Rajagriha, which lies at the base of the hill below the old fort. But something there is in his reign which grips attention more than conquests or buildings. During it, and under his rule, the founders of two great religions gave to the world their solutions of the problem of life. In all probability both Mahavira and Gautama Buddha were born in Bimbi-sara's days; certain it is that he must have heard the first teachings of Jainism and Buddhism preached at his palace doors. He is supposed to have reigned for nearly five and twenty years, and then to have retired into private life, leaving his favourite son, Ajata-sutru, as regent.

History of Parricides

And here tragedy sets in; tragedy in which Buddhist tradition avers that Deva-datta, the Great Teacher's first cousin and bitterest enemy, was prime mover. For one of the many crimes imputed to this arch-schismatic by the orthodox, is that he instigated Ajata-sutru to put his father to death.

Whether this be true or not, certain it is that Bimbi-sara was murdered, and by his son's orders; for in one of the earliest Buddhist manuscripts extant there is an account of the guilty son's confession to the Blessed One (i.e., Buddha) in these words: 'Sin overcame me, Lord, weak, and foolish, and wrong that I am, in that for the sake of [sovereignty] I put to death my father, that righteous man, that righteous king.'

If, as tradition has it, that death was compassed by slow starvation, the prompt absolution which Buddha is said to have given the royal sinner for this act of atrocity becomes all the more remarkable. His sole comment to the brethren after Ajata-sutru had departed appears to have been: 'This king was deeply affected; he was touched in heart. If he had not put his father to death, then, even as he sate here, the clear eye of truth would have been his.'

Apart from this parricidal act, the motive for which he gives with such calm brutality, Ajata-sutru seems to have been a strong, capable king. He had instantly to face war with Kosala, the murdered man's wife – who, it is said, died of grief – being sister to the king of that country. Round this war, long and bloody, legend has woven many incidents. At one time Magadha, at another Kosala, seems to have come uppermost. Ajata-sutru himself was once carried a prisoner in chains to his opponent's capital; but in the end, when peace came, Kosala had given one of its princesses in marriage to the King of Magadha, and had become absorbed in that empire.

But this was not enough for ambitious Ajata-sutru. He now turned his attention to the rich lands north of the Ganges, and carried his victorious arms to the very foot of holy Himalaya.

In the course of this war he built a watch-fort at a village called Patali, on the banks of the Ganges, where in after years he founded a city which, under the name of Pataliputra (the Palibothra of Greek writers), became the capital, not only of Magadha, but of India – India, that is, as it was known in these early days.

Patali is the Sanskrit for the bignonia, or trumpet flower; we may add, therefore, to our mental picture of the remaining four Sesunaga kings, that they lived in Trumpet-flower City.

For the rest, these two great monarchs, Bimbi-sara and Ajata-sutru, must have been near, if not actual contemporaries of Darius, King of Persia, who founded an Indian satrapy in the Indus valley. This he was able to do, in consequence of the information collected by Skylax of Karyanda, during his memorable voyage by river from the Upper Punjab to the sea near Karachi, thus demonstrating the practicability of a passage by water to Persia. All record of this voyage is, unfortunately, lost; but the result of it was the addition to the Persian Empire of so rich a province, that it paid in gold-dust tribute to the treasury, fully one-third of the total revenue from the whole twenty satrapies; that is to say, about one million sterling, which in those days was, of course, an absolutely enormous sum.

There is not much more to tell of Ajata-sutru; and yet, reading between the lines of the few facts we actually know of him, the man's character shows distinct. Ambitious, not exactly unscrupulous, but uncontrolled. A man who, having murdered his father, could weep over his own act, and seek to obliterate the bloodstain on his hands by confessions and pious acts. When Buddha died, an eighth portion of his bones was claimed by Ajata-sutru, who erected at Rajgrîha a magnificent tope or mound over the sacred relics.

But, if tradition is to be believed, he handed down the curse of his great crime to his son, his grandson, and his great grandson; for the Ceylon chronicle asserts, that each of these in turn were parricides. It is – to use a colloquialism – a tall order; but assertion or denial are alike unproven.

If it be true, there is some relief in finding that the last of these criminal kings – Maha-nundin by name – was ousted from his throne and killed by his prime minister, one Mahapadma-Nanda, who is said, also, to have been the murdered man's illegitimate son by a Sudra, or low-caste woman.

Whether this latter be true or not, certain it is that about the year 361 BCE, or thereabouts, the reign of the Sesunaga kings ends abruptly. The dream-vision of the steps of old Rajgriha with Scythian princelings – parricidal princelings – riding up to their palaces on processional horses, or living luxuriously in Trumpet-flower city, vanishes, and something quite as dream-like takes its place.

Nanda Dynasty

For in the oldest chronicles we are told that there were but two generations in the next, or Nanda dynasty – viz.: Mahapadma and his eight sons – yet we are asked to believe that they reigned for 159 years!

In truth, these nine Nandas seem in many ways mythical, and yet the very confusion and contradictions which surround their history point to some underlying reason for the palpable distortion of plain fact. They are said to have reigned together, the father and his eight sons. The name of only one of these is known, Suma-lya; but when Alexander the Great paused on the banks of the Beas, in the year 326 BCE, he heard that a king was then reigning at Pataliputra, by name Xandrames (so the Greek tongue reports it), who had an army of over 200,000 men, and who was very much disliked, because of his great wickedness and base birth. For he was said to be the son of a barber, and as such, 'contemptible and utterly odious to his subjects'.

This king must have belonged to the Nanda dynasty, and the story, if it does nothing else, proves that the family was really of low extraction. That it gained the throne by the assassination of a rightful king, is also certain. But revenge was at hand. The tragedy was to be recast, replayed, and in 321 BCE Chandragupta, the Sandracottus of the Greeks, himself an illegitimate son of the first Nanda, and half-brother, so the tale runs, of the eight younger ones, was, after the usual fashion of the East, to find foundation for his own throne on the dead bodies of his relations.

THE AGE OF GAUTAM BUDDHA, 320 BCE TO 400 CE
(Upendra Nath Ball)

From the sixth century before the birth of Christ; our information about the history of India are capable of arrangement in time order. They are not so vague and shadowy as in the previous ages. Two great religious teachers were born towards the end of the sixth century. The vast amount of literature of the two movements affords sufficient material for the history of the period. The first exact date in the history of India is 326 BCE when Alexander invaded the country. The more ancient dates have been calculated on the basis of literary traditions, reckoned back from the known dates.

The Sisunaga Dynasty

The first dynasty which has left any authentic account is that of Sisunaga. He was a chieftain of Benares and later on fixed his capital at Giribraja or old Rajgriha, in about 642 BCE. The fifth monarch of this family, Bimbisara, ruled Magadha from 582 to 554 BCE. He built the town of New Rajgriha, and extended his territory by conquering Anga (the modern Bhagalpur and Monghyr districts.) He was succeeded by his son, Ajatasatru, who remained king for about twenty-seven years. He built a fortress at the confluence of the Son and the Ganges, which afterwards developed into the imperial city of Pataliputra. He conquered the kingdom of Kosala, and the country of the Lichchavis. Ajatasatru was succeeded by his son Darsaka in 527 BCE and Udaya, his grandson, occupied the throne in 503 BCE.

The last king built the city of Kusumapura on the Gangres. He was succeeded by Nandivardhan and Mahanandin, who ruled for forty and forty-three years respectively. Mahanandin was the last king of the dynasty. He had, by a Sudra woman, a son named Mahapadma Nanda, who became the founder of the Nanda dynasty in 413 BCE.

Jainism

It was during the reign of Bimbisara that both Mahavira, and Buddha were preaching their religions. Mahavira Vardhamana was the founder of Jainism. He was born in a noble family of Vajsali, capital of the Lichchavis. He joined the order of Parsvanath, but could not remain long there, as the rules of the Order did not satisfy him. He became the leader of a new movement at the age of forty and preached his religion for about thirty years. His missionary activities were mainly confined to Magadha, Videha and Anga. He died at Pawa in the district of Patna. He was related to the kings of these countries, through his mother. Bimbisara and Ajatasatru accepted his teachings. At the time of his death the number of his followers was more than 14,000.

Jainism maintains a close connection with Hinduism. It does not go against the caste system, and Brahmans are very often employed in their religious ceremonies. The Jains also believe in the Hindu gods, and some of them do not object to be called Hindus. They however do not accept the authority of the Vedas, and they oppose the practice of animal sacrifice. Their doctrine of the duality of man's personality is their principal feature. Human personality comprises both material and spiritual natures, and they do not believe in the existence of a universal soul or a supreme deity. God, according to them, is the 'highest, the noblest, and the fullest latent in the soul of man.' Their highest virtue is *Ahimsa*, i.e., not to hurt any sentient object. They believe that even the so-called inanimate objects such as stocks and stone are endowed with soul (Jiva). So their Ahimsa extends very far.

The religion of Mahavira is a humane religion appealing man to practise love and charity, not only towards human beings, but also towards everything that surrounds our life. It is an austere religion demanding self-control and various other austerities. The followers of the doctrine have not only established hospitals for men but also for animals. They have erected rest houses and other institutions for travellers and pilgrims. Jainism has not gone beyond the borders of India on account of its close connection with Hinduism. There are two principal sects of the Jains, the Svetambaras and the Digambaras. The Svetambaras again have another branch called the *Sthanaka-vasi* who rejects the use of idols. Jainism is still a living religion, and there are a large number of Jains throughout India.

Gautam Buddha

While the teachings of Mahavira are respected by a large number of Indians the teachings of Gautam Buddha are followed by vast populations outside India, Gautam Buddha was a world-teacher, calling men from the troubles of their life to the enjoyment of eternal peace. He was the scion of a Sakya clan ruling at Kapilavastu on the borders of Nepal. His father Suddhodana was the chief of the clan. His mother was a daughter of the Raja of the Koliyans to the east. Whether the Sakyas and the Koliyans were Aryans or Mongolians is a matter of controversy. The accepted theory is that they were Kshatriya and Aryan. There are others who hold that they were Mongolians. Even if they were Mongolians, they were sufficiently Aryanized, and their social and political organization was purely Aryan. Gautam was the only child of his father and was brought up in luxury and pleasure. He married early in life, and at the age of twenty-nine a son was born to him.

At this time of his life he became contemplative. He was overburdened with the thoughts of age, sickness, death, and misery. The world was to him a snare, and he was anxious for a release from its troubles. He made up his mind to renounce his position, his wife, and his child, and went to Rajgir to spend his days as an ascetic. There lived in the caves of the hills several hermits renowned for their scholarship and piety. Gautam first attached himself to Alara and then to Uddaka. He learned from them all that Hindu philosophy had to teach. But this did not satisfy him. He then retired into the jungles of Uruvela near Bodh Gaya and spent six years in austere penance.

By fasting and mortification his body was emaciated, and yet he did not receive the peace of mind which he was seeking. He then gave up the practice of self-torture. His disciples left him and went to Benares. When sympathy was most needed his friends and disciples forsook. In this state of struggle while he was wandering about along the bank of the Nairanjara he received unexpected sympathy at the hands of Sujata, a village girl. He sat under a large tree throughout the day and towards the evening his doubts cleared away, and he became the *Buddha* or the enlightened. The great mystery of sorrow was solved, and he received the peace of mind. The passions lost their fire, and the world was no longer the abode of temptations. That was the supreme moment in the life of Gautama, and after receiving the enlightenment he was filled with love for humanity and began to preach his new doctrines.

First he went to Benares, and there he turned the Wheel of Law in the deer park. The site has been recently excavated. The Emperor Asoka erected a pillar at the place, which has been recently found at Sarnath, three miles from Benares. Benares has been associated with many sacred memories in India, and there it was that Buddha 'set rolling the chariot wheel of a universal empire of truth and righteousness'. From that time till his death he preached his Law. He moved about from place to place in the kingdoms of Magadha, Kesala, and in the territories of the Sakyas, the Koliyans, and the Lichchavis. He visited Kapilavastu more than once and received into the order his son, his wife, and his stepmother, besides a large number of friends and relatives.

The most famous resorts of the master during the four months of the rains were the *Velubana* in the vicinity of Rajgir, and the *Jetavana* near Sravasti. Throughout the year he used to wander about teaching his new gospel to the people and during the four months, June to October, he used to observe the *Vas*, where all his disciples met him and received instructions from him. This custom still exists among the Buddhists in Ceylon where people meet together at night to listen to religious discourses by the monks. Whenever Buddha visited any place he lived outside the city in some jungles, and if no food was supplied by the people he went about with a begging bowl from door to door till sufficient quantity of food was collected.

The Teachings of Buddha

In his first sermon at Benares he explained his teachings. The virtue lies in following the Middle Path, that is, on the one hand not to be addicted to the pleasures of sense, and on the other not to practise self-torture and mortifications which the ascetics advise. The Middle Path is summed up in the eight principles:

1. Right Belief.
2. Right Aims.

3. Right Speech.
4. Right Actions.
5. Right Means of Livelihood.
6. Right Endeavour.
7. Right Mindfulness.
8. Right Meditation.

There are four Noble Truths which everyone has to realize, viz., suffering, the cause of suffering, the cessation of suffering and the Path which leads to the cessation of suffering. This life is full of sorrow. We are always guided by our senses, this is the cause of suffering, and where we can conquer our passions there is an end of our sorrow. The eight-fold path leads to the attainment of this state of mind. This is the substance of his teachings. He thought neither ceremonialism nor penance was sufficient for the attainment of virtue. He presented a scheme of life which appealed to every reasonable man. His code of morality was sure to elevate people from narrow selfishness and baser elements of life. Ahimsa formed an important part of his creed. He did not disease about the next world or a Supreme Being. Self-culture is the key of hie entire teaching. He created an order of disciples who carried the gospel from place to place. But the progress of the movement was not much till the time of Asoka, the great Maurya Emperor, who sent missionaries to various parts of India and outside. Buddhism has made considerable progress since then, although its hold upon the land of its birth is almost nothing.

Gautam Buddha died at the age of eighty at Kusinara near the Nepal Terai in 487 BCE. He created a ferment in the country, by inviting men and women, of all classes to follow his teachings. His teachings have been gathered together in the three baskets (Tripitakas), viz., Vinaya Pitaka, Sutta Pitaka, and the Abhidhamma Pitaka. The social upheaval which Buddhism brought about in India lasted for several centuries. His teachings were afterwards absorbed by the Hindu teachers. A new philosophy embodying his doctrines but at the same time dealing with the ultimate problems of soul, reality, and God extinguished Buddhism in India in about the eighth century after the birth of Christ.

The Causes of Its Popularity

The popularity of Buddhism was due no doubt to its practical philanthropy, its social equality, and its deep morality and commonsense views. People were disgusted with the tyranny and superstitions of the Brahmans who fell off from their high ideal. Penances, self-torture, the sacrifices, and the unintelligent repetition of mantras had lost their charm.

Buddha spoke in the language of the people, and his discourses contained a practical philosophy. He drew the people to a brotherhood which helped considerably in uniting the nation. 'The success of Gautama's mission,' says Mr. E. B. Havell, 'must have been due partly to his own magnetic personality and the deep human feeling which inspired his teaching, and partly to the fact that he opened wide the doors of Aryan religion and satisfied the spiritual desires of the masses by offering them a religious law easy to understand and accessible to all, free from elaborated and costly ceremonial, raising the social status of the lower orders, giving them their spiritual freedom and making the life of the whole community healthier and happier.'

The Buddhist Order

Buddha gave a new interpretation to this old Aryan culture and tradition. The Sangha which he organized was an institution of great political importance. It trained the members of the brotherhood in conducting their business on a purely democratic basis. The great Councils which were held at the death of Buddha at Rajgir, or at Vaisali 100 years afterwards or at the time of Asoka, or of Kanishka, prove incontestably how Indians managed their affairs in a constitutional manner. These Buddhist Councils were not singular. Almost all religious movements had their own assemblies. Even now such meetings are not rare. The Buddhist order admitted men and women who renounced the world and devoted themselves entirely to the propagation of truth. The Jain order included the lay members as well. A candidate for admission into the Buddhist order after the preliminary ceremonies had to repeat the two formulas, kneeling before the president. The first of these was as follows:

'I go for refuge to the Buddha, I go for refuge to the Law, And I go for refuge to the Order.'

Then he had to repeat the ten precepts:

1. 'I take the vow not to destroy life.
2. 'I take the vow not to steal.
3. 'I take the vow to abstain from impurity.
4. 'I take the vow not to lie.
5. 'I take the vow to abstain from intoxicating drinks, which hinder progress and virtue.
6. 'I take the vow not to eat at forbidden times.
7. 'I take the vow to abstain from dancing, singing, music and stage plays.
8. 'I take the vow not to use garlands, scents, unguents, or ornaments.
9. 'I take the vow not to use a high or broad bed.
10. 'I take the vow not to receive gold or silver.'

The senior members of the order are called Samana, and Bhikshu and the novices Samanera. All of them were mendicants. They had to follow the injunctions of Buddha, which are summed up in the four earnest meditations, the four great efforts, the four roads to Iddhi or Saintship, the five moral powers, the seven kinds of wisdom and the Noble Eight-fold Paths. Of these injunctions the Noble Eightfold Paths are the most important. At the meeting of the Sangha the members took their seats according to seniority: The motions were carried after they were put three times either unanimously or if there were discussion by the vote of the majority including the absentee members. No vote was valid which was contrary to the Dharma or Law. The General Assembly of the Order was the only competent authority to decide disputes regarding the interpretation of Dharma.

The Buddhist movement was thus a protestant movement which [...] reorganized Indian society on a wider basis, and re-adapted the religious thoughts to the actual needs of the people. Its philosophy was not entirely new as it had some kinship with the Sankhya philosophy of Kapila. But its social doctrines gave the people a practical code for the guidance of their daily life.

The Political Condition of India at the Time of Buddha

The Aryan settlers lived in clans and their form of government was more or less republican. Generally a single chief was elected as the chief executive officer with the title of Raja, and whenever the supreme power became hereditary the result was the establishment of a monarch with unlimited authority. The reverse process of a monarch being converted into a republic is scarcely found. Videha is the only one instance in the Buddhist records of a tribe, once under a monarchy, going back to the republican form.

At the time of Gautam Buddha we find powerful monarchies existing side by side with republics with absolute or modified freedom. There were four kingdoms of great importance, viz., Magadha, Kosala, Kosambi, and Avanti. The small kingdoms were about a dozen in number but they had very little political importance, and they were gradually absorbed in the powerful neighbouring states. The number of aristocratic republics existing at the time is not easy to ascertain. The most important republics were those of the Sakjas and the Vajjians. The Koliyans were a sub-clan of the Sakya race. The Yajjias consisted of eight confederate clans of whom the Lichchavis and the Videhas were most important. The other independent clans were the Majlas of Kusinara and Pava. [...]

INDIA IN THE FOURTH CENTURY BCE
(Upendra Nath Ball)

Early Magadha

The **Buddhist literature** is peculiarly valuable as it presents a somewhat full account of the political and social condition of the sixth century BCE specially in the case of the United Provinces and Behar. We have already seen that the first historical name in the list of kings is that of Sisunaga, king of Magadha. He became the king in about 64 BCE. Bimbisara was the fifth king in his dynasty. There were about ten kings of this dynasty, continuing their rule almost up to the end of the fifth century BCE. In the time of Buddha the most important kingdoms in northern India were Magadha and Kosala. Magadha had absorbed Anga, and later on the territory of the Lichchavis. Kosala also annexed the Sakya country shortly after the death of Buddha, and it is believed Ajatasatru conquered Kosala and became the most important king by the end of the sixth century BCE. The eighth king Udaya built the city of Kusumpura near the old Fort of Pataliputra and removed Ids capital there. He was succeeded by Nandivanlhan and Mahanandin.

Persian Invasion

While Magadha was building, up its power in northern India, the King of Persia was extending his empire up to the banks of the Indus. Darius (521–486 BCE) sent an expedition under Skylax who succeeded in conquering the Indus valley for his master. Henceforth Persia enjoyed revenue from its Indian satrapy of 860 Euboic talents of gold dust, that is, about a million sterling.

The extent of this newly acquired territory cannot be exactly determined. It included Sindh and a greater portion of the Punjab on both sides of the Indus from Kalabagh to the Sea. The Indian satrapy not only contributed largely to the treasury of Persia but the Persian army was strengthened by the Indian recruits. When Xerxes fought against Greece he had a large number of Indian archers in his army. The Persian army contained an Indian contingent at the battle of Plataea (479 BCE). It is presumed that there was constant intercourse between Persia and India, and through Persia with other countries in the west. When Alexander invaded India in 326 BCE the Persian Empire extended up to the Indus.

Nanda Kings

From the time of Ajatasatru down to the invasion of Alexander we have to depend upon the Puranic lists for a connected account. But we gather very little beyond a list of names. The Sisunaga dynasty comes to an end in about 413 BCE when the throne of the last king

Mahanandin was usurped by Mahapadma Nanda, one of his sons by a Sudra woman. The Nanda kings ruled for 91 years. They were despised by the orthodox Brahmans, and no authentic account about them is therefore available. Mahapadma Nanda was succeeded by his eight sons. The Nanda kings were greedy and accumulated great wealth. The last Nanda king was overthrown by Chandragupta Maurya in about 322 BCE.

Alexander's Invasion

The most remarkable event of this time is the invasion of Alexander. But the Indian literature is quite silent about the incident. It is most probably because people considered it a mere raid by an adventurous chief with a view to plunder, or because it affected the western part of the Punjab and did not in any way interfere with the more important Indian kingdoms in the east. Alexander also died shortly afterwards and all the vestiges of his conquest were swept away by the Indian chiefs.

Persia under Darius then enjoyed an extensive empire from Asia Minor to the banks of the Indus. By the treaty of 887 BCE the Grecian cities accepted the Persian king as the arbiter of their destinies. When Philip of Macedon conquered Greece a congress of the Grecian states was held at Corinth, and they declared war against Persia in order to strike a blow at its supremacy. Philip was appointed Generalissimo of the expedition, but he was murdered before he could undertake it. As soon as his son Alexander came to the throne he announced his intention of carrying oat his father's plan.

He crossed the Hellespont in the spring of 334 BCE. In three and half years he subjugated Asia Minor, conquered Egypt and put himself on the throne of Persia at Susa in 330 BCE. Then he ran over Persian provinces in Central Asia, and in about three years he became master of Hyrcania, Drangiana, Bactria, Sogdiana and other Northern Provinces of the Persian Empire. He crossed the Hindukush in May 327 BCE and spent a year subjugating the hill tribes of Swat and Bajaur. A part of his army was sent under his generals Hephaiston and Perdikkas in advance towards India. He crossed the Indus at Ohind, sixteen miles above Attok in February 326 BCE. Between the Indus and the Hydaspes (Jhelum) was the kingdom of Taxila. Its king Ambhi was then at war with his neighbours. So he came with rich presents in order that he could enlist the help of Alexander against his enemies. He became the vassal of the Macedonian king and in return for his presents received from Alexander a large amount of money and many valuable things.

On the completion of this alliance between Ambhi and Alexander, the king of Abhisara who formed a plan of resisting the invasion in conjunction with Poros sent an embassy offering surrender. Alexander expected that Poros would follow the lead of his ally, and so demanded from him homage and tribute. But Poros was a brave and patriotic king. He prepared to meet Alexander on the field. The Greek army crossed the Hydaspes and met Poros in the plains of Karri. The Indians fought bravely. The elephants were an unmanageable element in the Indian army. When wounded by arrows they ran over both friends and foes alike. The Indians could not stand before the superior cavalry and infantry of the Greeks. They were mercilessly routed. Poros was captured and was received with honour by the conqueror. Alexander was so much impressed with his valour and dignity that he restored to him the conquered territory to the east of the Hydaspes. Then he proceeded towards the east, invaded the countries of the Glausai or Glaukanikoi, and subjugated thirty-seven towns and a large number of villages.

Other tribes submitted without any trouble. The conqueror proceeded still further, crossed the Akesines (Chenab), the Hydraotes (Ravi) and reached the banks of the Hyphasis (Beas). On the way he met with the military tribes known as the Kathaioi, Oxydrakai, the Malloi and the Adraistai. The allied tribes selected Sangala as their main stronghold and offered stout resistance to the invading army from there. After a fierce onslaught the stronghold was razed to the ground. The Greek soldiers refused to cross the Hyphasis in spite of exhortations by the king. Alexander was afraid of the Gangaridce in the east who had a vast force of large-sized elephants, with trained and equipped forces. So the orders for retreat were given in September 326 BCE. Alexander erected twelve altars on the Hyphasis to mark the furthest point of his march. But no traces of these altars can be found. It is believed that they were set up at the foot of the hills between Indaura in Rangra and Mirthal in Gurdaspore districts.

The retreat was as memorable as his march. The conquered countries between the Hydaspes and the Hyphapusis were put under the viceroyalty of Poros. His officers had built a fleet of 2,000 vessels for carrying the troops by the rivers and the sea. Alexander proceeded along the Hydaspes to its confluence with the Akesines. Then he followed the river up to its junction with the Hydraorites. There he confronted a big combination of the local tribes. The Mallois and the Oxydrakai were warlike peoples. They protested against the passage of the Greek troops through their territories. There was a fierce struggle with the Mallois in which Alexander was wounded. But the Indian troops could not stand long against the disciplined army of Alexander, and retreated into a neighbouring town.

The Oxydrakai however stood aloof while their allies were worsted. They be submitted to Alexander and saved themselves by offering tribute and presents. A Greek Satrap was appointed in the conquered provinces. The fleet then went down the Hydraotes to its confluence with the Hyphasis and then to the confluence of the four rivers with the Indus. King Mousi-kanos of Sindh was severely dealt with for not sending him envoy and presents. At first he submitted but later on he revolted at the instigation of his Brahman councillors. The king and his advisers were executed for this defection. Then other cities at the mouth of the Indus easily submitted. So practically the Western Punjab and Sindh came under his sway. He appointed his own governors and made arrangements for administration. He stayed for some time at Patala and from there he sent a part of his army under his admiral Nearchos along the coast by boats, and he led the other part to Persia through Gedrosia. He reached Susa in May 324 BCE and Babyon the next year. There he died of malarial fever at the age of 33 on the 28th June, 323 BCE.

Effects of the Invasion

Alexander spent about nineteen months on the east of the Indus and made necessary arrangements for the continuance of his rule in his absence. He appointed Satraps so that these officers might govern according to his orders. But as soon as he died his plans were upset. The vast empire fell into pieces.

Philippos, the Satrap of the Indus valley, had been assassinated before the death of the conqueror, Eudemos was appointed Resident in his place. But within a short time after the death of Alexander the Indian chiefs revolted. In 322 BCE the Punjab shook off its allegiance and by 317 BCE the nominal rule in Sindh was put an end to. India became her old self again. The Greek conquest did not produce any lasting effects. Alexander was in spirit an oriental monarch, but he had very little opportunity of proving his administrative capacity in managing his vast dominions from Macedonia to the Punjab. So

India did not undergo any change in her political life. Indian society remained undisturbed. There might have been some intermixture of blood inevitable in cases of military occupation. But as such cases of irregular unions were very few no change of manners and customs could have been expected.

The Greek mode of warfare was no doubt of a superior type, but the subsequent Indian wars did not present any marks of improvement. The Indians did not gain by experience. They did not learn the tactics of the Greeks. Art and literature were unaffected. Some historians think that Alexander opened up roads for future invasions from the west. 'They broke down the wall of separation between west and east,' says V.A. Smith, 'and opened up four distinct lines of communication, three by land and one by sea. The land routes which he proved to be practicable were those through Kabul, the Mulla Pass in Balochistan and Gedrosia. Nearchos demonstrated that the sea voyage round the coast of Makran offered few difficulties to sailors, once the necessary local information had been gained which he lacked.' But another scholar, Mr. E. B. Havell, is of opinion Alexander's expeditions did not lead to the opening up of new highways between east and west, rather the reverse. The Persians had entered India before this, and these routes were known to them. There is again no evidence that the Greeks or any other European peoples ever afterwards ventured to follow in the footsteps of Alexander.

The Greek colonists of Bactria and Parthia occupied some part of India later on. But they knew what other neighbouring tribes are expected to know. Whatever the Indians might have learnt from ta the Greeks that was not the result of the invasions of Alexander into India but it was on account of the existence of the Greek settlements in her neighbourhood. On the other hand, it is believed that Indian philosophy greatly influenced the Greek thoughts and culture. A number of Indian scholars went to Greece and Asia Minor and there the ideas of the East gradually percolated. 'The influence of Buddhist ideas in Christian doctrine may be traced,' says, V.A. Smith, 'in the Gnostic forms of Christianity, if not elsewhere. The motives of Indian philosophy and religion which filtered into the Roman empire flowed through channels opened by Alexander.'

Condition of India in the Fourth Century BCE

The invasion of Alexander has been important in another way. He was accompanied by a large number of scholars and historians who recorded various information regarding India. It is from the fragments of their writings that a full account of the civilization, manners, and customs of the people and their political condition has been drawn up.

India was then divided into a number of small states, mostly monarchies and some republics. About twenty years after the invasion Megasthenes stated that there were 118 distinct nations or tribes. There was no paramount power in India. The states were constantly at feud, one trying to absorb another. Ambhi of Taxila submitted to Alexander with a view to punish the king of Abhisara and Poros. The republics were strongly defended by the free Malavas and Kshudrakas (Malloi and Oxydrakai). The citizens of the republics were very jealous of their freedom and self-government, and they did not easily yield. As a matter of fast Alexander received the stoutest opposition from them. The Indians were strong and brave soldiers. But they lacked in combination and there was no good general among them to match with Alexander.

Although India was divided into a number of small states, there was full intercourse between the different parts of the country. Elephants were brought from such distant parts as Anga, Kalinga,

Saurashtra, and Bundelkhund. Gold, diamonds, pearls, and other gems came from such places in the south as Tamraparni, Madura, and Ceylon. Textile fabrics came from Benares, Madura and the Konkan. There were ordnances to regulate trade with foreign countries. Coins were in common use but they were of primitive type. Strabo the historian mentions some strange customs of the country. The poor parents used to sell their daughters at the marketplace after exposing their body in the flower of their age. The dead were thrown out to be devoured by the vultures. It was not universal for a man to have many wives. The widows were burned along with their dead husbands. The king of Taxila made a present of 3,000 oxen fattened for shambles. It is presumed from this that even at that time people used to slaughter cattle for entertaining distinguished guests.

Taxila then occupied an important position. It was the greatest centre of learning. Princes and sons of well-to-do Brahmans were sent there for finishing their education. Here three Vedas and the eighteen accomplishments were taught. The university of Taxila was specially reputed for its medical school. There were good arrangements for teaching all arts and sciences under distinguished professors.

The Punjab had attained a high degree of material civilization. The religion of the people was Brahminical, although there were followers of Zoroaster and worshippers of fire. The Greeks mention the names of Indra, Balarama and the Ganges as the gods worshipped by the people The Brahmans were no longer inferior to the Kshatriyas. They had assumed a position of authority. They were the chief councillors of the kings and even in the republic of the Malavas they received special treatment. Some trees were held sacred, the Brahmans used to take flesh but the taking of beef was a sin. This picture of Indian society is interesting as it continues almost in this state up to the present time.

THE MAURYA EMPIRE

From around 322 BCE, India was dominated by the Mauryan dynasty, founded by Chandragupta I. By the time of the third king, Ashoka, Mauryan control extended from Afghanistan to south India. The Mauryans were succeeded by the Shungas, followed by the Kanvas, who controlled a far smaller area. The political picture was complex. In the northwest were territories ruled by the Indo-Greeks, while across India were numerous small kingdoms, always ready to reassert their power. In the Deccan were the Andhras, also known as the Satavahanas; further south were the three dynasties of the Cholas, Cheras and Pandyas. In his overthrow of the Nanda dynasty, the first Mauryan king, Chandragupta I, was helped by his minister Vishnugupta, also known as Kautilya and Chanakya. Though far more sources are now available, some confusion about the origin of Chandragupta still exists. Some sources state that he was low-born, or the son of a Nanda king of Ayodhya, while Buddhist sources claim he was a *kshatriya*, that is, of the warrior caste, the second highest in the four-fold caste system. Literary sources include those of the Greeks, the *Arthashastra* of Kautilya, the *Mudra-rakshasa*, a play written by Vishakhadatta on Chandragupta Maurya, as well as the law books or Dharma Shastras and Buddhist and Jain texts. As pointed out earlier, however, the *Arthashastra* represents the ideal and was not composed in a single period.

The capital of the Mauryan empire was at Pataliputra, modern Patna, in the state of Bihar. Chandragupta Maurya further expanded and consolidated his empire. Seleukos Nikator was a commander of Alexander's forces and, after his death, a governor of part of Alexander's northwest territories. Soon he defeated other governors, and founded his own empire, next proceeding towards India. A battle was fought between the two and was won by Chandragupta. There was a marriage alliance and Megasthenes, a Greek ambassador, came to Chandragupta's court. He wrote the *Indica*, which today, though available only in fragments, is an important document, which provides insight on the economy and society of the time.

Chandragupta was succeeded by Bindusara, followed in turn by Ashoka, who ruled from 269–232 BCE. The rule of Ashoka is described in his edicts, inscriptions engraved on rocks and pillars from Afghanistan in the north to Karnataka in the south. One key edict narrates how Ashoka conquered Kalinga, yet the death and destruction that this conflict caused filled him with sorrow. After this, he vowed to end violence and to rule through *dhamma* (the Pali term for Sanskrit *dharma*).

Ashoka's edicts provide an idea of life in the empire during the third century BCE. Buddhist sources add to the picture. *Dhamma* is a word that Ball (whose text makes up this chapter) translates as 'Law of Piety'. This Pali term is used to define Buddhist precepts, but Ashoka's *dhamma* is not the same as that in Buddhism. Rather, it is a way of life, according to his ideas of what was right and correct. Ashoka converted to Buddhism, which spread during his reign. He sent Mahindra and Sanghamitra to Sri Lanka to reveal Buddhist truths. Ball refers to them as Ashoka's brother and sister, while in most sources they are his son and daughter. But not everyone converted to Buddhism as he suggested. There were also Jains, Ajivikas, who were a separate sect and not part of Jainism, and various Charvaka groups. Numerous Vedic and other deities were worshipped and Vedic literature such as the Upanishads continued to be composed. Art and architecture of the period include the highly polished stone pillars with animal capitals, erected by the king himself.

Ashoka's successors proved weak and the dynasty's last king, Brihadratha, was overthrown by Pushyamitra Shunga, who was the commander of his army. The reign of the Shunga dynasty was followed by that of the Kanvas. Vasudeva Kanva, a minister of the Shunga king Devabhuti, killed him and began to rule in 73 BCE. Menander, an Indo-Greek king, invaded the Gangetic plains in about 150 BCE, but was repulsed. The Andhras or Satavahanas, Kharavela, king of Kalinga, and the Kshatrapas and other local rulers of Gujarat were among other kings of the times.

Archaeologically the Mauryan empire is represented by urban centres with baked brick structures, terracotta ring wells for water storage and a variety of artefacts. Wood was also used and wooden palisades surrounded the ancient city of Pataliputra (Patna). Excavations at Kumrahar near Patna railway station revealed a hall with eighty pillars of polished buff sandstone. Apart from these, and the other monolithic stone pillars of Ashoka's reign, stupas surrounded by railings were erected. Cave dwellings for Buddhist monks and other ascetics were excavated in rocky hillsides.

The Mauryan empire has been one of the most studied periods in Indian history, with numerous books written on the subject. Ashoka is seen today as one of India's greatest kings. He not only created a vast empire, but put forward the ideals of good government, tolerance and respect for all sects and religions, kindness towards animals and the concept of ruling through *dhamma*, or idealistic principles. India's national emblem of three lions with the chakra below is derived from the capital of an Ashokan pillar found at Sarnath. And in the centre of India's flag is the chakra from the same capital, representing the dharmachakra, the wheel of dharma, symbolizing the teachings of the Buddha and the cycle of life. Ashoka's reign is also most important for the spread of Buddhism.

Only during medieval times did an empire as large as that under Ashoka exist again.

RISE OF AN EMPIRE IN INDIA

Shortly after the departure of Alexander a strong empire was established in India. The smaller kingdoms and states were brought together under one throne, and the north-west frontiers were protected against foreign invasions. India has several times been invaded by foreign armies on account of the existence of constant friction between her different states and races. The consolidation of the whole of northern India under one suzerain authority led to internal peace and prosperity and freedom from external raids.

The process of consolidation had commenced with the growth of the power of Magadha. Alexander heard of the powerful Gangaridae in the east, that is, of the powerful kingdom on the Ganges Valley. Magadha had extended its dominions up to Mathura by the time of Ajatasatru by annexing the kingdom of Kosala and other northern states. The Nanda kings were not popular. A young prince of the dynasty was in exile in the Punjab when Alexander was carrying on his campaigns. On the death of Alexander the Greek outposts in the Punjab were in danger. The Indians revolted against the Greeks under the leadership of Chandragupta, the exiled prince from Magadha. The Greek garrisons fell into the hands of Chandragupta and he became the master of the Punjab in 322 BCE. He took advantage of another revolution in Magadks. With the aid of a Brahman politician Vishnugupta, he deposed Dhana Nanda and slew him and occupied his throne. He thus became the monarch of the vast country from the Indus to the Ganges.

The smaller states were brought under the stern rule of a wise king. Anarchy and misrule disappeared and a strong government was established. He increased the army and overran the country between the Himalayas and the Narmada, and the Arabian Sea to the Bay of Bengal. His army consisted of 30,000 cavalry, 9,000 elephants and 600,000 infantry and innumerable chariots.

Invasion of Seleukos

On the death of Alexander his empire was divided among his generals. But they quarrelled among themselves for supremacy. Antigonos and Seleukos were the rival candidates for supremacy in Asia. In the beginning Antigonos managed to maintain his position, but he was defeated by Seleukos in 312 BCE, who was henceforth known as Seleukos Nikator or Seleukos the conqueror. It took him about six years in regaining his position in Persia and other countries.

In 305 BCE he led an expedition into India. He expected that like Alexander he would scatter the forces of the Indian chiefs. But he was met by the strong army of Chandragupta. The Greeks were defeated and Seleukos was forced to cede several provinces on the west of the Indus including the Paropanisadai, Aria, Arachosia, and Gedrosia, to up to the Hindu Kush mountains. Besides he had to give his daughter in marriage to Chandragupta. The treaty was concluded in about 303 BCE. The empire of Magadha reached its scientific frontier. Seleukos sent Megasthenes as an ambassador to the Court of Patailputra. Henceforth the two great kings of Magadha and Syria remained in amity.

Last Days of Chandragupta

Chandragupta may thus be called the first Emperor of India. He was the first successful monarch to bring about the unity of northern India and to maintain the independence of the country against foreign encroachments. The success of his administration is mainly due to the statesmanship of his minister Vishnugupta, better known as Chanakya or Kautilya. The country was visited by a severe famine in 298 BCE. The king abdicated in favour of his son Bindusara, and retired into the south along with some Jain ascetics, and the tradition goes that he starved himself to death after twelve years in Sravana Belgola on the border of Mysore.

The Literature of the Period

The history of the period is clouded with too many legends. The Brahman literature is silent about Chandragupta most probably because Buddhism prospered under the Maurya dynasty. But there can be no doubt that his exploits found an important place in the tradition of the country as in the 8th century CE his career was taken up as the plot of the well-known Sanskrit drama *Mudra-Rakshasa*. His name appears mostly in the Buddhist chronicles. Nothing has been found from the epigraphic records as yet discovered. The Rudradaman inscription at Girnar mentions Pushyagupta who was a governor of Chandragupta in the western provinces. Sir William Jones identified Sandracottus of the Greek writers with Chandragupta and since then the information supplied by the Greek writers have been connected with the historic materials of the Buddhist literature and the *Mudra-Rakshasa*.

The publication of Kautilya's *Arthasastra* written by the astute politician Chanakya has helped the scholars in making a comprehensive survey of the political conditions of the times. The *Arthasastra* is a treatise on the principles of administration in a monarchic state and there are occasional references to the republics. It describes no doubt an ideal state of things but the ideals set forth there may be taken as the picture of the existing state of things. The ordnance and regulations of the *Arthasastra* were the political principles recognized by the Indo-Aryan governments, and they are considered even now as breathing a spirit of sound statesmanship. That they were actually followed by Chandragupta and his descendants is corroborated by Megasthenes and other Greek writers who visited India at the time.

Nature of Chandragupta's Government

Pataliputra was the capital of the empire, and governors were appointed for the distant provinces. The city of Pataliputra was administered by a municipal governmental board of thirty members divided into six committees consisting of five members each. It is believed that this kind of municipal government might have been introduced into other cities of the empire. The central government was very strong and the provincial satraps were regular in their duties. The monarch was served by a highly organized staff of news carriers who reported to him about the doings of his officers. The vast army of trained soldiers was a dread to the evildoers.

The details about the provincial and village government are not available, but there is nothing to show that the old governments were altogether subverted or that the people in the villages were deprived of their communal rights. 'The government of Chandragupta,' says Mr. E. B. Havell, 'was a continuation and extension of a process of political amalgamation which had been going for centuries before Alexander's raid gave it a new impetus. The republican form of government which obtained among many of the Aryan tribes was not sup pressed, though in Kautilya it is regarded as a source of political. weakness. Neither were the traditional village communities or their powers of local self-government altogether ignored in the bureaucratic control set-up by the Mauryan imperial government for the purpose of removing the weakness of Indo-Aryan polity, which had been revealed by the success of Alexander's invasion.'

Chandragupta was an autocrat, but he had to depend upon the goodwill of the people. His ministers were all able men, and he could not override their advice. It was not merely because he was a powerful monarch that the throne remained so long in the possession of his dynasty. As long as a monarch rules in the interest of the people according to the tenets of the Dharmasastras and with the advice of wise and learned ministers his government remains acceptable to the people. The Arthasastra distinctly mentions the virtues requisite in a minister, who is not a mere tool in hands of the king. 'Chandragupta's will may have been law within his empire, but he was none the less a constitutional monarch bound by the common law of Aryavata,' says Mr. Havell.

The Central Government

The supreme control of the administration was vested in the King in Council. The number of members of the Council varied according to the requirements of the times. Each minister was severally put in charge of a department, and he was assisted by two subordinate ministers in his executive duties. The Council had the joint responsibility in the matter of finance, foreign affairs and other important subjects. The Council could carry on its deliberations in the absence of the king. The appointments of the provincial governors, the heads of the departments, and the principal officers of the state were made by the Council. The policy of government was framed by it, and if a member was absent from the meeting his opinion was given in writing. The resolutions were recorded, and signed and sealed by the ministers according to the order of precedence. Here we have all the formalities of a constitutional government. 'All kinds of administrative measures are preceded by deliberations in a well-formed council', says Kautilya.

Duties of the king

The king had to lead a regulated life. The day and the night were each divided into eight equal parts (*nalikas*) each, and he had to look to fixed duties in each part. Thus in the first part of the day he despatched watchmen, and attended to the accounts of receipts and expenditure. In the second part he looked to the affairs of citizens and the people. The third part he spent in bath, dinner, and study. In the fourth part the revenues were received and the king attended to the appointment of high officers. In the fifth part he attended to correspondence with the ministers and gathered information from his secret service. The sixth period he kept for himself, for amusements or deliberation. In the seventh period he looked after the elephants, horses, chariots, and infantry, in the eighth he considered with the commander-in-chief the plans of military operations.

His night was also equally divided. In the first part he received secret emissaries, the second he spent in bathing, supper, and study. The third, fourth, and fifth parts of the night he spent in his bedchamber. He was roused up in the sixth part, and in the seventh part he had to consider the administrative measures, and to send out spies. In the eighth part he received benedictions from the priests, saw the chief household officers and then went to court. This timetable could be altered when necessary, according to the urgency of business.

Kautilya insists upon attending personally to the business of the petitioners, specially to the business of God, of heretics, Brahmans, cattle, sacred places, minors, the aged, the afflicted, the helpless and the women according to the nature of these works. When attending to the business of physicians and ascetics be must sit round the sacred fire in company with his high priest and teacher.

'In the happiness of his subjects lies his happiness; in their welfare his welfare; whatever pleases himself he shall not consider as good, but whatever pleases his subjects he shall consider as good' (*Arthasastra*, Book 1, Chapter 19).

Functions of the Government

The Government had many functions besides maintaining peace and order. Legislation did not form a part of the state duties. The Dharmasastras were the principal law books, and the scholars versed in the Vedas and the sciences were the interpreters of law. The administration of justice was carried on by three scholars acquainted with Sacred Laws and three ministers of the king. The courts were held at places where several districts met.

There were a large number of officials for the collection of revenue, for collecting news, and for the superintendence of the industrial domains. The state had a regular staff for carrying on agriculture, mining operations, manufactures of cotton, liquor, arms and ammunition, chariots, and various other commodities; for the management of forests, supervision of commerce and for the protection of elephant forests and looking after the elephants and horses in the royal stable and the cattle and other useful animals. There were also special officers for maintaining weights and measures, issuing passports, and collecting tolls. The conduct and activities of these officers were systematically watched by the secret service men and reported to the king. They were severely dealt with for offences of misrule or dishonesty. The reports of the spies were not accepted until corroborated from other sources.

The kingdom way divided in to four Provinces which were sub-divided into districts and villages. The Collector-General was the chief officer of the Revenue Department. For a group of five or ten villages there was an accountant called *Gopa*. The officer of the province was known as *Sthanika*. Special officers were also deputed by the Collector-General to inspect the work of the provincial and the village officers and to collect the special religious tax known as *Bali*. The duties of the *Gopa* were very important. He had to fix the boundaries of the villages, to keep a register of the householders and their lands with descriptions of the plots of grounds such as cultivated, uncultivated, forests, cremation grounds, pasture lands, places of pilgrimage, and various other information. He had also to note the number of men following the different professions, and to keep an account of the villages regarding their character, occupation, income, and expenditure. The register that the *Gopa* had to keep was a full survey of the economic and social condition of the people, and was expected to supply accurate information to the state! The system could have been followed in a perfectly organized state, where people also have sufficient knowledge of public duties.

Municipal Government

The *Sthanika*, supervised the work of the village officers like the modern district officer. Besides the collection of revenue these officers were entrusted with the several duties of administration. The arrival and departure of persons of doubtful character were regularly watched and all cases of corruption and dishonesty reported by the spies. The cities had a similar staff of officials. Chandragupta made an improvement upon the old system of city government. The Greek ambassador Megasthenes informs us that Pataliputra was managed by a municipal board consisting of thirty members. The board was subdivided into six Committees of, five members each for the management of separate departments. An enumeration of the committees with their respective duties will show how the machinery of municipal administration was organized.

The first committee was something like a *Board of Labour* which fixed the wages, enforced laws for the use of pure materials, and in a general way looked after the welfare of the artisans. There were strict laws for the preservation of the efficiency of the craftsmen. The second committee watched the interests of the *Alien and the Visitors*. Elaborate arrangements were made for lodging them, and giving medical and other aids when necessary. This shows that there were a large number of foreigners residing in Pataliputra in that time. The third committee dealt with *Vital Statistics*, and kept the register of births and deaths. The fourth committee a *Board of Trade and Commerce* which regulated sales, and weights and measures. It also granted license to traders who had to pay taxes according to the nature and amount of business. The fifth committee was a *Board of Industries* regulating manufactures and sale of commodities. There was a strict regulation to separate the old goods from the new so that customers were not deceived. The sixth committee was entrusted with the task of collecting a tithe of the value of goods. All sellers had to pay a duty, the evasion of which was punishable with death.

It is presumed that the administration of other cities such as Taxila, and Ujjain, followed the lines of Pataliputra. The Municipal Board also performed certain other duties in their collective capacity such as the supervision of the markets, temples, harbours, and the public works. Kautilya mentions that there was an officer in charge of the capital known as *Nagaraka*. He gives a detailed description of the way in which the people in the capital lived. The regulations regarding the sojourn of the strangers were very strict, and the sumptuary laws extended over all the departments of a household.

Organization of the Army

The army was organized on the old method. It consisted of the infantry, the cavalry, the elephantry, and the chariotry. Chandragupta greatly increased the strength of his army, which included 600,000 foot soldiers, 30,000 horses, 8,000 chariots, 9,000 elephants.

The administration of the army was vested in a Board of thirty members divided into six departments managed by five members each. The departments were as follows: 1, Admiralty; 2, Transport, Commissariat and Army service; 3, Infantry; 4, Cavalry; 5, War-chariots, and 6, Elephants. The troops were either hereditary or hired. The commander-in-chief had the entire control of the army and directed the operations in the field. The king used to consult him about the defence of the country. There were forts of various kinds scattered throughout the country. A fortress of the *Sthaniya* type was set up in the centre of 800 villages, of *Drona-mukha* type in the centre of 400 villages, of *Kharratiko* type in the centre of 200 villages, and of *Sangrahana* type in the centre of ten villages. Besides, there were fortifications in the extremities of the kingdom, on mountains or in islands. These forts were constructed on sound scientific principles. Each fort had twelve gates, and a secret land and water way. Inside the fort there ran three royal roads from west to east and three from south to north. Besides, there were special roads for chariots, and elephants, and roads leading to other forts and important places. The harbours and shipyards for river and ocean-going vessels were constructed at suitable places. It is on account of this efficient organization of the army that Chandragupta succeeded in consolidating his empire and in warding off the Greek invaders.

Sources of Income of the State

The principal sources of revenue were according to income of the Kautilya, forts (*durga*), country-parts (*rashtra*), mines (*khani*), buildings and gardens (*setu*), forests (*vana*), herds of cattle (*vraja*), and roads of traffic. Under the head of forts were tolls, fines, duties on the trade guilds, the profit of coinage, and such things. Produce from brown lands, government share in the produce, religious taxes, taxes paid in money, road access, and income of ferries and other state services were put under the head of country-parts. Income from gold, silver and other minerals came under the head of mines. Income from flour, fruit and vegetable gardens was considered as *setu*. Forests used for games, timber or elephants also were a source of revenue. Cows, buffaloes, horses and other animals came under the head of herds. Land and the water ways were the roads of traffic.

All these yielded income to the state. To put them in the phraseology of finance the main sources of revenue were the revenue from the crownlands, forests, and gardens, income from the mines and industries, license duties on trade and manufactures, [assessments] of various kinds, and taxes on land. If the income at any time were not sufficient for the various charges of the government then the king could raise benevolences.

There is a controversy over the question of land revenue. We found that in the fifth century BCE land belonged to the community and not to the state, which was entitled to a share of the produce for services rendered, and not on account of any right in the land. But it seems the king acquired a proprietary right as he extended his territory and made new conquests. He reclaimed forests and created new settlements over his crown lands. The income from these lands was strictly his revenue. It seems however that there were villages of various types, e.g., villages exempt from taxation, villages supplying soldiers, villages paying taxes in kind or gold, and villages supplying labour or dairy produce in lieu of taxes (*Arthasastra*, Book II, Chapter 35).

People enjoyed land not always as a tenant of the king. To some the king was the head of the tribe. In their cases, the land was the property of the community. Even when the king gradually asserted his rights as a landlord we do not find that the old occupants were ejected from their lands. It has been held as a gross violation of rights to interfere with the property of the people. The cultivators of the crown lands paid the king as much as they could without entailing any hardship upon themselves with the exception of their own private lands that were difficult to cultivate (*Arthasastra*, Book II, Ch. 24). The expression 'private lands' clearly shows that people had proprietary right in some lands, and that the ultimate property in land was vested in the state is a thing of later history. There was a regular system of keeping the accounts and for their audit. Embezzlement of funds and dishonesty on the part of revenue collectors was a grave offence and the culprits were severely punished.

General Condition of the People

The Greek ambassador Megasthenes has left much valuable information regarding the country. The greatest city of India was Pataliputra at the confluence of the Sone and the Ganges. It was about ten miles in length and two miles in breadth and surrounded on all sides by a ditch 600 feet in breadth and thirty cubits in depth.

There were 570 towers above the ramparts and sixty-four gates of the city. The people were free and not one of them was a slave. The king was attended by women servants in the palace, and when he came out these attendants accompanied him. The king provided irrigation works for the improvement of agriculture and facilities were provided for industrial developments. The roads were in good order, and milestones were set up at the interval of ten Stadia (20221/2 yards). The north-western frontier was connected with the capital by grand trunk road.

All the information available bear testimony to a high degree of civilization in India People were generally honest. Crimes were rare. Megasthenes heard of very small thefts in the capital of 400,000 persons, amounting in the aggregate not more than 200 *drachmas* (about £8). The pay of the officers ranged from 48,000 silver *panas* a year for the heir appoint to fifty *panas* for a labourer. The king constructed many works of public utility out of the public revenue, and provided land and other necessary things for construction of other works such as reservoirs, places of pilgrimage and groves by the people. The rules of co-operation among the people in public works and trade and industry were very strict. This shows that the public life was highly organized.

Chandragupta built an empire unique in its kind in India. It may be that he borrowed some ideas from the neighbouring empire of Persia, which at one time extended from the Mediterranean to the banks of the Indus. But the ideals of Chandragupta's government were purely Indo-Aryan. The remains of architecture found in the excavations at Kumrahar do not conclusively prove that the Indian buildings were modelled on Persian style. The marks of intermixture of culture may not be wanting, and this is nothing extraordinary. The neighbouring peoples are sure to influence each other.

Bindusara (297–272 BCE)

Chandragupta was succeeded by his son Bindu sara in 297. The details about the administration of Bindusara are not available. It is inferred from his title of Amitrochates (*Sanskrit Amitraghata*) which means slayer of foes that he was a brave and successful soldier. He maintained the empire in good order. Most probably the Deccan was conquered by him.

The only conquest made by Asoka was Kalinga, but his empire extended up to Mysore. Chandragupta ruled the country from Kathiawar to Magadha and so it is concluded that the rest of Asoka's empire must have been conquered by his father. Antiochos, the son of Seleukos, sent an embassy under Deimachos, and Ptolemy Philadelphus of Egypt sent another under Dionysios to the court of Pataliputra. The fame of the Indian empire spread far into the Western countries in the time of Chandragupta and the foreign kings maintained the old relations. Bindusara was anxious to extend the relations with the West by importing Greek philosophers.

ASOKA THE GREAT

Asoka was the Viceroy of Taxila and Ujjain during the reign of his father Bindusara. He was selected as *Yuvaraja*, or heir-apparent on account of his ability and fitness. He was residing at Ujjain when his father fell ill and he was summoned from there to the bedside of the dying king to step into the throne. The succession, however, was contested by his eldest brother Susima in vain and after four years the coronation of Asoka took place in 269 BCE. He ruled the country for about forty years from 272 to 232. BCE. It was a peaceful administration which made the people happy and prosperous.

Kalinga War

In the ninth year from his coronation or the thirteenth year of his reign Asoka invaded Kalinga, the country between the Mahanadi and the Godavari. The people of Kalinga did not easily yield, and the war has been commemorated in the Rock Edict XIII from which we learn 'One hundred and fifty thousand persons were thence carried away captive, and many times that number perished.'

The war, however, marked the turning point in the life of the emperor. The slaughter, death, and imprisonment of the large number of persons brought remorse into his heart. At this critical period he met the Buddhist monk Upagupta, and his teachings produced a great impression upon him. Henceforth he became a follower of Buddha. He remained a lay disciple for two years and a half, and then he joined the Order and strenuously exerted himself for the attainment and spread of the *Dhamma*. He gave up war and considered the spread of the *Dhamma* as true conquest.

His Proclamations

The exertions of Asoka succeeded in making the precepts of Buddha acceptable throughout the land. He sent missionaries in all directions, and inscribed the teachings on rocks and pillars at the wayside places.

These inscriptions supply the most important in formations for a history of his administration. The Kadian literature has no reference to this great monarch, and we gather some idea of his life and character from the Ceylonese chronicles, the *Dipavamsa* and the *Mahavamsa* written in the third and fourth centuries of the Christian era. In about this time Buddha Ghosa, a Brahman from Behar, went to Ceylon and collected the traditions there which he embodied in Pali in his commentaries on the *Vinaya*. The other source of information is the *Asoka-Avadana* written in Sanskrit, preserved in Nepal. All these books are full of legendary accounts, and it is a difficult task to compile a correct narrative from them. The historical importance of the inscriptions therefore cannot be exaggerated. They are a genuine record of the instructions of the be king to his officers and subjects. Although they do not contain sufficient details they enable us to form a correct estimate of his administration and character.

The edicts have been found inscribed on rocks in such distant places as Shahbazgarhi and Mansera in the north-west frontier, Girnar in Kathiawar, Dhauli in Orissa, Jaugad in Ganjam, Kalsi near Mussoorie, and Sopara in the Bombay Presidency. These rock edicts are fourteen in number. The minor rock edicts found at Bairat in Rajputana, Rupnath in the Central Provinces, Sahasram in Bengal, and Siddapura in Mysore were probably issued earlier in about 257 BCE. The Bhabru Edict, which was discovered on the top of a hill near Bairat, was addressed to the Buddhist Order all the same time as the Minor Rock Edict No. 1. Asoka issued instructions to his officials in the newly conquered province of Kalinga in two special edicts in about 256 BCE. A few inscriptions have been found in the caves of Barabar Hill near Gaya which record the presentation of cave dwellings to the Ajivikas, a sect of Jains, in the thirteenth and twentieth years of his reign (257 and 250 BCE).

In the twenty-first year of his reign Asoka went on a pilgrimage to the places associated with the memory of Buddha. He was companied by Upagupta and a large number of Buddhist Bhikshus. He erected pillars in the places he visited, and on some of those pillars he recorded the information of his visit. The pillars at Rummindei and Nigliva are two such commemorative monuments in the Nepal Terai. The seven Pillar Edicts were issued in the twenty-seventh and twenty-eighth years of his reign (243 and 242 BCE) for the benefit of the people within his kingdom. Pillars bearing edicts have been found at Delhi, Meerut, Allahabad, Lauriya-Araraj, Lauria-Nandan Garh and Rampurwa in the Champaran district of Behar, and at Sanchi in Bhopal State. A Buddhist Council was held at Pataliputra in 240 BCE and shortly afterwards edicts were issued denouncing schism in the Church. The inscriptions discovered at Sarnath and Sanchi bear evidence of an active propaganda to stop Church dissensions. Two more inscriptions have been found at Allahabad which were probably recorded in the twenty-seventh year of his reign or later.

Extent of the Empire

An idea of the extent of the empire may be formed from the distribution of the edicts, from the internal evidence of the inscriptions, and from literary and historical traditions. The whole of India excluding the extreme South and Assam, Afghanistan, Beluchistan, and probably Khotan were comprised within his empire. His powers extended over Nepal, Kashmir and other border lands. Although he was the supreme ruler over this vast empire it is believed that there existed a number of autonomous states within it owing allegiance to the sovereign power. These states enjoyed freedom in their internal affairs, but in all other matters they submitted to the emperor.

Form of Government

Asoka was a benevolent monarch always anxious to do good to his people. 'Work I must for the public benefit and the root of the matter is in exertion and dispatch of business, than which nothing is more efficacious for the general welfare. And for what do I toil? For no other end than this, that I may discharge my debts to animate beings, and that while I make some happy in this world, they may in the next world gain heaven.' (Rock Edict VI) He was so studious about the welfare of the people that he enjoined his official reporters to keep him informed of the people's business at all hours and in all places. He kept strict watch over the activities of his officials and the Buddhist monks. The subjects were looked upon as children, and the officials as skilful nurses.

In the Pillar Edict IV he says: 'Commissioners have been appointed by me to rule over many hundred thousand persons of the people, and to them I have granted independence in the award of honours and penalties, in order that they may in security and without fear perform their duties, and bestow welfare and happiness on the people of the country and confer benefits on them.' The Kalinga Edict contains a passage which shows that the officers had to consult the people periodically in an Assembly specially called for the purpose. A separate Assembly was called at each of the provincial capitals, at Tosali, Ujjain and Taxila. The Assembly at Tosali was called every five years and at Ujjain and Taxila every three years. It was practically a parliamentary system of government. The king ruled according to the Law of Piety. He directed his officials to follow the Law of Piety and to pursue the public welfare in the way desired by the people.

People's rights to justice were safeguarded in a passage in the Kalinga Edict: 'There are again individuals who have been put in prison or to torture. You must be at hand to stop unwarranted imprisonment or torture. Again, many there are who suffer acts of violence. It should be your desire to set such people in the right way.' Provisions of Habeas Corpus in England do not protect the rights of the people in a better way. His solicitude for the people was extended to the border tribes as well. He issued instructions to the officials at Sampa: 'If you ask what is the king's will concerning border tribes, I reply that my will is this concerning the borderers that they should be convinced that the king desires them to be free from disquietude.

I desire them to trust me and to be assured that they will receive from me happiness, not sorrow, and to be convinced that the king bears them goodwill, and I desire that (whether to win my goodwill or merely to please me) they should practise the Law of Piety, and so gain both this world and the next.'

The resolutions and promises of the king were immutable, and the instructions to the officials were not private. They were recited at every Tishya Nakshatra festival and at suitable intervals. The people were fully informed of the wishes of the king and the way in which they would be governed. Such public announcements were made with a view to ensure confidence in the government.

The officials were warned not to disregard the king's instructions and especially to avoid certain dispositions which render success impossible, viz., envy, lack of perseverance, hardness, impatience, want of application, idleness, and indolence. Such instructions would not be quite out of place even in the most advanced states, of the modern times. A systematic attempt was thus made to introduce good government throughout the empire, in the old territory as well as in the newly acquired provinces.

The lieges, commissioners and the district officers were required to attend the General Assembly every five years. In these meetings they discussed the public questions, and specially they received instructions from the Buddhist teachers in the Law of Piety. He had a special staff of high officials known as Dharma Mahamatara (Censors of the Law of Piety). These officers were appointed in the fourteenth year of the reign with a view to promote the establishment of piety, the progress of piety, and the welfare and happiness of the people in the country as well as on the borders; to prevent wrongful imprisonment or punishment; to administer relief to men with large families, or smitten with any calamity or advanced in years; and to superintend the female establishments of the king's brothers, sisters and female relatives. The king thus provided for the material and spiritual welfare of the people. He stopped with a sternness an oppression on the part of the officials. The poor, sick and the aged received help. Hospitals were established both for men and beasts. Medicinal herbs, and roots and fruits were planted in the country, and whenever they were not found in the country were imported from other countries. Trees were planted on the roads, and wells were dug for the use of men and beasts.

Asoka issued injunctions against the slaughter of animals. He forbade animal sacrifices and slaughter of animals for feasts and food. In the Pillar Edict V he mentioned the names of animals which were specially exempted from slaughter. On a number of specified days animals could not be castrated or branded.

His principles of government are summed up in the Pillar Edict I: 'For this is the rule – protection according to the Law of Piety, regulations by that law, felicity by that law, and security by that law.'

The king's resolutions and instructions were not mere pious wishes. He recounts with pleasure the good deeds he performed in the Pillar Edict VII:

'By what means there can mankind be induced to obey? by what means can mankind develop the growth of piety according to expectations? by what means can I raise up at least some of them so to develop the growth of piety?

'Therefore, thus sayeth His Majesty King Piyadasi:

'This thought occurred to me: I will cause sermons on the Law of Piety to be preached, and with instructions in that law will I instruct, so that men hearkening thereto may obey, raise themselves up, and greatly develop the growth of piety.

'For this purpose I have sermons on the Law of Piety to be preached, I have disseminated various instructions on that law, and I have appointed agents among the multitude to expound and develop my teaching.

'Commissioners have been appointed by me over many thousands of souls with instructions to expound my teaching in such and such a manner among the lieges.

'Considering further the same purpose, I have set up pillars of the Law, I have appointed Censors of Law, and preached sermons on the Law of Piety.

'On the roads I have had banyan trees planted to give shade to man and beast, I have groves of mango trees planted, at every half kos, I have had wells dug; rest houses have been erected; and numerous watering places have been prepared here and there for the enjoyment of man and beast.

'That so-called enjoyment, however, is a small matter.

'With various blessings have former kings blessed the world even as I have done, but in my case it has been done, solely with the intent that men may yield obedience to the Law of Piety.

'My Censors of the Law of Piety are occupied with various charitable institutions with ascetics, house holders, and all the sects; I have also arranged that they should be occupied with the affairs of the Buddhist clergy, as well as with the Brahmans, the Jains, the Ajivikas, and in fact, with all the various sects.

'The several ordinary magistrates shall severally superintend their particular charges, whereas the Censors of the Law of Piety shall superintend all sects as well as such special charges.

'These and many other high officials are employed in the distribution of the royal alms, both my own and those of the queens; and in all the royal *households both at the capital and in the provinces these officers indicate in diverse ways the manifold opportunities for charity.*

'*The same officials are also employed by me in the distribution of the alms of my wives' sons and of the queens' sons, in order to promote pious acts and the practice of piety. For pious acts and the practice of piety depend on the growth among men of compassion, liberality, truth, purity, gentleness, and goodness.*

'*Whatever meritorious deeds I have done, those deeds the people have copied and will imitate, whence follows the consequence that growth is now taking place and will further increase in the virtues of obedience to father, and mother, obedience to teachers, reverence to the aged, and kindly treatment of Brahmans and ascetics, of the poor and wretched, yea, even of slaves and servants.*

'*This growth of piety among men has been affected by two means, namely, by pious regulations, and by meditation. Of these two means pious regulations are of small account, whereas meditation is of greater value.*

'*Nevertheless, I have passed pious regulations forbidding the slaughter of such and such animals, and other regulations of the sort. But the effect of meditation is seen in the greater growth of piety among men, and the more complete abstention from injury to animate creatures and from slaughter of living beings.*'

Spread of Buddhism

This edict was ordered to be written in the twenty-eighth year of his region and inscribed on stone pillars and tablets throughout his dominions. The religion of Buddha was preached by the Bhikshus among the people. It was gradually changing the thoughts of the people, it is not easy to say what progress it made during the previous two centuries and a half. Asoka's efforts in preaching the precepts to the people proved extremely successful. Buddhism became the universal religion in India. Missionaries were also sent to other lands. The proclamations of the king and his patronage to the missionaries who went to every corner of India immensely furthered the Buddhist movement. The gospel was carried to far off Syria, Egypt, Macedonia, Epirus, Cyrene, and to the neighbouring countries, such as Ceylon, and among the Cholas and the Pandyas in the South, the Andhras, the Pulindas and the Bhojas and the Pitinikas in the Southern Peninsula, the Yonas (Yavanas) and the Kambojas in the north-west.

The Ceylonese Chronicles confirm the information of the Inscriptions. Tissa, the son of Moggali, was the president of the third Buddhist Council held at Pataliputra in about 340 BCE. He sent missionaries to Kashmir, Gandhara and to the Himalayan region probably under the orders of the king. The Northern Chronicles mention Upagupta as the chief missionary. Most probably the two names refer to the same person. Each party consisted of a leader and four assistants. In the topes at and near Sanchi names of the three great missionaries, Majjhima, Kassapa-gotta and Dundubhissara have been discovered. Both the chronicles and the inscriptions on the urns tell us that these teachers were sent to the Himalayan region. The Chronicles do not contain any information regarding the dispatch of missionaries to Greece or other Western countries.

The most important event according to the Chronicles, was the mission of Mahendra, Asoka's brother, and of his sister Sanghamitra to Ceylon. Sanghamitra carried branch of the sacred Bodhi Tree from Gaya and planted it at Anuradhapur. This incident has been represented in two bas-reliefs on the Sanchi Gateway. King Tissa of Ceylon became a convert to Buddhism. He helped Mahendra and his sister to spread the religion in the island. An Order of monks and another of nuns were formed, and the brother and the sister spent the rest of their lives there. It is told that the Stupa at Mihintale was erected over the ashes of Mahendra.

Pilgrimage to the Sacred Places

In company with Upagupta the king went on a pilgrimage to all the places connected with the memory of Buddha in 249 BCE. The party proceeded from Pataliputra to Nepal through Mozafferpur and Champara along the route marked by monolithic pillars at Bakhira, Lauriya-Araraja, Lauriya-Nandangarh, and Rampurwa.

First he visited Lumbini Garden where Buddha was born. An inscribed pillar commemorating the events was erected on the spot. Then the party went to Kapilavastu, the capital of the Sakyas, among whom Buddha spent his childhood. Other places visited were Bodh Gaya where Buddha attained nirvana, Sarnath near Benares where he preached his first sermon, Sravasti on the Rapti, where he spent a number of years, and Kusinara, the place of Mahaparinirvan or the great decease. In all these places Asoka erected memorial pillars, and distributed largesses. The king gave up the tours of pleasure in which hunting and other amusements were practised, and instead undertook tours devoted to piety in which the ascetics, Brahmans and elders were visited, endowments and largesses were given to them, the questions of the country and the people were studied, and the law of piety was proclaimed and discussed. The rulers and governors of the present day may very well follow this ideal.

The Law of Piety

Asoka always exalted the Law of Piety, which consisted in the kind treatment of slaves and servants, obedience to father and mother, charity to ascetics and Brahmans, and respect for the sanctity of life. He exhorted the people to shun manifold worthless and corrupt ceremonies and to live according to the Law of Piety in order to obtain happiness in this world and in the next. He always appealed to the practical aspect of the Law: 'Even for a person to whom lavish liberality is impossible, the virtues of mastery over the senses, purity of mind, gratitude, and fidelity are always meritorious' (Rock Edict VII).

The Law was the ultimate standard of all actions. Nothing was considered to possess merit unless it was according to the Law of Piety. An undue emphasis was however laid upon the pleasures of the next world, which injured the position of Buddhism as an intellectual and moral creed. It made a compromise with Brahmanism. Buddha gradually became the Supreme Deity, ruling over the Devas whose influence upon the destinies of mankind he himself had denied. It is generally believed that Buddhism lost its purity when it was preached among the peoples in different countries. Asoka rightly said that even the small man could win heavenly bliss by exertions. 'Let small and great exert themselves to this end' is a doctrine of hope and it was on account of this popular message that Buddhism became universal within such a short time.

Religious Toleration

Although Asoka was an ardent disciple of Buddha he had respect for other religious teachers. One of the fundamental principles of his creed was respect for ascetics, Brahmans, and the teachers. He bestowed the cave dwellings in Barabar Hill near Gaya on the Ajivikas, a sect of naked ascetics of the Jain faith. His main object was to promote the 'Growth of the essence of matter in all sects in order to show reverence to one's own sect. He who does reverence to his own sect, while, disparaging all other sects from a feeling of attachment to his own, on the supposition that he thus glorifies his own sect, in reality by, such conduct inflicts severe injury on his own sect.' He was of opinion that the sects of other people deserved reverence for one reason or another.

People no doubt gave up worshipping the false gods as a result of the efforts of Asoka, but they were never coerced to follow the State religion. Missionaries were appointed to preach the tenets of the Law of Piety, and the proclamations were issued to educate people about the virtues of Law. The officers who were appointed to look after the religion of the people had to ensure the security of all the sects. There has been really no religious war in India. Buddhism became a recognized system of philosophy, and Buddha is considered by the Hindus as one of the ten *avatars*. Asoka's toleration was thus quite in keeping with the Indian spirit.

The Third Buddhist Council

A Council of the Buddhist monks was held at Pataliputra in 326 BCE according to the Ceylonese Chronicles. No epigraphic evidence is available to confirm this tradition. This council was convoked 236 years after the death of Buddha in order to remove heresy among the monks and to prevent disorder. The first Buddhist Council was held at Rajgriha immediately after the death of Buddha, and the second council was held at Vaisali 100 years after that. Tissa, the son of Moggali, was brought from Mathura to conduct the business of the third council. All the priests in India assembled, and Tissa examined the faith of each. Dissenters to the number of 60,000 were expelled from the order, as they did not conform to the teaching of the Master. A thousand priests were selected to form a Convocation which was in session for nine months. The whole body of the scriptures was recited and verified in the council. The king issued edicts forbidding schism in the church after this council. The inscriptions found at Sarnath appear to be an edict of this type.

The Character of Asoka

Asoka ruled his empire for about forty years. His administration bears an impress of his remarkable character. He was a real 'patriot king' answering to the ideal of Plato. The Ceylonese Chronicles are responsible for the legend that he had to wade through blood by killing ninety-nine brothers in order to ascend the throne. They also portray him as a cruel and bloodthirsty ruler in the early part of his life. But the inscriptions contradict these legends. He had his brothers and sisters living, and he was not unmindful of their interests. He was a good soldier, and no doubt he had to shed blood to maintain his position. But that he was extraordinarily cruel is not supported by facts. He had more than one wife. At least two of them enjoyed the status of queens.

He was sincere in his profession. His toleration for other religions was not due to any political motive. He was convinced that every religion contained truth, and thus we find that he laid stress on the essence of matter, and did like to dwell upon ceremonies and other details. At the Kalinga war he resolved to give up war, and never afterwards he is seen to wield arms. He has been compared to Akbar, but in this matter he stands much higher. Akbar fought till the end of his life, and his religion evaporated immediately after his death. But Asoka did not fight after he had taken a vow and his religion endured for a long time to come. Asoka inherited a vast empire which fell into pieces as soon as he died, but his creed remained an active faith of the people for several centuries afterwards, and his foreign missions have been fruitful. While Buddhism is practically extinct in India, it is practised by vast populations outside the country.

India is a country of diverse races and different religions. Asoka laid the foundation of a strong nationality by his benevolent catholicity which promoted the essence of all creeds and all races. His creed acknowledged the equality of all persons, small or great. A king who did not recognize wealth and social position as the criteria of nobility was really a saint. Asoka appeared in the garb of a monk in a true spirit of humility, and all his activities show that he was filled with a desire to serve God, humanity, and the living creatures He succeeded in putting an end to the slaughter of animals, and useless ceremonies. The kingdom of Magadha was turned into a *Bihar* or monastery. Most of the intelligent people joined the Buddhist order. The result was not quite satisfactory to the future growth of Buddhism. Buddhism aimed at the restoration of a rational spirit in the conduct of life. His followers gradually were led to regulate their life according to a stringent set of rules, and thus they were deprived of freedom of thought and of action.

The strict moral code brought about a reaction which proved disastrous to Buddhism. Asoka, however, was not to blame for this. He had never any such intention to curb the spirit of freedom. But the Buddhist Councils were greatly responsible for setting up those regulations which were meant to give the people a standard of high morality and broad social life. Asoka had respect for different creeds and different teachers. So the spirit of his religion could not have condemned differences of opinion regarding manners and customs among the followers of Buddhism. The missionaries brought about the ruin of their own religion by trying to introduce a dead uniformity which did not afford any scope for rational difference. Unity of spirit does not presuppose uniformity of conduct. Asoka was fully conscious of this fact. He could not however bring the monks round to his views, who were afraid of heresy and schism in the church.

The Condition of Society

The Indian society was considerably changed by the Buddhist Bhikshus who were sent out to preach the Law of Piety. The pleasures and amusements of the people were replaced by charity and good living on any festive occasion slaughter of animals was a custom. Asoka forbade this practice. Thousands of animals were killed for the royal kitchen alone, the number was gradually reduced and ultimately no animals were killed for food. Asoka claims that his instructions were carried throughout his dominions. There is nothing to contradict this statement. But shortly after his death animal sacrifices were resumed by the people.

His proclamations were issued in the language of the people. Generally, they were put up at such places by which people passed. It is presumed that education among the people was widely spread, otherwise they could not have read the proclamations. The inscriptions were written in Prakrit language in Brahmi or Kharoshthi script. The edicts in the North-West Frontier at Shahbazgarhi and Mansera were probably inscribed by Persian scribes and hence they were done in the Kharoshthi style. But in the mainland the alphabets were all varieties of the Brahmi characters. It shows that Brahmi was in use since a long time, and made considerable progress. The Buddhist prose literature could not have been preserved by memory alone. Indians were thoroughly familiar with writing. The education of the people was not confined to the school room. It was really given in the public places where all social, religious, and political questions were discussed. The Indian folk could take active interest in deep philosophical questions. Asoka desired his officers to consult the people on other matters as well. Indian society of the time thus presents all the features of a living and growing organizm.

Art and Architecture

The monolithic pillars (Dhwaja-Stambha), the stupas and the railings round them with decorations in bas-relief are the remains of the Indian art and architecture which have been discovered by the archaeologists. The other monuments of the artistic genius of the people are the cave dwellings in Barabar Hill. These remains prove that Indian art reached a high state of technical development during the period.

The lions on the top of the pillars at Sarnath, Bakhira and Lauriya-Nandangarh, the elephants carved from the rock at Dhauli are specimens of fine sculptures. These were the works of the skilled royal architects who were specially protected by law. 'The arts in the age of Asoka,' says V.A. Smith, 'had undoubtedly attained to a high standard of excellence. The royal architects were capable of designing and erecting spacious and lofty edifices in brick, wood, and stone, of handling with success enormous monoliths, of constructing massive embankments with convenient sluice gates, and of excavating commodious chambers in the most refractory rock. Sculpture was the handmaid of architecture, and all notable buildings were freely and richly adorned with decorative patterns, an infinite variety of bas-reliefs, and numerous statues of men and animals. The art of painting was no doubt practised, as we know it was practised with success in a later age, but no specimen that can be referred to the Maurya period has escaped the tooth of time.'

The monolithic pillars, according to Mr. Havell, were the prototypes of the royal or tribal ensign which at the Vedic sacrifices were set up to mark the sacrificial area. The so-called bell-shaped capital is really the mystic world-lotus with turned down petals. The pillar and the capital with lotus or the lion are the emblems of world dominion, like a state umbrella, the umbrella is a lotus with turned down petals. The idea of these pillars was not borrowed from Persia as some people suggest but the existence of similar pillars in Persia indicates their common origin in the ancient Aryan practices.

The Stupa was a symbol of the cosmos, the solid hemispherical dome representing the heavenly vault. In the time of Asoka the stupa became an object of worship for the members of the Buddhistic Sangha. The railings round the stupas at Sanchi and Bharhut contain pictures in bas-relief describing current events or legends connected with the life of Buddha. The workmanship was not so elegant as in the pillars and the caves. Most probably they were executed by a lower grade of craftsmen.

The buildings of the period were mainly wooden structures. Carpentry was of a finished type as revealed by the recent discoveries at Pataliputra. 'The beads and other jewellery and the seals of the Maurya period and earlier ages, which have been frequently found, prove that the Indian lapidaries and goldsmiths of the earliest historical period were not inferior to those of any other country,' says V.A. Smith. In other matters India attained a very high stage of material civilization.

The progress of Indian culture and civilization was ensured by the good government of Chandragupta Maurya and his successors. Asoka appears in history as the most important ruler of India. He stands unsurpassed in his deep insight, grand ideas, and noble personality by any other monarch. His administration marks the high water level of Indian civilization. It shows what a wise and good king can do for his own people, and what people can achieve under a ruler who is thoroughly identified with them in race, sentiment, and culture. It is on account of great reverence for his personality that his last days have been shrouded in legends. He died in his old age in 232 BCE.

BREAK-UP OF THE MAURYA EMPIRE

Successors of Asoka

The Maurya Empire did not long survive Asoka. His successors did not possess his ability, wisdom, and statesmanship. Moreover, the states which were conquered by the Maurya Kings were allowed to retain their government. As subordinate states they reasserted their independence on the death of Asoka who served as a bond of unity. The central government at Pataliputra depended entirely upon the personality of the king. On the death of Asoka there was probably a scramble for the throne of Magadha. The names of three of his sons are found. Tivara, the most favourite, predeceased his father. Kunala, was blinded, according to folklore, by his step-mother Tishyarakshita. Another son, Jalauka, became the king of Kashmir and conquered the plains as far as Kanauj. He was a worshipper of Siva and was hostile to Buddhism. His name occurs only in the Kashmir traditions.

The throne of Magadha, however, was occupied by his grandson Dasaratha. His name appears in an inscription in the Barabar Hills, which records an endowment given by him to the Ajivikas. According to the Puranas he ruled for eight years Buddhist and Jain traditions mention the name of another grandson Samprati, son of Kunala. According to *Asoka-Avadana* the ministers placed the government in the hands of Samprati when Asoka became very old. He was succeeded by Brihaspati, Brishasena, Pushyadharman, and Pushyamitra. The Jain traditions are not consistent. Some point Pataliputra as his capital, while other traditions mention Ujjain as his place of government. He was a great patron of Jainism and erected a large number of temples are throughout western India. It seems he ruled from Ujjain over the Western parts and Dasaratha from Pataliputra over the Eastern provinces. The legends of Khotan refer to the story of an exiled prince, perhaps Kunala, occupying the throne of Khotan. These stories have not been corroborated.

The distant provinces gradually fell off from the empire. Kalinga was the first to revolt under Kharavela in 212 BCE. The provinces to the west of the Indus became independent under local chiefs. When Antiochos III of Syria invaded that region in 206 BCE Subhagasena, a chief of Kabul, was compelled to offer tribute to him. The Andhras who lived between the Krishna and the Godavari declared their independence in about 200 BCE. Brihadratha, the last king of the Maurya Dynasty, was assassinated by the commander-in-chief, Pushya-Mitra, in 185 BCE. The family of Asoka was not fully extinct. The surviving princes became local Rajas in Magadha and their descendants were found in the seventh century CE when Hiuen Tsang visited India. The rulers of the Konkan in the sixth, seventh and eighth centuries were connected in some way with the old Maurya dynasty.

The Sungas

Brihadratha was a weak king. Bana relates in his *Harshacharita* that as he could not keep his coronation oath his commander-in-chief Pushyamitra usurped the throne. The people supported the usurper probably because they were tired of the bad government of the later Maurya Kings. Pushyamitra ruled for thirty-six years. His dynasty is known as the Sungas. The new king ruled over the reduced territories of the Mauryas. The Narmada was the southern boundary of his kingdom, but the western boundary was indefinite. Most probably the Punjab seceded from the empire by that time.

Towards the end of his reign (about 155–53 BCE) a Greek adventurer from Bactria, named Menander, invaded India. He advanced as far as Central India and threatened Pataliputra. The western provinces up to Mathura and Saurashtra were annexed to his dominions. But the Sunga king gathered forces and repelled the invasion. Menander was forced to retire. He was the last European invader who ventured to attack India by land. He made Sakala (i.e., Sialkot) his capital in India.

The outlying provinces of the Sunga Empire were well-governed. The crown prince Agnimitra ruled over the southern provinces as Viceroy with Vidisa (modern Bhilsa) as his headquarters. The name of Agnimitra has been immortalised in the famous drama of *Malavika-Agnimitra* by Kalidas. Pushyamitra celebrated the Rajasuyayajna in order to get himself recognized as the Raj Chakravarti (Lord paramount) of northern India. The sacrificial horse was let loose throughout this country in charge of his grandson Vasumitra. A band of Yavanas, probably remnants of Menander's army, challenged the horse on the banks of the Sindhu between Bundelkhund and the Rajputana States, but they were completely routed. The ceremony was performed with great pomp, in which Patanjali was present.

The Buddhist writers allege that Pushyamitra persecuted the Buddhists. A number of monks were executed and their monasteries burned most probably because these Buddhist missionaries were creating discontent in the country as they had lost their old position. The Buddhist rules might have been enforced with some severity which the people did not long tolerate, and naturally therefore the king dealt rather harshly with the supercilious and oppressive monks. The missionaries are generally carried away by their enthusiasm to spread their faith. The injunctions of Asoka to respect other religions might have been overridden by the monks, and the king was therefore forced to take strong measures to maintain official neutrality.

Pushyamitra was succeeded by his son Agnimitra, and ten kings of the dynasty altogether ruled at Pataliputra. The last king Devabhuti, who was a man of licentious habits, was killed in an intrigue contrived by his minister Vasudeva in 73 BCE. The Sunga kings thus ruled northern India for 112 years. The most important of these kings was Pushyamitra, the founder of the dynasty. The ninth king Bhagavata is said to have ruled for thirty-two years, but no other information about him is available.

These kings were Hindus and the ceremonies they performed were according to the old Hindu traditions. Hinduism and Buddhism grew side by side. Evidences of a few Hindu ceremonials do not prove that Buddhism decayed, or that Buddhism was discouraged. […]

It is believed that the Sungas were originally feudatories of the Mauryas at Bidisa, important as a central city connecting the western coast with Sravasti, Pataliputra, and Paithan. On the downfall of the Mauryas the Sungas rose into prominence, and made the kings of Bharhut, Kausambi, and Ahichhatra their feudatories. In the second century BCE both Panchala with capital at Ahiccatra, and Vatsa with capital at Kausambi were ruled by branches of the same royal family. The kings of Mathura were also feudatories of the Sungas, till the region passed into the hands of the Sakas. Besides there were a number of independent kingdoms or tribal states in northern India in this period. There were the Yaudheyas in southern Punjab and the Arjunayanas in Central India. In the Punjab there were the Udumbaras in the Gurdaspur District, the Kulutas in the Kulu valley of the Kangra District, and the Kunindas in the Sutlej valley in the Simla Hills. These independent kingdoms continued in power even when they had to submit to some suzerain ruler.

The Kanvas

The Brahman minister Basudeva founded a new dynasty known as the Kanvas. They were only for kings ruling altogether for forty-five years. According to the Puranas Vasudeva ruled for nine years, Bhumimitra fourteen years, Narayana twelve years, and Susarmana 102 years. It is inferred from the short reign of these kings that they were not undisturbed in the enjoyment of their power. There were constant struggles over succession to the throne. Susarmana was overthrown and slain by an Andhra King from the South in 28 BCE. The Andhras were growing in power and taking advantage of the disturbances at Pataliputra, invaded the country and removed the last Kanva king from the throne.

The Andhras

The Andhras were a Dravidian people living between the Godavari and the Krishna. They were an ancient race having a strong and independent government when Chandragupta ruled at Pataliputra. Megasthenes describes that there were thirty towns and numerous villages in the Andhra territory. Sri Kakulam on the Krishna was the ancient capital of the Andhras. The Maurya kings subjugated the country and Asoka referred to the Andhras in one of his edicts as a dependent people. Shortly after the death of Asoka the people shook off the government of the Mauryas, and their country was ruled by the kings known as the Andhras or Andhrabhrityas. The Andhra kingdom existed for 450 years down to about 225 CE. Simuka was the reputed founder of the dynasty and there were thirty kings. They were generally known as Satavahana or Salivahana kings and sometimes the appellation Satakarni is associated with their names.

The Andhra kingdom made rapid progress. The second king Krishna (Kanha) extended their power up to Nasik in the west. The third king Sri Satakarni came into conflict with Kharavela, king of Kalinga, in 218 BCE. The latter, however, succeeded in maintaining his position. We do not know anything of the Andhra kings till we find that one of these kings slew the last Kanva king in 28 BCE. The identity of this king has not yet been possible. The seventeenth king Hala is credited with the authorship of the vernacular poem *Saptasataka* or 'seven centuries'.

The twenty-third and the twenty-fourth king of the dynasty, Gotamiputra Satakarni and Vasishtiputra Pulamayi, were engaged in war with the foreign settlers in the Western provinces. The Indo-Parthians penetrated into India up to Kathiawar, and there were a number of local governors with the title of Satraps. The two great Satraps of the Kshaharata family, Bhumaka and Nahapana, consolidated their position in the new settlements. Nahapana assumed the title of Mahakshatrapa and Raja. Gautamiputra Satakarni exterminated the Kshaharatas in about 124 CE and celebrated his victory by giving liberal donations to Brahmans and Buddhists. The next king Vasishtiputra Pulamayi was defeated by the Saka Satrap Rudradaman I of Ujjain in about 135 CE, Rudradaman gave his daughter in marriage to Pulamayi but he did not hesitate to reconquer the lost territories of the Kshaharatas from his son-in-law. Vasishtiputra Pulamayi died about 163 CE.

The next important king of the dynasty was Gautamiputra Yajna Sri. He recovered some of the lost provinces and is believed to have extended his powers far and wide. He issued silver coins in the western districts and leaden coins in the eastern parts. He had a long reign of about twenty-nine years. Some of his coins bear the figure of a ship which suggests that his army might have crossed the seas in extending his dominions. The later kings of the dynasty were of no importance and nothing is known about the sad end of these rulers.

They disappear from history after 225 CE. According to the *Geography* of Ptolemy the capital of the Andhras in about 130 CE was at Paithan.

The country under the Andhras was in a prosperous condition. The people were mostly Buddhist although of the people under the Brahmanism was in a flourishing state. Princes and chiefs, merchants, goldsmiths, carpenters, corn dealers, and men of other professions carved temples and monasteries out of solid rocks at Karli and other places for the use of the Buddhist Bhikshus. Monasteries were also dug out in the caves on the seashore. Most of the historical information of the times are derived from the inscriptions found in these places. We gather from the *Periplus of the Erythraean Sea* that the country was enjoying material prosperity. The cities of Broach, Sopara, Paithan, and Tagara were important for trade. Foreign vessels used to call at Broach, then known as Barygaza, and goods from the country were stocked there for export. Paithan was the greatest city in the Dakshinapatha. The important articles of export were rough stone, ordinary cotton, muslin, mallow-coloured cotton, and spices and unguents; and the articles of import were wine, and glass and spices and beautiful girls for the royal harem. India was industrially ahead of the European countries in the first century of the Christian Era.

The people had a perfect corporate life. They had their trade and industrial guilds, municipal corporations, and village communities. 'There were in those days,' writes Sir R.G. Bhandarkar, 'guilds of trades such as those of weavers, druggists, corn dealers, oil manufacturers, etc. Their organization seems to have been complete and effective, since, as already mentioned, they received permanent deposits of money and paid interest on them from generation to generation. Self-government by means of such guilds and village communities has always formed an important factor of the political administration of the country. A *Nigama Sabha* or town corporation is also mentioned in one of Ushavadata's Nasik inscriptions, which shows that something like a municipal institution existed in those early days. The rate of interest was from five to seven and half per cent, per annum, which is a sufficient evidence of the efficiency of government, and the confidence of the people in their own institutions. Inscriptions in different places bear testimony to the fact that people of different provinces could move from long distances without great difficulty. There must have therefore been good inter-provincial roads.

THE INDO-GREEKS AND
THE INDO-PARTHIANS

The northwestern boundaries of India were fluid. At times Persian or Greek rule extended through Afghanistan into India, while at other times local kings retained power. Some Mauryan kings also controlled Afghanistan. During the period after 250 BCE Greeks, Parthians and Scythians or Shakas struggled for control in Bactria which provided a base to extend their rule into northwest India.

The Indo-Greeks or Bactrian Greeks included several kings who ruled over Bactria in the period after Alexander. At the time Ball (whose text makes up this chapter) was writing, only 35 kings were known. By contrast Irfan Habib, in his book *Post-Mauryan India* (2002), states that there were more than 40 over a period of just 200 years.

The Parthian or Arsacid dynasty is named after Arsaces. He conquered Parthia, a region of Iran, from the Greeks in 238 BCE, later extending their territories into Bactria. One branch of the dynasty was known as the Pahlavas.

The Shakas, a branch of the Scythians, were known in Achaemenid Iran and seem to have been horse breeders of Central Asia. Greek sources state they ruled over Bactria, but to date no coinage attests to this.

All three described above proceeded from Bactria to India.

Despite new excavations, and additional coin finds at Ai Khanum and elsewhere, the chronology of these rulers remains uncertain. However, the Shakas also ruled in western India, where they founded the Shaka era of 78 CE, and here the sequence of kings can be established.

THE INDO-GREEKS

The Hindukush was the boundary of the of the Maurya Empire on the north-west, and Afghanistan and Beluchistan were included in the territories of the Mauryas since 303 BCE when Seleukos entered into an alliance with Chandragupta. The other Asiatic conquests of Alexander to the west of the Hindukush remained in possession of Seleukos, who consolidated the dominions. Seleukos was assassinated by his son Antiochos Soter in 280 BCE. Antiochos Soter succeeded by his son Antiochos Theos, a young man of twenty-four, a drunken sensualist, and murderer of his brother Seleukos (in about 261 BCE). This young king created a large number of enemies by his bad government. He remained on the throne for fifteen or sixteen years. The Bactrians and the Parthians of the north-eastern provinces of the empire revolted against Antiochos in about 250 BCE.

Rise of Bactria

Bactria was a rich and prosperous country on the other side of the Hindukush. It was watered by the Oxus and was inhabited by an intelligent people well known for their civilization and culture. Bactria (modern Balkh) formed an important satrapy of the Persian emperors. The Greek writer Strabo says that there were about 1,000 towns in Bactria. After the conquest of Alexander, the Greeks settled in large numbers in this rich valley, and the civilization of the country was therefore a happy blend of Greek and Bactrian cultures. The Greek settlers brought with them their institutions, manners, and customs.

When the misrule of Antiochos Theos became intolerable, they rose in rebellion under their governor Diodotos, and declared themselves independent. The new king of Bactria was a Greek and the Greek rule in the province continued for about a century more. The names of about thirty-five Indo-Greek kings and two queens are supplied by the large number of coins found in the Punjab, north-west frontier, and Afghanistan. An outline of their history has been constructed with the help of these coin legends. The information is therefore scanty and incomplete.

It seems there was constant struggle for the throne of Bactria. Diodotos was succeeded by his son of the same name after a short reign of five years in 245 BCE. There was a rebellion in 230 BCE led by Euthydemos, native of Magnesia, in which Diodotos II lost his throne.

The king of Syria made an attempt to regain the revolted provinces when Euthydemos was the ruler of Bactria. Antiochos III carried on a long war with both Bactria and Parthia, which terminated in 208 BCE and independence of both the kingdoms was recognized. The integrity of Bactria was not interfered with, as it was considered impolitic to weaken a settlement of the Greeks in view of the constant menace of a Scythian invasion from the North. Antiochos crossed the Hindu Kush, invaded Kabul Valley and obtained a large indemnity from Sobhagasena, the independent king of that region (206 BCE). At the time of recognizing the in dependence of Bactria he gave his daughter in marriage to Demetrios, son of Euthydemos. Demetrios followed in the footsteps of his father-in-law, and succeeded in conquering Kabul, the Punjab, and Sindh (190 BCE). While he was away in India another rebellion took place in Bactria under the leadership of Eucratides. Henceforth Bactrian history is occupied with the wars between the descendants of Euthydemos and of Eucratides.

Eucratides was not supported by the various tribes and states of Bactria, but it seems he ultimately succeeded in defeating the partisans of Demetrios (175 BCE), and even obtained from him some of his Indian possessions. Demetrios, however managed to retain his hold upon his other conquests for some time to come, and the two families ruled over one province or another till they were swept away by the flood of Saka invasion. Bactria was invaded by Mithridates I, the king of Parthia, during the reign of Eucratides, and was in occupation under him for years. Shortly afterwards Eucratides was inhumanly murdered by his son Apollodotos (156 BCE). These internal causes weakened Bactria, and it became an early prey for the Saka hordes. Heliokles was probably the last Greek king of Bactria. When Bactria was conquered by the Sakas a number of Greek princes retained their power in India.

The Greek Princes in India

Apollodotos and Menander conquered several provinces of India, and Strabo says that they carried on their conquest very far. Silver coins of these two princes were found at Barygaza in the first century of the Christian Era. Menander is identified with Milinda of the Buddhist book 'Milinda-panha'. He probably had his capital at Kabul and invaded India in 155 BCE. He advanced as far as Kathiawar in the South, Nagari near Chitor, and Saketa in Oudh. His attack upon Pataliputra was repelled. Sakala (Sialkot) and Mathura were the headquarters of these Greek princes.

References to Greek invasions are found in such books as Kalidas's *Malavika-Agnimitra*, Patanjali's *Mahabhashya*, and the *Gargi Samhita*. It has been gathered from the evidences of coins that the provinces of Kabul and Gandhar, which were originally conquered by Demetrios, were later on snatched away from him by Eucratides. The Greek rule in Gandhar was terminated by the Saka invasions, but the Kabul valley remained in the hands of the Greeks till 25 CE, when the last Greek king Hermaeus was succeeded by the Kushan chief Kujula Kadphises. The only one stone inscription which mentions the Greek princes is that found at Besnagar in Gwalior. The inscription records the erection of a standard by one Heliodoros, a Greek ambassador of king Antialcidas at Besnagar, in honour of God Vishnu in the fourteenth year of the reign of king Bhagabhadra, probably a successor of Pushyamitra. This Antialcidas was evidently a member of the family of Eucratides. The inscription is very interesting in as much as it shows how the Greeks assimilated the culture of Hindus. The names of many other Greek kings are found in the coins, but no connected history can be made up with the help of these bare information.

THE INDO-PARTHIANS

Almost simultaneously with the Bactrians the people of Parthia revolted against Antiochos Theos. They were a race of mounted shepherds skilled in the use of bow and arrow. They did not adopt the Greek culture and retained their habits unchanged. Their country was not very fertile. It was beyond the Persian deserts to the south-east of the Caspian Sea. The leader of the revolution was a national hero called Arsakes. The war of independence continued for several years. They declared their autonomy in 248 BCE but the war did not come to an end till the death of Antiochos in 246 BCE. The kingdom grew in power and importance and became an empire by acquiring the provinces of the Empire of Syria. The independence of Parthia was formally recognized when Antiochos III failed to reduce the recalcitrant provinces.

The Parthian Empire

The territories of Parthia were extended on all sides in the reign of Mithridates I (171 to 136 BCE). He invaded Bactria and came to India. The general of Demetrios in India was defeated and Mithridates annexed not only the provinces to the west of the Indus, but it is believed that he also conquered the nations In between the Indus and the Hydaspes (Jhelum) and the Parthian Empire extended from the Euphrates to the border of India. The successors of Mithridates were engaged in suppressing a Saka rising for several years, and in the reign of Mithridates II (123-88 BCE) they succeeded in stemming the tide. The Sakas had two settlements, one to the north of Bactria and the other in the province of Drongiana between Persia and India, later known as Sakastan or Seistan. The Parthians were engaged in suppressing the Sakas of Seistan and ultimately a subordinate kingdom arose in this struggle. There was another subordinate kingdom, that of the Pahlavas, a branch of the Parthian people. They lived in Seistan, Arachosia (Kandahar) and Gedrosia (Northern Beluchistan) and they came to India in large numbers. Coins have been found in India bearing Parthian names. It is believed that these names are of the Pahlava Satraps of the Parthian kings. The Sakas of Seistan came along with the Pahlavas, and thus we find that the Parthians, the Pahlavas and the Sakas were mixed up in India. The coins bearing the inscription 'King of Kings' are referred to the Pahlavas and Saka Satraps, who probably borrowed the title from their superior lords of Parthia. The title is an adaptation of the title *Kshayathiyanam Kshayathiya* of the Persian emperors. The later Kushan kings also adopted the title.

The Saka Invasion

The Sakas were nomad hordes of Scythians who originally belonged to China. On account of the growth of population in the latter country there were successive waves of emigrations from it to Western Asia and to Europe. One branch of these people settled in Central Asia to the north of the Jaxartes. But when another wave came from China the settlers in Centra Asia moved southwards. The kingdom of Bactria was swept away by this flood, and swarms of the Sakas came to the valley of the Hilmand, where perhaps there was an earlier settlement of their people. There they came in conflict with the Parthians, which has been already alluded to.

Hordes of these Sakas, Pahlavas, and Parthians came to India through Kandahar and crossing the Bolan Pass passed over Beluchistan to Sindh and from there went up the valley of the Indus. They occupied the Punjab, and spread eastwards as far as Mathura Tire Kabul valley was then under the occupation of the Greek princes from Bactria. In India these invaders ruled as governors of the Parthian monarchs. They were known as Satraps. Takshasila and Mathura became capitals of these Satrapies, and later another horde occupied the peninsula of Surashtra where they continued in power till 390 CE. The kingdoms of these Sakas in the Punjab and northern India were conquered by a later horde of the Scythians known as the Yuch-chis or the Kushans, who came by the Kabul Valley.

Satraps of Takshasila and Mathura

Our information is mainly derived from the coins. In the Saka line the names of the following monarchs and Satraps are known: Maues, Venones, Azes, Azilises, and Satraps Liaka, Patika, Rajuvula, Sodasa, Kharahostes Jihunia etc. And in the Parthian line we gather the names of Gondopharnes, Abdagases, Arsakes, Pakores and Sanabares.

The Greek prince Strato I was ruling in the Kabul valley and the Punjab when Heliokles was overcome by the Scythian hordes. He was succeeded by his grandson Strato II. The Sakas drove the Greeks from the Punjab and occupied Takshasila which was their capital, but the Greeks remained for some time in the Kabul Valley, of which Kapisa was the capital. At Mathura the Sakas displaced the Greeks as well as the Hindu rulers. The first known Satrap of Takshasila was Liaka as subordinate to King Moga or Maues. Patika was the son of Liaka. At Mathura the names of the two Hindu Rajas, Gomitra and Ramadatta, are known from the coins. They were displaced by the Satraps Hagana and Hagamasha. These Satraps were followed by Rajuvula, or Ranjuvula, who was succeeded by his son Sodasa.

A monument of the Saka Satraps at Mathura was discovered by Pandit Bhagwan Lal Indraji, bearing inscriptions in Kharoshthi. It is lion-faced capital of a pillar in red sandstone. From the inscription the names of the Satraps of Mathura and other places have been found. We also learn from the same source that the Satraps of Mathura, Takshasila, and Kapisa were Buddhists.

The Western Satraps

Hordes of the Sakas also went to Kathiawar, Malwa, and the Deccan, and they carved out kingdoms for themselves. There were two distinct kingdoms of these 'Western Satraps', one with capital at Nasik and the other at Ujjain. The first known name of the Satrap at Nasik is Bhumaka Kshaharata, and next is that of Nahapana. Nahapana assumed the title of Mahakshatrapa. The kingdom of these Kshaharata Satraps included Kathiawar, Southern Rajputana and the Deccan up to Nasik and Poona. The time of the beginning of their settlement is not definitely known. Probably the kingdom was established sometime in the first century after the birth of Christ. It was conquered and annexed to his dominions by the Andhra King Gautamiputra in about 126 CE.

The second satrapy at Ujjain was founded by Chastana late in the first century CE. His grandson Rudradaman I greatly extended the dominions. Here conquered the territories of the Kshaharata Satraps from the Andhra King Pulamayi II. His dominions thus included Kathiawar, Cutch, Sind, Malwa, the Konkan and some other districts. The Satraps of Ujjain continued in power till they were conquered by Chandragupta II in about 390 CE.

The Indo-Parthian Kings

Mithridates I (171–136 BCE) raised Parthia from a small state to a vast empire extending from Babylon to the Punjab. The capital of this empire was Ctesiphon. The distant provinces could not possibly be managed effectively by the central government. Besides, the Parthian kings had to deal with the nomadic invasions. Two kings, Phrastes II and Artabanus, died between 130 and 120 BCE while engaged in resisting the Scythian invasions. In this disturbed state of the Parthian government a Saka chief named Maues established himself at Takshasila as the king of the Punjab (120 BCE). At the same time a Parthian named Venones became feudatory chief of Seistan and Arachosia. He was succeeded by his brother Spalirises, and by Azes, son of Spalirises. The government of Arachosia was in the hands of Venones and his family for about twenty-five years.

Within a short time, Parthia succeeded in restoring order. Mithridates II re-established its supremacy over Seistan, Arachosia, and the Punjab. Azes, the governor of Seistan and Arachosia, was transferred to Takshasila, in place of Maues (about 90 BCE). The Punjab was governed by Azes and his family for a long time. Azes was in power for about fifty years, and became practically independent. He was succeeded by his son Azilises and then by his grandson Azes II.

In about 20 CE Gondopharnes succeeded Azes II, conquered Sindh and Arachosia and became independent. He shook off the Parthian control. He enjoyed a long reign and died in 48 CE. Gondopharnes was a Parthian. In the legends of the Christian church it is related that St. Thomas, the apostle of the Parthians, was sent to the Court of Gondopharnes, and the king became a convert to Christianity. There is, however, no historical evidence to support this story, but it may not be altogether false.

On the death of Gondopharnes his kingdom could not maintain its unity. His nephew Abdagases became king of the Punjab, and Orthagnes assumed the government of Sindh and Arachosia. Orthagnes was succeeded by Pakores, but the name of any successor of Abdagases is not known. The Kushans came to India by this time and they conquered the Punjab, Arachosia and Sindh in turn and built up an empire with the scattered states and the divers races. The Parthian kingdom of Ctesiphon remained under the descendants of Arsakes till they were superseded by the Sassanians in 226 CE.

Hellenic Influence upon India

The invasions of Alexander, Seleukos, and Antiochos were mere raids. They came as storms and passed away shortly after. Such temporary disturbances could not have produced any change in

the civilization of India. Megasthenes, the Greek ambassador at
Pataliputra, has left records of the unadulterated culture of the
Indians. They did not borrow anything from the foreigners. Their
art, architecture, and literature bear no traces of foreign influence.
Demetrios of Bactria was the real founder of a Greek line of kings in
Afghanistan and the Punjab. He was called 'the king of the Indians',
and his successors remained in power in these provinces for about
200 years. The last Greek prince, of whose name we know, was
Herraeos. He was overthrown by the Kushans in about 25 CE. During
this long period the Indians came under the influence of the Greeks
and it is expected that their civilization was affected thereby. The
Greeks settled at Takshasila or Taxila, Kapisa, Mathura and other
large towns. But there no evidence to prove that they influenced the
Indian in an appreciable manner.

The coins of the Indians were not very polished. They used
punch-marked, cast, or rudely struck coins. But the coins of the
Greeks were polished and struck with the two dies bearing the effigy
and title of the king on one side, and some other device on the other.
The Indians adopted the style of these coins in later ages. But the
Greek princes had to accept the Indian standard of weight for their
coins. Their language was not understood by the common people. So
their coins were imprinted on one side in Greek and on the other in
Kharoshthi. In some cases they adopted Indian device. In architecture
we do not find any change. The Greek sculpture may have appealed
to the imagination of the Indians, for we find more sculptures after
the Greek connection. The literature of the Indians does not show
any sign of Greek influence. It is believed that the Indians learnt to
produce dramas later on from the Greeks. But it cannot be said with
confidence that the dramatic literature of the Indians owes entirely
to foreign inspiration. The Indian dramas reached such excellence

that it is hardly believed that they were not Indian in spirit and in execution.

The manners and customs of the people remained unaffected. The Indians at that time were not an exclusive people. They accepted the Greeks in their own society. The Greeks adopted their manners. The monument of Besnagar shows that there were Greeks who worshipped Hindu Gods. The Hindu philosophy went on undisturbed in its own course. It is however believed that the Greek sculpture suggested to the Buddhists to introduce the figure of Buddha in their artistic representations. Before this Buddha was indicated by symbols such as Bodhi tree and other things. But later on we find that the figure of Buddha was portrayed.

In summarizing the effects of Greek civilization upon India V.A. Smith says: 'The conclusion of the matter is that the invasions of Alexander, Antiochos the Great, Demetrios, Eukratides, and Menander were in fact, whatever their authors may have intended, merely military incursions, which left no appreciable mark upon the institutions of India. The prolonged occupation of the Punjab and neighbouring regions by Greek rulers had extremely little effect in Hellenizing the country. Greek political institutions and architecture were rejected, although to a small extent Hellenic example was accepted in the decorative arts, and the Greek language must have been more or less familiar to the officials at the king's courts. The literature of Greece probably was known slightly to some of the native officers, who were obliged to learn their masters' language for business purpose, but that language was not duly diffused, and the impression made by Greek authors upon Indian literature and science is hardly traceable until after the close of the period under discussion.'

THE KUSHAN DYNASTY

The Kushanas, a branch of the Yuezhi (a.k.a. Yueh-chi or Yuch-chi), were the next entrants into India from the northwest. Displaced from China, the Yuezhi moved into Central Asia and Bactria, and one of their five main branches moved to India. The Kushanas are known from numerous coins and inscriptions, yet their chronology remains uncertain. In the 1990s the discovery of an inscription at Rabatak in Afghanistan provided new insights, revealing the name of a previously unknown king, Vima Taktu. The inscription also provides additional information on the later Kushana ruler, Kanishka. The approximate chronology is as follows: Kujula Kadphises, who conquered Kabul around 50 CE; Vima Taktu, ruled 90–113 CE; Vima Kadphises, 113–128 CE; Kanishka I, the most powerful of the Kushana rulers, 128–150 CE. They were followed by Huvishka; Vasudeva I, Kanishka II and Vasishka, the last of whom ruled from 247–267 CE. The Kushana empire declined after this. Today this chronology is the one most accepted, based on an analysis by Robert Bracey (2017). Earlier Rosenfield, in *The Dynastic Arts of the Kushans* (1993), had also calculated a date of 128 CE for the beginning of Kanishka's reign.

The date of Kanishka is still the subject of debate. Among other historians Irfan Habib, in *Post-Mauryan India* (2002), places Kanishka's date of accession in 160 CE, while R.S. Sharma and several others believe it to be 78 CE. A slightly different chronology is put forward in the extracts below.

Kanishka ruled from two capitals, Purushapura or Peshawar in the northwest, and Mathura in the Gangetic plains. Even at the height of the Kushana empire, local kingdoms continued to exist, and they must have offered their allegiance to the Kushanas. Elswhere in India other kingdoms and dynasties flourished. The Satavahanas or Andhras were in the Deccan, the Shakas in western India and the Cholas, Cheras and Pandyas further south. Right across India there were urban centres, craft production and widespread trade, including trade with China and Rome. Arikamedu, on the southern coast, is among the sites that have both Roman amphorae and Roman coins. *The Periplus of the Erythraean Sea*, a Greek text of the first century CE by an unknown author, also provides an account of ports and trade.

As for Kanishka, Ball (whose text makes up this chapter) puts forward the view that he was of a Yuezhi branch known as the Little Yuezhi. However, this theory is no longer valid, as the Rabatak inscription and other sources reveal Kanishka to be a direct descendent of Vima Kadphises.

During this time Mahayana Buddhism developed, while under the Kushana multiple religions were practised. Their coins depict images of Greek, Zoroastrian and Hindu deities, along with those of the Buddha and Bodhisattvas. New forms of art emerged at Gandhara and Mathura, with Buddhist images being sculpted in both areas. Those in Gandhara had Graeco-Roman influence, while in Mathura the images were more rounded, in an indigenous style. Craft production and widespread trade increased, not only in the north of India but also in the south.

Literary works of Ashvaghosha and others are described below. Charaka, the famous physician of the first century, composed the *Charaka Samhita*, while Susruta was a surgeon who composed the *Susruta Samhita*.

60-375 CE

Migration of the Yuch-chis

India was visited by a fresh race of invaders in the first century CE. The north-west frontier has always been a vulnerable point. Invasions have come through the passes on this side from the earliest times. We have already seen that the Aryans, the Persians, the Greeks, the Sakas, and the Parthians came in successive waves and settled in the region watered by the Jaxartes, and from Central Asia, who originally came from China, which was seething with population from very remote times. The Sakas came from the same country earlier and settled in the region watered by the Jaxartes, and partly in Drongiana. They were followed by a smaller tribe called Wu-sun.

By the middle of the second century BCE about a million people of north-western China left their home in search of means of subsistence. They were goaded by privation at home and came westwards. They first overcame the Wu-sun on the way and then came into conflict with the Sakas who were forced to give way and migrated towards India. But the Yuch-chis were left undisturbed for a long time. The Wu-sun tribe gathered their forces and drove them further south. The Yuch-chis in their turn pressed upon Bactria, and occupied the region on both sides of the Oxus. The fertile country of Sogdiana and Bactria afforded ample food. So in the course of time they gave up their nomad habits and became peaceful citizens. They became a fully developed nation before the beginning of the Christian era. But their unity was not maintained as they were divided into five principalities.

Kadphises I

One section of these people known as the Kushan became prominent by the middle of the first century CE. Its chieftain Kujula-kara-Kadphises, or Kadphises I became the supreme lord of the five principalities. He carried his arms across the Hindu Kush to find fresh fields for the increasing number of his people. In the course of his long reign he conquered Kabul, Ki-pin (Gandhara including Taxila) and the other territories of the Indo-Greeks. The Parthians also did not escape from his wide arms. He thus acquired a vast empire including modern Bokhara, Afghanistan and the Western Punjab upon the Jhelum. He died in about 77 or 78 CE at the age of eighty.

Kadphises II

His son Wima Kadphises or Kadphises II succeeded to the throne of his father Kadphises I. The Saka era which commenced in 78 CE probably marks the accession of Kadphises II to the throne. His coins have been found in distant places throughout northern India. It is believed from this that he conquered as far as Benares in the east and the Narmada Valley in the south. The Saka satraps of Malwa also acknowledged his supremacy.

Kadphises had also to avert another danger from the north. The kings of China cast their longing looks towards the west. The Emperor Wu-ti sent an embassy under Chang-kien to establish relations with the kingdoms of Western Asia (140–86 BCE). But by the first quarter of the Christian era these relations were stopped. Fifty years afterwards the Chinese led a fresh campaign under their General Pan-chao. They conquered Khotan and Chinese Turkistan, and reached the shores of the Caspian Sea. The approach of the Chinese was a menace to the Kushan empire. Kadphises II challenged Pan-chao. He demanded the hands of a Chinese princess. Pan-chao treated this offer with contempt. Kadphises II then sent an army consisting of 70,000 cavalry across Taghdumbash Pamir under his viceroy Si. But his troops were exhausted in crossing the difficult mountain passes, and they were easily defeated. Kadphises II had henceforth to pay tribute to China.

As Kadphises I died at the age of eighty Kadphises II could not possibly have reigned more than thirty years. It is therefore presumed that he died in about 110 CE. His governors most probably managed the government for some time after his death. A large number of anonymous coins issued in this time have suggested this theory.

Kanishka

Another section of the Yuch-chis known as the Little Yuch-chi settled in the Khotan region. The section which settled in the Oxus region was called the Great Yuch-chi. In about 120 CE Kanishka, son of Vajheska, of the Little Yuch-chi section, came into the throne of Kadphises II. He is the most well-known of the Yuch-chi kings of India. A new era was started during his reign, and it was continued by his successors The exact date of the commencement of this era has not yet been determined. Coins and inscriptions bearing the years 3 to 99 of this era have been found. The Orientalists are not yet agreed about the nature of this era.

Kanishka built up a vast empire. He not only established his supremacy over the old dominions of the Yuch-chis, but annexed Kashmir and subjugated Khotan, Yarkand and Kashgar. The Chinese annals refer to the loss of Chinese Turkistan to the empire in 152 CE. The Buddhist chronicles have also narrated the exploits of Kanishka beyond the Pamirs. The conquest of Turkistan is therefore established on credible authority: Hostages were exacted from one of the princes, who were provided with residences in the Punjab and the

Kabul provinces. It is told that Kanishka was smothered by his officers in Khotan, as they were weary of these troublesome campaigns.

Purushapura or modern Peshawar was the capital of Kanishka. It occupied a central position. He could watch the events of India as well as the provinces on either side of the Khyber from this place. In India his empire extended up to Benares on the least and Sindh in the south. He had also to subjugate the Parthians. His government was strong and efficient. It presents all the signs of prosperity and internal order. During his absence in Turkistan, first his elder son Vasishka and then the younger son Huvishka carried on the government. Vasishka probably died before his father, and Huvishka succeeded him. The excavations at Peshawar and Taxila have produced many valuable remains of the Kushan period. One of them is a headless statue of Kanishka.

Images of various Gods, Zoroastrian, Greek, Mithraic and Indian, appear on the coins of Kushan kings. The coins of Kanishka bear these images as well as that of the Buddha. The Buddhist chronicles tell of the conversion of Kanishka to Buddhism. A Buddhist Council was held at Kundal-Vana near the capital of Kashmir. The delegates to the council all came from the Hinayana School. About 500 delegates attended. Vasumitra was elected president, and Asvagosha vice-president. The council prepared huge commentaries on the *Tripitaka*, including the *Mahavibhasha*, which is described as an encyclopedia of Buddhist philosophy.

Hinayana and Mahayana

Buddhism underwent a great transformation during the first two or three centuries of the Christian era. The early Buddhism was based upon the 'Indian ideas of unity, of rebirth, of the survival and transmission of Karma, or the net result of human action, and of the blessedness of escape from the pains of being' (V.A. Smith). Devotion to duty and charity for all living creatures were added to these philosophic views. Buddhism was thus an intellectual, moral, and social movement. But when it was carried beyond the frontiers of India it underwent changes according to the traditions of the people among whom it was preached.

The Western world during the period was being unified under the Roman Caesars. The personality of Jesus Christ was working as the bond among the different races. There was intercourse between India and the Western world through trade, and the Buddhist Missionaries also came in contact with the new type of the Christians. It was during this time that 'nascent Christianity met full-grown Buddhism in academies and markets of Asia and Egypt, while both religions were exposed to the influences of surrounding paganism in many forms and of the countless works of art which gave expression to the ideas of polytheism. The ancient religion of Persia contributed to the ferment of human thought, excited by improved facilities for international communication and by the incessant clash of rival civilizations.'

Buddha now appears as a Divine Being surrounded by a hierarchy of Bodhisattvas. The old Buddhism was rather cold and did not appeal to the devotional sentiments of the people. The Indian mind has been always of a synthetic type where *Bhakti* (devotion) is mixed up with *Jnana* (knowledge) and *Karma* (action). The old Buddhism had very little scope for *Bhakti*. So in the course of time Buddhism assimilated all the elements of a progressive religion. It seems therefore that foreign intercourse, as well as an internal movement all helped in transforming Buddhism. Henceforth we find two main sections of Buddhists; one called *Hinayana* or the Little Vehicle professing to follow the old ideas, and *Mahayana* or the

Great Vehicle adopting the new, ideals of the divinity of Buddha, and the existence of Bodhisattvas acting as mediators between man and Buddha. Nagarjuna, a contemporary of Kanishka, was the chief exponent of the *Mahayana* School.

Gandhara Art

Changes in the sculpture of India are also noticed in this period. No image of Buddha appears in Sanchi or Bharhut but images of Sakyà, Bodhisattva or Buddha appears in the first century CE. The sculpture of the time of Kanishka and his successors was executed in the style of Gandhara where Greek art was applied to Buddhist subjects. The inspiration was Indian but the technique Greek. The copious' sculptures of this period have been discovered. Elaborate drapery is a distinguishing feature of these sculptures. The art spirit of India was however not confined to the Gandhara style. Remains of genuine Indian style have been discovered at Sarnath, Amaravati, and Mathura. The bas-reliefs at Amaravati are excellent productions and they have received universal admiration, The styles of Mathura and Sarnath are free and vigorous. They are marked by a dignity of expression and grand conception.

Kanishka was a great builder. He erected a tower at Peshawar over the relics of Buddha, 400 feet high. He built a town in Kashmir, and Mathura was beautified by a large number of buildings and sculptures, A statute of Kanishka, executed in the pure Indian style, has been found at Mathura. This is now preserved in the museum at Lucknow. The excavations at Taxila, which bear remains of the different strata of civilization, Maurya, Greek, Parthian, and Kushan, have established the view that Gandhara art is associated with the time of Kanishka. Gandhara sculptures are not found in the Parthian or early Kushan strata.

Literature of the Kushan Period

The literature of the period became also very rich by the writings of such eminent writers as Vasumitra, Ashvaghosa, and Nagarjuna. Ashvaghosa was the most remarkable of them. He was a poet, musician, scholar, theologian, and monk. He was first living in Pataliputra, and was carried off from there by Kanishka. He wrote in Sanskrit and not in Pali. His *Buddha Charita* is written in pure Sanskrit and in elegant style. This shows a turning point in the development of Indian culture. Charaka, the famous physician and author of *Susruta*, was living in the Court of Kanishka.

The rich literature and abundant architecture and sculptures of the times are evidence of a flourishing people, and it shows that the national life was in its full tide.

Date of Kanishka

A great deal of controversy has arisen over the date Kanishka. Many scholars have tried to find out the date with the help of the coins. Some considered the unknown era as the Vikrama, the Saka, or the Laukika era, beginning with 58 BCE, 78 CE, or omitting certain digits. The literary and archaeological evidence however proves that Kanishka could not have come to the throne earlier than 120 CE. Sanskrit made sufficient progress in his time and there is no evidence of the existence of such Sanskrit in the first century CE or earlier. The excavations at Taxila prove that Kanishka could not have come before the first quarter of the first century. The unknown era is now considered to be a special era started by Kanishka or his subjects.

Successors of Kanishka

Kanishka was succeeded by his son Huvishka, who founded a city called Huskapura in Kashmir. He was the last king to rule over the vast empire. In the time of Vasudeva I the empire broke up. The history of the fall of the Kushan empire is rather obscure. Kushan chiefs continued to rule over smaller principalities in different parts. The western provinces were absorbed in the Persian empire shortly after 226 CE. Some Kushan chiefs retained their power in Kabul till the fifth century when the Hunas overpowered them.

The Kushans, like the previous foreign tribes who settled in India, assimilated the Indian culture. The name Vasudeva indicates that he was a worshipper of Vishnu. But an accurate history of the social and religious conditions of the people is impossible from the scanty materials available.

Relations with Foreign Countries

The Indians maintained trade relations with Greece and Egypt through Asia Minor. Palmyra in Syria was the principal commercial depot between 105 and 273 CE. The eastern trade with the West passed through this distributing centre. Commerce was carried on with Persia, Mesopotamia, and Asia Minor by land. The *Periplus of the Erythrean Sea* gives a good account of the trade along the coast. This has been already referred to in connection with the Andhra kings. Merchants sailed from Mouza in Arab and reached Muziris or Cranganore on the Malabar coast in forty days during July and August, and returned in December or January. There were three principal trade routes with the West, one through Persia, the Caspian Sea, the Black Sea, and then to Constantinople; the second along the coast to the mouth of the Euphrates and thence to Palmyra; and the third along the coast to the Red Sea, and then through Egypt to Alexandria. The Indian goods were paid in Roman coins, and we find the Indians later on adopted the Roman style of aurei in their coinage.

Trade with the eastern countries were maintained during the period. Remains of Hindu and Buddhist civilization have been found in Cambodia and Siam. The principal route of trade with China was by land.

THE INDIAN RENAISSANCE

The Gupta dynasty, with its capital at Pataliputra, was the next major dynasty to rise to power in northern India. Local kingdoms had reasserted their power after the decline of the Kushanas, while in central India the Satavahanas had also declined; they were replaced by the Vakatakas, Ikshvakus and Chutus. The Chutus had their capital at Banavasi, but in the fourth century CE the Kadambas defeated them and took over the region. East of them, with their capital at Kolar, were the Western Gangas and further east still the Pallavas, with their capital at Kanchipuram. In the far south the Cholas and Cheras were in decline. The Pandyas ruled at Madurai. Kingdoms in northeast India included Kamarupa, Manipur and Tripura.

Chandragupta I, founder of the Gupta era in 319–320 CE, was the first important Gupta king. He had been preceded by Sri Gupta and Ghatotkacha. His son Samudragupta extended the empire, making conquests in all directions; the next king, Chandragupta II, consolidated the territory. The Chinese pilgrim Faxian visited during the reign of Chandragupta II and provided an account of conditions in the kingdom. There were more Gupta kings too, but in the sixth century the dynasty started to decline. One of the reasons for this was the invasion of the Hunas (Huns) from Central Asia.

Samudragupta, the greatest conqueror, was not only proficient in the art of war, but was also depicted playing the veena, a musical instrument. The reign of the Gupta kings was a time of great literature, art, architecture and developments in science.

Literature in Sanskrit reached a height with the works of Kalidasa. Varahamihira wrote books on astronomy and Aryabhatta on mathematics. The latter's work was extraordinary; he even calculated the value of pi and the earth's diameter, and explained the rotation of the earth. More Puranas too were composed, the sacred texts that lay the foundations of Hinduism today. However, it would not be correct to say that the principles of the *Manusmriti* were followed. Rather, kings ruled according to what was expedient. The earliest temples extant today date from the Gupta empire. However, the wonderful paintings and sculptures of Ajanta and Ellora belong to the Vakataka kingdom.

As the Guptas declined, once again, numerous small kingdoms arose. Among these rulers, King Harsha of the Pushyabhuti dynasty gained prominence in north India. His reign, the extent of his empire and the various kings he defeated are described in the passages below. Prominent dynasties at this time included the Chalukyas, located in the Deccan. Their king, Pulakeshin II, defeated Harsha in 618–19 CE.

Education was provided for upper caste males, but there was no standard system of education, as suggested by Ball (whose text makes up this chapter). The Buddhist universities included Nalanda and Vikramshila and education was also provided at temples and gurukuls, the latter being where a guru taught male students, either at his own home or in an ashram. Women and lower castes were excluded from formal education.

Different religions were practised at the time of Harsha, but it is likely he was a Buddhist of the Mahayana sect. The Buddhist pilgrim from China, Xuanzang, visited at this time, and Ball provides an account of his description of India and of the state of Buddhism at the time of Harsha. Many small kingdoms again arose after Harsha's death in 647 CE.

AN AWAKENING OF THE NATION

No state in India rose into prominence for about a century after the fall of the Andhras in the South, and of the nation. the Kushans in the north-west. India was divided into a number of small states without any cohesion or any bond of unity. Each of these states was busy in setting its own house in order. The people also began to arrange their social and religious institutions in their ancient spirit, which, they thought, were contaminated by foreign connection. The *Manu Samhita* was developed into a code of social and moral laws in this period. We do not come across any literary or epigraphic records of Indian history till we come to the second quarter of the fourth century. Pataliputra then rises from centuries of oblivion into the capital of an empire once again. With the rise of the Gupta Kings India enters into a new life. The social and political institutions, art, architecture, and literature all feel the impulse of a rejuvenescence.

Indian civilization reached its zenith during the administration of the Guptas. It seems after centuries of foreign interference the Indian people devoted their entire energy to the restoration of the ancient glory of their country. The progress which India made during these three centuries of good government under Indian kings was due mainly to a strong desire [of the Kushans] to live according to the noble traditions of the past.

Sources of Information for the Period

The Gupta kings helped by their exploits in re-uniting the people under the aegis of a strong paramount power, and in maintaining the country safe from foreign invasions. Their achievements were recorded in inscriptions which have been collected from several places and the literature of the times both Indian and foreign bear ample testimony to the peace and prosperity which the people enjoyed. The inscriptions were compiled in a volume by Dr. Fleet in 1888 and some more inscriptions have been discovered an edited since then. We owe to them the chronology of the Gupta kings, and an account of their government and territory. The Sanskrit literature and the memoir of the Chinese travellers have supplemented the inscriptions. The memoirs of Fa-Hien are especially valuable in this connection. Other information has been supplied by the dumb monuments of art and architecture.

THE GUPTA KINGS

Chandra Gupta

Early in the fourth century a Raja of Pataliputra married Kumara Devi, a princess of the Lichchavi clan. The Raja named Chandragupta was son of Ghatotkacha and grandson of Maharaja Gupta after whom the dynasty is called. The marriage was considered by the Guptas as the turning-point in their career, as they always referred to it with pride.

The Lichchavis were a clan enjoying a republican form of government since early times. They were conquered by the kings of Magadha later on, but it seems on the fall of the Maurya power they reasserted their independence. Chandragupta most probably acquired some power and prestige by this marriage. He extended his territory along the Gangetic valley up to Prayag and assumed the title of Maharajadhiraja. By his conquests he became the master of South Behar, Tirhoot, Oudh and some other adjoining districts. He held a formal ceremony of coronation as Emperor in 319 CE from which he started a new era called the Gupta era.

Samudra Gupta

Chandragupta was succeeded by his son Samudra Gupta in 330 or 335 CE. He has been described in one of the inscriptions as the exterminator of all kings, having no antagonist in the world, his fame extending up to the four oceans, and an equal of gods, a giver of millions of cows and gold, and a restorer of the *Asvamedha* sacrifice. The English historians call him an Indian Napoleon. He realized, as no other Indian king ever afterwards, the necessity of consolidating the empire by either conquering the hostile states or subjugating them. When India was divided into a number of small states then it was easy for the foreigners to enter into the country by overpowering the weak chiefs of the frontier provinces, and then to conquer the other states.

Chandragupta Maurya first set up an obstacle in the way of foreign invasions by building a strong empire but the fall of the empire after the death of Asoka weakened the defence of the country. The Greeks, the Parthians, the Sakas, and the Yuch-chis came one by one and settled themselves in different parts of India. It was not possible for any one small state to withstand these invasions. The distant provinces of the South and the East escaped these invasions not so much on account of their military strength, but very likely because the force of the invading army was gradually exhausted in traversing such a long distance. Weaker states in the vicinity of a kingdom are often a source of great danger. No state can feel itself safe when it can be overrun by the people of a neighbouring state, or a foreigner may invade it through weak states adjoining it. A system of confederation was attempted by Chandragupta and his successors. But a combination of the states under the hegemony of powerful kingdom has nowhere endured. India has not been exception in the matter.

Samudra Gupta made another attempt, and he succeeded in establishing a strong empire which lasted so long as it was guided by a strong monarch. But it fell into pieces when the central government became weak.

Samudra Gupta's Policy of Conquest

Samudra Gupta undertook his campaigns not under the principle that 'kingdom-taking' is the business of the king's but with a view to build up a strong kingdom which might stand against foreign invasions. Kingdom-taking as such could not be a principle with him as he maintained the autonomy of many of the kingdoms he conquered. Napoleon might have this avarice, and many of the modern states of Europe are not free from the greed of land, but the Indian king does not seem to have anything else behind his policy of conquest except the spirit of national defence. The inscription on the Asoka pillar at Allahabad records that he captured twelve kings of the South, and then liberated them by forming an alliance with them. He however exterminated the kingdoms of northern India, and admitted the kings of the forest countries into his service. He made the frontier kings his tributaries that they might pay allegiance to him. He established royal families but they were deprived of sovereign rights. The peoples of the outlying countries such as the Daivaputras, Shahis, Shahanushahis,

Sakas and Murandas, and the people of Simhala also formed alliances with him by sending rich presents. All these indicate that his only motive was the strengthening of the military position of the country. He conquered the neighbouring countries, and made alliances with the distant states. [...]

Campaigns of Samudra Gupta

The places mentioned in the inscriptions have not all been identified, neither is it possible to arrange his campaigns in time order. Harishena has put the places in the famous inscription at Allahabad according to their situation. It is presumed that he conquered the kingdoms in northern India, which were lying close to his kingdom, before he undertook his campaigns in the Conquest of South. The names of the kings of Aryavarta who the Northern Kingdoms. were violently exterminated are Rudradeva, Matila, Nagadatta, Chandravarman, Ganapatinaga, Nagasena, Achyuta, Nandin, Balavarman, and many others. The exact position of the territories of these kings could not be traced. The capital of Ganapatinaga only has been identified with Padmavati or Narwar, which exists even now in the territories of the Scindhia.

After completing the conquests in the North, Samudra Gupta led his campaigns into the South. First he came upon South Kosala in the valley of the Mahanadi and overthrew its king Mahendra. He then subjugated the forest kingdoms lying on the way. This region was known as Mahakantara, and its principal chief Vyaghra Raja. Mahendra of Pistapuram (modern Pithapuram), and Svamidatta of Kottura on the Mahendragiri hills in the Ganjam, Mantaraja of Kerala (on the banks of the Kolleru or Colair lake), Hastivarman of Vengi between the Krishna and the Godavari, and Vishnu Gopa of Kanchi or Conjeeveram fell one by one before his conquering arms. He then turned westwards and fell upon Ugrasena of Palakka, perhaps in the Nellore district. From there he marched northwards, subjugated the kingdoms of Kubera of Devarashtra (Maharashtra) and Damana of Erandapalla (Khandesh). Two other kingdoms, Kusthalapura and Avamukta, have not been identified. These kingdoms he did not annex, he simply demanded from the conquered kings in the South an acknowledgment of submission.

The frontier kings did not wait for the king to send his troops to demand submission. On orders being sent they agreed to pay taxes, to render obeisance to him, and to carry out his orders. There were a large number of kingdoms and republics on the borders of his empire. The following kingdoms are mentioned in the inscriptions: Samatata (Bengal between the Hooghly and the Brahmaputra), Davaka (North Bengal), Kamarupa (Assam); Nepal in the Himalayas, and Kartripura (probably Kumaon, Almora, Garhwal, and Kangra).

Samudra Gupta dealt fairly with the republics, and was satisfied by simply receiving their submission. The Yaudheyas and the Madrakas were the tribes in the Punjab. The Arjunayanas, Malavas, and Abhiras lived in the Eastern Rajputna and Malwa. The situation of the territory of the Prarjunas, Sanakanikas, Kakas and Kharaparikas is not yet known.

Limits of the Empire

The empire of the Gupta kings can be definitely known by ascertaining the position of the frontier kingdoms. So it is clear that it extended up to the Hooghly on the east, the Himalayas on the north, the Chambal on the west, and the Narmada on the south. It was a vast empire including the most flourishing parts of the country. The kingdoms and republics on the border, or in the south acknowledged his supremacy in one way or another either by paying tribute, paying allegiance, or carrying the orders in any other way. Samudra Gupta thus bound all the states of India in a chain of subsidiary alliance, and made himself the Lord Paramount of the whole country.

Relations with Foreign Kings

As Samudra Gupta succeeded in establishing a strong empire, the states in the neighbourhood of India solicited friendship with him. They sent him rich presents and offered their services to the king, whenever occasion required. The allies included the Daivaputras, Shahis, Shahanushahis, Sakas and Murundas, and the people of Simhala and other islands.

The king Meghavarna of Ceylon sent an embassy to get permission from Samudra Gupta to build a monastery at Buddha Gaya for the Buddhist pilgrims from Ceylon. The permission was readily granted. A splendid building was accordingly erected near the famous Bodhi tree. Hiuen Tsang saw the monastery accommodating about 1,000 monks of the Sthavira School of the Mahayana.

Samudra Gupta performed the *Asvamedha* ceremony in pomp and splendour to proclaim to the kings and potentates of India that he was the Lord Paramount of the Indian states. No other Indian king performed the ceremony since the days of Pushyamitra, as no other king really occupied the position of the supreme lord. The Asvamedha sacrifice by itself cannot be taken as a sign of the revival of Hindu ceremonies. But there is ample evidence of the growing popularity of Hindu culture and ceremonies.

Personal Accomplishments of Samudra Gupta

Samudra Gupta peacefully reigned for about fifty years. He was as much renowned for his personal accomplishments as for his generalship and kingly virtues. He was a patron of learning and was himself a poet. His various poetical compositions won for him the title of 'king of poets'. He was also well known for his choral skill and musical accomplishments. He could play skilfully upon *vina*, a rather difficult art. Of all the Gupta kings Samudra Gupta is the best fitted to be called the greatest monarch of the times. He extended his dominions, formed strong alliances, and established peace in the country. Harishena, his poet laureate, rightly says, 'his many wonderful and noble deeds are worthy to be praised for a very long time'.

Chandragupta II Vikramaditya

He was succeeded by his son Chandragupta in about 375 CE. He as sumed the title of Vikramaditya. The empire was extended by him by annexing Surashtra which was then in possession of the Saka Satraps. Samudra Gupta received an embassy from the Satrap Rudra Sena, but Chandragupta resolved to drive the foreign rulers from India. He attacked Rudra Simha, dethroned him, slew the Satrap, and annexed his dominions in about 388 CE. He also annexed Malwa and Guzerat, and extended his dominions up to the Arabian Sea. Connection with Western world was established through the ports, but it cannot be said that his Court and subjects were there by brought under the influence of Western ideas, Broach, Sopara, and Cambay were the principal ports on the west coast. Ujjain was an important distributing centre which was connected with all the important places within the country. The possession of these places must have increased the income of the state.

Chandragupta II enjoyed a long reign of about forty-six years. The Gupta dominions reached their furthest limits under his- strong and vigorous rule. He was a brave soldier, and used to fight with lions in order to display his strength and courage. It seems he removed his headquarters to Ajodhya in Oudh, as Pataliputra was not central enough for a capital. Ujjain was the capital of the western provinces, and here developed a great literature which India is now proud of. There was also a splendid observatory at Ujjain, which was attended by a good number of famous astronomers such as Aryabhatta and Varahamihira.

Visit of Fa-Hien

It was during the reign of Chandragupta II that the Chinese pilgrim Fa-Hien visited India. He came to India to collect authentic texts of the *Vinaya-pitaka*. He left China in 399 CE. He came by the south of the Gobi desert through Sha-chow and Labnor to Khotan, Then he came across the Pamirs to Udayana or Swat. From there he visited Takshasila (Taxila) and Purushapura (Peshawar). He spent ten years in India from 401 to 410 CE and visited all the important places in northern India such as Mathura, Kanouj, Sravasti, Kapilavastu, Kusinara, Vaisali, Pataliputra, Rajgir, Gaya, Benares, Kausambi, Champa, and Tamralipti. He lived at Pataliputra for three years, and at Tamralipti for two years, from where he sailed for Ceylon. The voyage from Tamralipti to Ceylon took him two weeks. After staying for two years in Ceylon he returned to China via Java.

The account of India as recorded by Fa-Hien is extremely interesting. It is from his writings that the historians have collected so much information regarding the social, moral, and economic condition of the people, although he does not mention the names of any of the kings. He calls the Gangetic plains to the east of Mathurà *Madhya-desa* or Mid-India. The countries to the west the places visited by Fa of Mathura constituted western India. The kings of Hien. Western India were all Buddhists. He found most of the ancient places in the Himalayan region deserted. Sravasti, the ancient capital of Kosala, contained about 200 families. Kapilavastu and Kusinara were de populated, and so were also Rajgir, Gaya, and Kausambi. But other towns and cities were in a prosperous condition. The cities of Magadhai were in a flourishing condition, and they were very large. Pataliputra was the capital of Magadha. He saw the remains of Asoka's palace, still standing, which he heard was built by supernatural beings. There were monasteries both belonging to the Mahayana and the Hinayana Schools. The number of Sramanas in these two monasteries was about 600. Students from different parts of the world came there for study. The celebrated Brahman savant Manjusri was then residing at the Mahayana monastery at Pataliputra. He was held in highest reverence by the Sramanas and the Bhikshus.

Buddhism was still the religion of a large number of the people. He saw numerous monasteries on the banks of the Jumna, and the kings of western India were all Buddhists. The Sramanas received from the kings and the people all marks of respect. At Pataliputra he witnessed the processions of chariots carrying the image of Buddha. These chariots were four-wheeled and five-storied. The procession drew a huge concourse of people, who spent the night in great rejoicing. The kings, nobility and rich citizens of India considered it an act of religious merit to endow monasteries, and to make gifts of land, gardens, and houses for the use of Sramanas. They recorded their grants in copper plates, and these grants could on no account be forfeited. Inscriptions corroborating this statement have been found. The Kakanada-bota Inscription at Sanchi records the grant of a village and a sum of money for the maintenance of five Bhikshus by Amrakardava, who was probably an officer of Chandragupta II.

Fa-Hien was struck with the good government of Madhya-desa. The revenue was derived from the crownlands, people had not to pay any taxes. There was no restriction upon the movement of the people. They were not required to take any passports as in China. Capital punishment or any corporal punishment did not exist. Fines were imposed according to the gravity of the offence. Rebellion was sometimes punished with amputation of the right hand. Men in the service of the king received fixed salary. The government did not interfere with the rights of the people. The people were free and prosperous.

'Throughout the country no one kills any living thing, or drinks wine, or eats onions or garlic, they do not keep pigs or fowls; there are no dealings in cattle no butcher's shops or distilleries in their marketplaces.' Only the Chandals or low-class people who lived outside the city did not observe these rules. They were looked down upon by the people, and whenever they entered the city they had to strike a piece of wood in order that others might not be defiled by their touch.

The pilgrim saw a large number of hospitals in the city of Pataliputra endowed by the people and the rich citizens. The patients received free treatment and free food. The physicians were very attentive in their duties and the patients were admitted irrespective of their creed or caste.

The picture drawn by Fa-Hien represents the true life of the people. The government of the kings was not oppressive, on the other hand everybody was happy under them. The kings of Mid-India were not Buddhists but they followed the tradition of Asoka and other catholic rulers in maintaining a spirit of benevolent neutrality. The people were also very zealous in promoting social good by endowing hospitals and monasteries. The spirit of *Ahimsa* still continued as an active force. Brahmans respected Buddhist Sramanas and Buddhists reciprocated their feelings for Brahman scholars. There was not antagonism between Brahmanism and Buddhism.

Kumar Gupta I

Chandra Gupta II was succeeded by his son Kumar Gupta I in about 413 CE. Kumara reigned for forty years, and the empire remained intact throughout this long reign. He also celebrated the Asvamedha in imitation of his grandfather, but the occasion of the sacrifice is not known. He might have conquered some new territory, or might have subdued some rebellions, and to commemorate his victory the great sacrifice was performed. India was visited by a tribe called the Pushyamitras towards the end of his reign Another nomadic horde called the Hunas from Central Asia was approaching towards. India in the middle of the fifth century, Kumar Gupta I died in 455 CE and was succeeded by his son Skanda Gupta.

Skanda Gupta

The last great king of the Gupta dynasty was Skanda Gupta. He had to meet two dangers that threatened the empire. First he had to deal with the Pushyamitras, most probably a tribe of the north. These people possessed great power and wealth, and it was very difficult for Skanda Gupta to subdue them. It is stated in the Bhitari Stone pillar inscription that the prince had to spend a night on bare earth while engaged in war with them. The enemy was defeated and Skanda Gupta retrieved the tottering fortune of his dynasty.

The Hunas from Central Asia came as it were in a whirlwind. The nomadic hordes were driven off by the strong arms of Skanda Gupta, and India was saved for the time being. The victory over the Hunas, which was achieved in the early part of his reign, has been celebrated in the stone pillar dedicated to the image of Sarngin at Bhitari. The Junagadha Rock Inscription which is dated 458 CE mentions the defeat of the Hunas, and it can be inferred from this that the Huna invasion was repulsed a year or two before 458 CE.

Skanda Gupta however could not enjoy peace very long. The Hunas returned in larger number in about 465 CE. Skanda Gupta could not repel the attack, and the empire was shattered, although the Gupta kings retained their power for some time in the eastern parts. On the previous occasion Skanda Gupta could mobilize all his resources and utilize the services of his governors throughout the empire. But it is probable that when the Hunas came later he did not receive the help of all his subordinate chiefs and governors. He had to reduce the weight of coins to meet the extraordinary expenses of the war. But nothing did avail. The result was disastrous. The Hunas had already conquered the kingdom of Kabul then under the Kushans, and the kingdom of Gandhar. They made Peshawar their base and from there penetrated into India. The western provinces of the empire were occupied. Skanda Gupta thereafter ruled from Pataliputra over reduced territories. He died in 480 CE.

Successors of Skanda Gupta

Skanda Gupta had no son. He was succeeded by his brother Pura Gupta. The only event which is known in his reign was the attempt to restore the purity of the coinage which was debased by Skanda Gupta under the stress of war. He died in 485 CE. His son Narasimha Gupta Baladitya Narasimha succeeded him. The Hunas had become more formidable by defeating and slaying king Firoz of Persia in 484 CE. The invasion into India was led by a chieftain named Toramana. By 500 CE he established himself as ruler of Malwa, and made the local rulers his tributaries. Hiuen Tsang says that Baladitya, king of Magadha, defeated the Hunas. But there is no such mention in the inscriptions. He also says that Baladitya built a beautiful temple, 300 feet high, in the University town of Nalanda. Nara Simha Gupta Baladitya died in 505 CE and was succeeded by Kumar Gupta his son Kumar Gupta

II. By the middle of the sixth century the dynasty of the Guptas ceased to rule Magadha. A branch of the imperial dynasty appeared later as local rulers of Magadha, who shared their government of the province with another clan known as the Maukhari.

The Hunas

The Hunas, as we have already seen, were a nomadic tribe living in the steppes of Central Asia. When they were pressed for subsistence one stream went into Europe and another came southwards into the Oxus Valley. In Europe they occupied the territory between the Volga and the Danube. They became very terrible under their leader Attila. But on his death in 453 CE they again became disunited and their empire was shattered into pieces by another horde of nomads from Northern Asia. The section of the Hunas who invaded India was known as the Ephthalites or the White Hunas. They first attacked in 465 CE but were repulsed by Skanda Gupta. The king of Persia suffered a fatal defeat at their hands in 584 CE, and thereafter they invaded India with redoubled vigour which Skanda Gupta could not with stand. They penetrated into India as far as Malwa, under Toramana who appears in some inscriptions as Maharajadhiraja. Toramana came to Central India towards the end of the fifth century. The local Rajas became his tributaries. He died in about 510 CE and was succeeded by his son Mihirakula.

The Hunas by this time had acquired an extensive territory. Bamyin near Herat was the capital of the empire. The Chinese envoy Song-Yun, who visited the place in 519 CE, says that the Huna king received tributes from forty countries, extending from the frontier of Persia to Khotan. Mihirakula was a subordinate chief of the great Huna king of Bamyin. Sakal (modern Sialkot) was his capital. He was a cruel tyrant, and the sufferings of the people under his savage rule knew no bounds. The Indians once more made up their mind to drive the foreigners away. Raja Yasodharman of Central India, who ruled from the Himalayas to the Western Ocean, brought about the overthrow of the Huna chiefs, with the aid of Narasimha Baladitya of Magadha in 530 CE. Mihirakula was taken a prisoner but was kindly released by Baladitya. He retired into Kashmir, and managed to retain his power over Gandhara with the help of the Raja of Kashmir. He died before 540 CE, and the people rejoiced at his death. The Hunas could not recover their position in India after the death of Mihirakula, and their dominion in Asia was conquered from them by the Turks and the Persians combined between 563 and 567 CE.

Smaller Kingdoms on the Fall of the Gupta Empire

Yasodharman

A number of smaller kingdoms assumed independence on the decline of the Gupta Empire. Mention has already been made of Yasodharman. He has been described in the Mandasor inscription as the Raja of Central India, and that he overthrew Mihirakula in 533 CE. His territory extended from the Brahmaputra to the Mountain Mahendra and from the Himalayas to Western Ocean. Further informations regarding the Raja of Central India are not available. There was another Raja named Vishnudharman who lived towards the Vindhyas, and who was probably in subordinate alliance with Yasodharman.

Buddha Gupta and Bhanu Gupta

The Eran Stone pillar inscription mentions a king Buddha named Buddha Gupta who was on the throne of Western Gupta and Bhanu Gupta Mahoa in 484, and another king named Bhanu Gupta in

510 CE. They were most probably connected with the early Gupta kings of Magadha. Toramana invaded India after Buddha Gupta and before Bhanu Gupta.

Valabhi kings

Bhatarka, entitled *Senapati*, was probably a general of the Gupta kings in Kathiawar. His son Dharasena I was also a *Senapati*, but another son Dronasimha assumed the title of Maharaja. Two other brothers Dhruvasena and Dharapatta succeeded him. Gahasena, son of the latter, followed him and then his grandson Dharasena II who was the Maharaja of Valabhi in 571 CE. The Valabhi kings do not seem to have been in dependent from the beginning. They asserted their in dependence after the destruction of the Huna power. They remained in power till 770 CE.

Valabhi was a rich and prosperous city when Hiuen Tsang visited India. It was the residence of two great Buddhist teachers Gunamati and Sthiramati. The Chinese traveller, I-tsing, compares Nalanda in Bihar and Valabhi in Kathiawar, the two important centres of learning in India, with the famous Universities of China. Valabhi is identified with Wala, the chief town of a state of the same name in Kathiawar. One of the later kings of this dynasty, Dhruvabhata, was defeated by Harshavardhana, and was compelled to marry his daughter. His uncle Siladitya was a pious Buddhist. He was a Raja of Mo-la-po or Western Malwa. Both Siladitya and Dhruvabhata were conquered by Harsha.

CIVILIZATION OF THE GUPTA PERIOD

The civilization of the Gupta period was a revival of Aryan culture and of Aryan polity, which owing to the disturbed conditions of Hindustan and the corruption of Aryan ideals, were becoming decadent and stood in need of revision. The profound peace which a firm central government established. opened the highways of commerce, promoted a great activity in all the arts of peace, and brought about a general revival of Aryan learning – philosophy, science, poetry, and the drama – all of which sectarians include under the vague designation of 'Hinduism'. The great works of art have been destroyed by the Mahomedan conquerors; some only are still to be found in the distant places. But the literature and philosophy still exist to increase the glory of ancient India.

Revival of Sanskrit

Asoka issued his Edicts in the vernaculars of the people, and the literature of the times found a convenient medium in Pali. The inscriptions in India were written in Pali till we come to the middle of the second century CE. The ancient epics and the other literature of the Aryan ancestors were assiduously cultivated by the people. The inscriptions of the Gupta period were all written in high-flown Sanskrit. Kalidasa, the greatest poet of India, wrote his famous poems and dramas during the first half of the fifth century when Chandragupta II and then Kumar Gupta adorned the throne of Magadha. There were many other poets and scholars besides Kalidasa. The famous dramas *Mrichchakatika* and *Mudra Rakshasa* were written in this age. The *Vayu Purana* and the *Manu Samhita* received their present forms. Mathematics and astronomy made very great progress. Aryabhatta and Varaha Mihira wrote books in these abstruse sciences which are still admired by the scientists. The age is marked by a great intellectual upheaval.

Education

The intellectual movement was not confined to a few. It was fostered in the famous centres of learning. Takshasila was a famous university near modern Rawalpindi from before the invasion of Alexander. Chandragupta Maurya and Chanakya received their education there. Benares and Ujjain then rose into importance. Nalanda in Bihar developed into a great university after the decease of Buddha. A great mango garden was offered to Buddha by a number of merchants to hold his religious discourses there. King Sakraditya of Magadha built there a monastery, and then many other kings and rulers erected monastery after monastery.

The Gupta kings supported these monasteries, and we are told that Narasimha Gupta Baladitya looked upon the place with great favour. Nalanda was the biggest and the best university in India when Hiuen Tsang visited the country. Its fame carried far beyond the borders of India. The university of Valabhi was also an important centre of learning. Education made the highest progress in Magadha and Malwa. I-tsing says that the University of Nalanda was supported out of the produce of 200 villages which were given as endowment to it by the people. There were 10,000 students reading in the University, which contained eight big halls, 300 rooms and a large number of chapels. If 10,000 students could come to one university for the completion of their study there must have been a network of schools for elementary education.

Art and Architecture

The plastic and pictorial arts felt the same impulse of life as literature and science. Innumerable monasteries and temples were erected to express the sense of spiritual hankering of the people. Their devotion took shape in the various beautiful structures which however have been destroyed by the unsympathetic invaders of later ages. We learn from the inscriptions that temples were dedicated to Vishnu, votive columns were erected in honour of the Sun, monasteries were given over to the Buddhist Sangha, and even temples were built for the spiritual culture of the Jainas. The remains of most of these edifices cannot be traced. But whatever have been discovered bear ample testimony to the richness of the creative genius of the Indians.

The excavations at Sarnath have yielded very valuable results. Buddhist monasteries and statues of Buddha of the fifth and sixth centuries have been discovered. Statues and other sculptures have been found in various places of northern India. They all bear the marks of an independent style with very little foreign influence. The figures of the gods, goddesses, of Buddha and the Bodhisattvas, with their characteristic decorations are purely Indian. The temples and the monasteries represent the Indian ideals. The temples were mainly of the type of the Mount of Vishnu to represent the rajasic aspect of the civilization. The people were imbued with a spirit of self-assertion, and it was expressed in grand and superb edifices, beautiful sculpture, and splendid paintings, and in rich literature. The cave-monasteries at Ajanta, the sculptures found at Sarnath, the frescoes on the walls of the Ajanta temples still stand as so many monuments of the artistic genius of the period.

In the year 456 CE a breach in the great Sudarsana Lake in Kathiawar was restored by an officer under Parnadatta, the governor of the province, when Skanda Gupta was the monarch of Pataliputra. The lake has a history of its own. Pushyagupta, the governor Chandragupta Maurya, first devised the scheme of creating a reservoir by damming a small stream near Girnar for irrigation purposes. But he could not complete the work, which was done in the reign of Asoka by the Persian governor Raja Tushaspha. During the great storm of 150 CE the embankment gave way, and the lake overflooded the country. The embankment was rebuilt by order of the Saka Satrap Rudradaman of the Western provinces, and was made three times stronger. Again in 456 CE the Sudarsana Lake burst during the heavy rains, and the streams which fed it became furious. Chakrapalit, an officer under governor Parnadatta, repaired the embankment. The lake thus stood as the witness of the care which the rulers paid to the works of public utility. The spirit of good government continued from the early times down to the fifth century CE. Unfortunately many such evidences of the devotion of the Indian kings to the public good have not been discovered.

Social Condition

Buddhism, Hinduism, and Jainism flourished side by side. There was no antagonism between them. We have seen that at a monastery at Pataliputra there dwelt a Brahman savant, and he was held in highest veneration. The number of Hindu temples increased and there was a revival of Hindu ceremonials. The social institutions gradually developed on the modern lines. The caste system was an established institution but it had not yet attained its rigidity. Inter-marriages were allowed although they were not looked upon with favour. People were not bound to follow a fixed occupation according to the caste rules. The Mandasor Stone inscription of Kumar Gupta relates how a band of silk weavers who came from Lata to Dasapura took up other occupations. While some excelled in their own business, others either took up archery, or became soldiers, or followed the profession of astrologers and bards or took up some business according to their inclination.

The economic condition of the country was very satisfactory. The description of the city of Dasapura in Scindhia's dominions gives a vivid idea of the wealth, grandeur, and beauty of the industrial cities. Dasapura was surrounded by mountains clad in big forests and two streams passed by it. There were numerous lakes adorned with water lilies, and many flower trees stood on their banks. The houses were long and many storied. Big gardens were attached to these houses, a fixed occupation and they all presented a look of joy and happiness. Each trade had its own guild or corporation. These corporations were well-organized, and they were not confined to one place. They created and managed endowments. The prosperity of the country must have been the result of good government Industries did not depend entirely upon royal patronage. Their development was greatly due to non-interference and the excel lent condition of the roads and communications.

The Gupta period has been described as the Golden Age of India, and the epithet is not at all inappropriate. The coins of the Gupta Kings were also polished and bore beautiful designs. The system of sale and exchange was of an advanced type. Trade with foreign countries was carried on an extensive scale. This state of things however did not long continue. The fall of the Empire was followed by dark days and depression in all other departments.

HARSHA-VARDHANA
606-647 CE

Rise of Thaneswar

A number of small states came into existence on the downfall of the Gupta kings. The Hunas settled in the north-western Punjab, and the smaller Rajput states gradually rose into prominence.

Towards the end of the sixth century Prabhakar-Vardhan, king of Thaneswar, defeated the Hunas and some Rajput princes in his neighbourhood, and made an attempt more to consolidate the whole northern India under one king. He was connected with the ancient Gupta kings through his mother Mahasena-Gupta. Naturally therefore he wanted to attain the glory of his illustrious ancestors. He carried on successful wars against the Malavas, the Gurjaras and the Hunas. In 604 CE he sent his elder son Rajya-Vardhana assisted by his younger son Harsha to repel the attack of the Hunas on the north-west frontier. While the Prince was engaged against the enemy the king fell ill, and Harsha returned to the capital. On the death of his father Harsha managed the affairs of the state till the return of his elder brother. As soon as Rajya-Vardhan had assumed his powers as king, he received the news of the murder of the king of Kanouj by the king of Malwa. Graha Varman Maukhari, the king of Kanouj, was the husband of his sister Rajyasri who was cruelly treated by the murderer. Rajya-Vardhan hastened to the rescue of his sister, defeated the king of Malwa, but he was treacherously murdered by Sasanka, the king of Gaur (Central Bengal), an ally of his enemy. Rajyasri fled to the Vindhyan forests in this state of confusion (606 CE).

Harsha Vardhana

Prince Harsha was invited by the councillors of the state to occupy the throne as he was the eldest of all the claimants. The son of Rajya-Vardhana was an infant. For six years Harsha was busy in bringing order out of chaos and anarchy which ensued the death of his brother. The first task of the new ruler was the recovery of his sister who in a desperate condition was about to burn herself alive. With the help of some ab original chiefs Harsha succeeded in finding her whereabouts. In the meantime, Sasanka, the murderer of his brother, escaped. When he made his position secure he performed his coronation ceremony in 612 CE. He became the king of Thaneswar and Kanouj, and made the latter his capital. His sister was associated with him in the administration of the country. He was a young of seventeen when he succeeded his brother.

Harsha's Expedition

After restoring order in his own kingdom he set out on an extensive tour of conquest with a view to bring the whole of India under one Government. His military strength was immense. His force consisted of 5,000 elephants, 20,000 cavalry and 50,000 infantry when he started his campaign. In the course of first five years, and a half he brought under subjection the country in the north-west, and a large part of Bengal. By that time his forces had also increased to 60,000 elephants and 100,000 infantry.

In about 620 CE he led an expedition against the Chalukya king of the Deccan, Pulakesin II. Harshavardhan found in the Chalukya king a formidable foe, suffered a defeat in his hands and was forced to recognize the Narmada River as the southern boundary of his territory. This was the only defeat he suffered in his long career of victory.

His campaign against Valabhi and the other kingdoms of Guzerat was very successful. Dhruvabhat II, the king of Valabhi, was an ally of the Chalukya kings. He was forced to sue for peace, and to marry the daughter of Harsha in about 633 CE. The kings of Anandapura, Cutch and Kathiawar also recognized the supremacy of the king of Kanouj. His last campaign was directed against Ganjam on the Bay of Bengal in 643 CE.

Extent of Harsha's Empire

His empire extended from the Himalayas to the Narmada, and from the Punjab to the borders of Assam. The administration of the country was left in the hands of the local Raja, all of whom acknowledged him as their suzerain. In the great assembly at Kanouj eighteen Rajas attended his Court. The Raja of Assam had also to acknowledge him as his superior monarch.

Mode of Government

Harsha ruled his vast territory on a purely personal basis. He was constantly on the move except during justice and supervising the work of the local rajas. The usual accommodation for the emperor was provided in an improvised travelling palace, made of boughs and reeds, at each halting place. The tents of the later times did not then come into use. These temporary habitations were set fire to at the departure of the emperor. The march of the emperor was accompanied by the music of the golden drums.

His administration was marked by justice and benevolence. The revenue was derived mainly from the rent of the crown lands, which was assessed at about one-sixth of the produce. The officials received grants of land in lieu of their pay. The labourers were duly paid for their services rendered to the state. Taxes were not heavy, and the subjects were not forced to render free personal services. The king was liberal in charity towards all religious communities. He used to distribute all his accumulated treasure to the religious teachers of different sects and to the poor and the needy at the end of every five years. The king thus lived for the people and the people did not live for the king. The system of punishment was not of an advanced type. Imprisonment was the ordinary penalty. Mutilation of limbs was generally the penalty for serious offences, but this was very often commuted into banishment. Fines imposed for minor offences. Ordeal by water, fire, weighment, or poison was an effective method of ascertaining the truth.

Education

There is evidence to prove that education was widely spread, especially among the Brahmans and the Buddhist monks. But learning was not the monopoly of any one class of men. There was an organized system of education.

At the first stage children were taught the alphabets and a book called Siddah-vastu containing 12 chapters. At the age of seven they commenced the study of the 'Five Sastras', viz., 1, Sabdavidya (Etymology), 2, Silpa Sthana Vidya (science of arts and crafts), 3, Chikitsa (medicine), 4, Hetu Vidya (Logic) and 5, Adhmyatma Vidya (Principles of philosophy and theology). Education was therefore of a comprehensive type training young men in the art of living as well as in the art of thinking and expressing their thoughts.

The method of teaching was oral. The teachers were earnest and industrious. They inspired their pupils to exert themselves. The dull and the inert were infused with enthusiasm by their able teaching. The pupils used to live with their teachers up to the age of thirty. After completing their education the pupils used to pay Dakshina (reward) to their teachers. The Buddhist Bhikshus were very useful in spreading knowledge from place to place. The Buddhist monasteries were centres of learning. The monasteries at Takshasila, Nalanda, and Vikram Sila were the most famous universities of the time. Takshasila was reputed for its school of medicine and Ujjain for astronomy. Nalanda was the centre of Buddhist teaching of all schools.

Harsha was a great patron of learning. The poet Bana was the greatest ornament of his Court. He wrote the Harsha-charita, a historical romance describing in high-flown language the exploits of his hero. Harsha himself was a poet. His drama *Nagananda* is considered to be one of the best dramas written in Sanskrit. *Ratnavali* and *Priyadarsika* are his two other productions.

Harsha's Religion

The members of the royal family to which Harsha belonged followed different religions according to their individual choice. One of his ancestors, Pushya-bhuti, was a worshipper of Siva. Harsha's father was a Sun worshipper. His brother and sister were Buddhists of the Hinayana School. Harsha was an eclectic in faith. He paid his devotions of Siva, to Sun as well Buddha.

Towards the end of his life he was inclined more towards Buddhism. Both he and his sister showed their preference to Mahayana philosophy under the influence of the Chinese pilgrim, Hiuen Tsang, who spent a few years with him. Although he liked the Mahayana Buddhism most he did not withdraw his support from other religions. Hindus, Buddhists, and Jains uniformly received benevolence from him. He was not particularly harsh upon any one creed. He punished a number of people who made an attempt upon his life at the instigation of jealous Brahmans. The guilty Brahmans were deported, but no one was punished for avowing any faith. He maintained his position as an impartial monarch. His toleration was not of the negative type but it found expression in an active support of all movements which aimed at the spiritual welfare of the people.

Harsha's Death

Shortly after the departure of Hiuen Tsang, king Harsha died in 647 CE. He left no heir, and his minister Arjuna or Arunasva usurped the throne. Harsha maintained friendly relations with China, and exchanged embassies with that country. Wang-hiwn-tse was in command of the Chinese embassy when Harsha died. The members of the escort of the envoys were massacred by Arjuna. But the envoys escaped to Tibet. The Tibetan king, Strong-tsan Gampo married Chinese princess, and was an ally of the king of China. He sent a strong army against Arjuna. Tirhut was annexed and Arjuna taken a prisoner to China. With in a short time after the death of Harsha-Vardhana his vast empire was again torn into pieces. A number of smaller principalities arose on its ruins.

Condition of India in the Time of Harsha

The best account of the time is derived from the Chinese traveller Hiuen Tsang who visited India between 630 and 644 CE. His *Travels* is a source of authentic information for the social, political, and religious conditions of almost all the parts of India. His biography written by his friend Hwni-li supplies many additional details. The official Chinese histories also contain reference to Indian events of the period. Besides we have the invaluable book of Bana presenting the career of the emperor in high-flown Sanskrit.

Itinerary of Hiuen Tsang

Hiuen Tsang was a great scholar. After mastering of all the literature on Buddhism available in China, he started on a pilgrimage to India to learn Buddhistic philosophy in the land of the Master. He left China in 629 CE and crossed Central Asia with great difficulty. He came to Kapisa at the foot of the Hindu Kush, passing Ferghana, Samarkand, Bokhara, and Balkh on the way. From Kapisa he visited Langhan, Nagarhar, Gandhar and Udyana beyond the Indus. Then he crossed the great river and reached Taxila. Kashmir and the important towns in the Punjab were next visited. Proceeding eastward to Magadha, and visited the important places connected with the life of Buddha, such as Kapilavastu, Kusinara, Sravasti, Benares, Gaya, Rajgir and other places. He spent a considerable portion in the monasteries, and studied from the monks Buddhist scriptures.

At the great monastery of Nalanda he had the privilege of reading under Silabhadra. He became known as the Master of the Law. He was invited by Kumara, the king of Kamrupa, and then he came to Harsha, who held him in great veneration. He also went to many places in Central India, Bengal, and the Deccan. From the Deccan he went to the Malabar coast, and then completed his itinerary by visiting Guzerat and Sindh. He returned to China by Central Asia in 645 CE. He carried a large number of manuscripts and Buddhistic relics from India, and devoted the latter portion of his life in writing the *Travels* and translating the books he collected.

Kanouj and Harsha

A full account of the places, including history and extant traditions, have been recorded in the *Travels*. A connected history of India would have been impossible but for the information left by the Chinese traveller. The description of Kanouj and Harshavardhana is a very pleasant one. At the time of Fa-Hien there were only two Buddhist monasteries at Kanouj but Hiuen Tsang saw about 100. From this it seems Buddhism made some progress in the capital. Harsha forbade the use of animal food and capital punishments. He erected thousands of stupas on the banks of the Ganges, established travellers' rest-houses throughout his dominions, and erected Buddhist monasteries at sacred places of the Buddhists.

We further learn from him that Harsha held a convocation at the end of every five years and gave away in charity everything except the materials of war. He used to summon all the Buddhist monks together once a year, and organize discussions on religious questions. The learned and the honest scholars were amply rewarded, but the immoral and careless members of the Order were banished from his presence and the country. The king used to distribute food to 1,000 Buddhist monks and 500 Brahmans daily wherever he might be in the course of his tour.

Cities and Houses

The description of the general features of the cities and buildings of India given by the pilgrim is very interesting. The quadrangular walls of the cities, he says, 'broad and high, while the thoroughfares are narrow tortuous passages. The shops are on the highways and booths line the roads'. Butchers, fishermen, public performers, executioners, and scavengers were treated by the people with contempt. They had their habitations marked by a distinguishing sign, and they were forced to live outside the city and they had to sneak along on the left when going about in the hamlets.

The city walls built of bricks while walls of houses and enclosures wattled bamboo wood. The ordinary houses thatched with grass, and differed very little from the structures in the villages of India found at present. The Buddhist monasteries, on the other hand, were of remarkable architecture. They had a tower at each of the four corners of the quadrangle, and three high walls in a tier. The rafters and roof beams were carved with the strange figures, and the doors, windows and walls were painted in various colours. The houses of the laity were sumptuous inside and economical outside.

Dress and Personal Characteristics

People of India in general have changed very little in their dress since the day of Hiuen Tsang. The contact with the West has effected some changes in cities and among the educated people only. We find in the accounts of Hiuen Tsang: 'The inner clothing and outward attire of the people have no tailoring; as to colour a fresh white is esteemed and motley is of no account. The men wind a strip of cloth round the waist and up to the armpits and have the right shoulder bare. The women wore a long robe which covers both. Generally silk (Kausheya), muslin, calico, kshiauma (a kind of linen), and wool were used. Close-fitting jackets were used in North India where the climate was very cold. There were also some non-Buddhists who wore peacock's tails. Some people adorned themselves with a necklace of skulls. There were also some people who were quite naked, and there were some who covered their body with grass or boards.' The Kshatriyas and Brahmans, goes on the description, 'are clean-handed and unostentatious, pure and simple in life and very frugal. The dress and ornaments of the kings and grandees are very extraordinary. Garlands and tiaras with precious stones are their head- adornments, and their bodies are adorned with rings, bracelets, and necklaces. Wealthy mercantile people have only bracelets. Most of the people go bare-footed and shoes are rare.' The people were pure in habits and they must have a wash before every meal.

Language

Hiuen Tsang has made a statement to the effect that the Sanskrit alphabet was invented by the god Brahma. The story has been repeated by several Buddhist writers. There is another tradition that a king named Brahma invented the letters and hence the Brahmi script, and another king Kharostha invented the script called after him Kharoshthi.

The Chinese pilgrim mentions forty-seven letters in the alphabet. The people of Mid-India were 'pre-eminently explicit and correct in speech, their expressions being harmonious and elegant, like those of the devas, and their intonation clear and distinct, serving as rule and pattern for others.' This holds good even up to the present time. 'The people of neighbouring territories and foreign countries repeating errors until these became the norm and emulous for vulgarities,' observes Hiuen Tsang, 'have lost the pure style.'

The state of education has already been described. There were separate custodians of the archives and records. The official annals recorded in detail the calamities and good fortune of the people. These annals were collectively called Nilapita (Dark-blue store).

The State of Buddhism

Different schools had arisen who held different views with regard to the teachings of Buddha. The religion was pure or diluted according to the spiritual insight and mental capacity of its adherents. There were eighteen schools of Buddhism, each famous for the defence and propagation of some peculiar doctrine. The Buddhist Church was principally divided into two sections, Hinayana (small vehicle) and Mahayana (great vehicle). The tenets of the two systems widely different. 'The Mahayanists had,' says Watters, 'a more expansive creed, a different standard of religious perfection, and a more elaborate cult than the Hinayanists. As to particular tenets, they differed very much from the early Buddhists in such matters as opinions about Arhats and Bodhisattvas, their views of the relation of Buddha to man were kind, of the efficacy of prayer and worship, and of the elasticity of the Canon.' The Hinayanists practised quiet thoughts, walking up and down and standing still while the Mahayanists practised Samadhi and Prajna.

There was a regular gradation among the members of the Brotherhood. 'The Brother who expounds orally one treatise (or class of scripture) in the Buddhist Canon, whether Vinaya, Abhidharma or Sutra, is exempted from serving under the Prior; he who expounds two is invested with the outfit of a Superior; he who expounds three has Brethren deputed to assist him; he who expounds four has lay servants assigned to him; he who expounds five rides an elephant; he who expounds six rides an elephant and has a surrounding retinue. Where the spiritual attainments are high, the distinctions conferred are extraordinary.' Occasionally discussions were held in the assembly of the Brethren to test intellectual capacity and to judge moral character. There was a gradation of penalties for offences against the Vinaya. A reprimand for slight offences, for grave offences, cessation of oral intercourse with the Brethren, and expulsion from the community for serious offences were generally the rule.

The caste system, as observed by Hiuen Tsang, had become rigid. The Brahmans strictly observed ceremonial purity, and kept their principles and lived continently. The Kshatriyas formed the second order. They had held sovereignty for many generations and they were marked by benevolence and mercy. The Vaisyas or the traders belonged to the third order. They bartered commodities and carried on trade far and near. The fourth class was that of the Sudras. They were agriculturists cultivating the soil. The members of a caste married within the caste. Relations, by the father's or the mother's side, did not intermarry, and a woman never contracted a second marriage. There were also menial castes and numerous classes or people according to their trade and occupation. In the Buddhist literature Kshatriyas formed the first order, but the Brahmans gradually rose into prominence and occupied the first position. The Sudras also had risen from the position of servants to that of agriculturists. That shows that they acquired property, and became important members of society. Other customs indicate the strict observance of purity among the people.

The Army

The kings were generally Kshatriyas. But occasionally other castes occupied the throne by rebellion and regicide. The soldiers formed a distinct caste, and they were adepts in military tactics. In peace they guarded the sovereign's residence and in war they became the intrepid vanguard. The army consisted of foot, horse, chariot, and elephant soldiers. The commander-in-chief rode on an elephant and the officers on chariots. The infantry soldiers bore shield and spear and some sword. They were perfect experts in the use of all these implements of war.

The Character of the People

Hiuen Tsang gives a high tribute to the character of the Indian people. 'They are of hasty and irresolute temperaments, but of pure moral principles. They will not take anything wrongfully, and they yield more than fairness requires. They fear the retribution for sins on other lives, and make light of what conduct produces in this life. They do not practise deceit and they keep their sworn obligations,' says the pilgrim.

His description of the administration of justice is very interesting, as it shows the nature of the people and the humane treatment of the criminals.

'As the government is honestly administered and the people live together on good terms the criminal class is small. The statute law is sometimes violated and plots made against the sovereign; when the crime is brought to light the offender is imprisoned for life; he does not suffer any corporal punishment, but alive and dead he is not treated as member of the community (lit. as a man). For offences against social morality and disloyal and unfilial conduct, the punishment is to cut off the nose, or ear, or a hand, or a foot, banish the offender to another country or into the wilderness. Other offences can be atoned for by a money payment.' The innocence or guilt of an accused person was determined by ordeal of either water, fire, weighing or poison. This system of justice compares favourably with the system of any other country on the face of the earth at that time. The offenders against social morality were so treated that they might not spread the contagion. There was no compromise with crime but at the same time there was no inhumanity. Revenge did not cry out 'tooth for tooth' or 'nail for nail'. Capital punishment did not exist. Hiuen Tsang justly remarks that government was honestly administered, and as the people lived together on good terms the criminal class was small. This is the picture of a happy and contented people.

Revenue and Taxation

The most important information supplied by the pilgrim is with reference to the relations between the government and the people. The government was generous and the official requirements few. Families were not registered and individuals were not subject to forced labour contributions. There was four-fold division of royal land: one part was for the expenses of government and state worship, one for the endowment of great public servants, one to reward high intellectual eminence, and one for acquiring religious merit by gifts to the various sects. People followed their hereditary profession, and managed their patrimony as taxation was light and forced service sparingly used. Only one-sixth of the produce was paid as rent. Duties paid by the traders at ferries and barrier stations were light. The

government servants were paid according to their work. Ministers of
state and common officials all had their position of land, and were
maintained by the cities assigned to them.

From these accounts it appears that the king devoted more than
half of his revenue to promotion of learning and to religious purposes.
Protection and general administration of the country did not cost
more than half the revenue. Trade and commerce was lightly taxed,
and the main source of revenue was the rent from land, which
again was only one-sixth of the produce. The people were naturally
therefore happy and prosperous. They had full control over the fruits
of their labour.

Products of India

In concluding the general survey of India, Hiuen Tsang describes
the general products of the country. He mentions various kinds
of fruits and flowers, herbs, and trees. Mango, tamarind, plum,
apple, myrabolam, plantain, were in abundance. From Kashmir
downwards, pears, plums, peaches, apricots, grapes were planted
here and there. Pomegranates and sweet oranges were grown in
all the countries. The principal agricultural products were rice,
wheat, ginger, mustard, melons, pumpkins, etc. Onions and garlic
were little used, and those who used them were ostracized. The
common food of the people consisted of milk, ghee, granulated
sugar, sugar-candy, cakes, and parched grain with mustard seed
oil. Fish, mutton, and venison were occasional dainties. The flesh
of oxen, asses, elephants, horses, pigs, dogs, foxes, wolves, lions,
monkeys, and apes was forbidden, and those who took such food
became *pariahs*.

The Kshatriyas used the wines from the vine and the sugar cane,
the Vaisyas a strong distilled spirit, the Buddhist monks and the

Brahmans drank syrup of grapes and sugar cane. The low mixed castes had no distinguishing drink.

The household utensils were mostly of earthenware, very few of brass. Generally they did not use spoons, or chopsticks except in cases of sickness. They took their food with their fingers.

Gold, silver, bronze, white jade, and crystal links were found in abundance in the country. Rare precious substances could be had in exchange for merchandise. Gold and silver coins, cowries and small pearls were the media of exchange in the commerce of the country.

APPENDIX:
ALEXANDER THE GREAT'S INVASION OF INDIA, ACCORDING TO RUFUS

Quintus **Curtius Rufus** wrote an account of Alexander the Great in Latin, and here the section on his invasion of India is presented. Who Curtius was, and when exactly he lived, is uncertain. We know of more than one person named Quintus Curtius, but none of them is mentioned as having written this history. Language and style indicate a date in the first three centuries of the Roman empire and, according to current scholarship, as Heckel (2001) explains, Rufus probably lived at the time of the emperor Claudius or possibly Vespasion. This account is less known than the works of the Greeks, but equally fascinating; it is also the only complete account of Alexander in Latin. The primary sources on Alexander no longer exist, but there are later accounts based on these.

There are numerous manuscripts of Curtius's history, the earliest version of which dates from the ninth century. Unfortunately Books 1 and 2, and some parts of Books 5, 6 and 10, are missing from the version we have.

Curtius was the name of both a consul and a rhetorician in the Roman Empire. These two, according to Heckel and others, may have been the same man, and also the composer of this work. If this is correct, Curtius died in 53 CE. He uses earlier Greek and Latin sources and puts together a compelling narrative.

R.B. Steele (1918) points out that Curtius has reworked the story of Alexander to give it a 'Roman colouring'. Heckel observes that Curtius writes as a 'Roman of the senatorial class', though a hypocritical one, and is sensational and emotive in his work. Curtius also puts forward a moralist viewpoint; he believes Alexander's good fortune corrupted him, though some positive aspects of his character are retained. While there have been criticisms of Curtius's approach to history, other reports are favourable: it is said that Alfonso V of Aragon was cured of an illness by reading his work! There are contradictions in this narrative and the geography is not always correct; the Ganga does not flow into the Erythraean Sea (Red Sea), now the Arabian Sea, but into the Bay of Bengal.

We do get an account of ferocious battles, however, in which men, elephants and horses are injured and killed. A forested land is described, some areas full of snakes, others with peacocks. There is also a strange kingdom where deformed children are killed and beauty is most valued.

The speeches of the king and of Coenus, as well as the lament of Alexander's exhausted and wounded soldiers, unwilling to proceed with further conquest, are among the most moving parts of this account.

HISTORY OF ALEXANDER THE GREAT

Description of India

Alexander, not to foster repose which naturally sets rumours in circulation, advanced towards India, always adding more to his glory by warfare than by his acts after victory.

India lies almost entirely towards the east, and it is of less extent in breadth than in length. The southern parts rise in hills of considerable elevation. The country is elsewhere level, and hence many famous rivers which rise in Mount Caucasus traverse the plains with languid currents. The Indus is colder than the other rivers, and its waters differ but little in colour from those of the sea. The Ganges, which is the greatest of all rivers in the east, flows down to the south country, and running in a straight bed washes great mountain-chains until a barrier of rocks diverts its course towards the east. Both rivers enter the Red Sea. The Indus wears away its banks, absorbing into its waters great numbers of trees and much of the soil. It is besides obstructed with rocks by which it is frequently beaten back. Where it finds the soil soft and yielding it spreads out into pools and forms islands. The Acesines increases its volume. The Ganges, in running downward to the sea, intercepts the Iomanes, and the two streams dash against each other with great violence. The Ganges in fact presents a rough face to the entrance of its affluent, the waters of which though beaten back in eddies, hold their own.

The Dyardanes is less frequently mentioned, as it flows through the remotest parts of India. But it breeds not only crocodiles, like the Nile, but dolphins also, and various aquatic monsters unknown to other nations. The Ethimanthus, which curves time after time in frequent meanders, is used up for irrigation by the people on its banks. Hence it contributes to the sea but a small and nameless residue of its waters. The country is everywhere intersected with many rivers besides these, but they are obscure, their course being too short to bring them into prominent notice. The maritime tracts, however, are most parched up by the north wind. This wind is prevented by the mountain- summits from penetrating to the interior parts, which for this reason are mild and nourish the crops. But so completely has nature altered the regular changes of the season in these regions that, when other countries are basking under the hot rays of the sun, India is covered with snow; and on the other hand, when the world elsewhere is frost-bound, India is oppressed with intolerable heat. The reason why nature has thus inverted her order is not apparent; the sea, at any rate, by which India is washed does not differ in colour from other seas. It takes its name from King Erythrus, and hence ignorant people believe that its waters are red.

The soil produces flax from which the dress ordinarily worn by the natives is made. The tender side of the barks of trees receives written characters like paper. The birds can be readily trained to imitate the sounds of human speech. The animals except those imported are unknown among other nations. The same country yields fit food for the rhinoceros, but this animal is not indigenous. The elephants are more powerful than those tamed in Africa, and their size corresponds to their strength. Gold is carried down by several rivers, whose loitering waters glide with slow and gentle currents. The sea casts upon the shores precious stones and pearls, nor has anything contributed more to the opulence of the natives, especially since they spread the community of evil to foreign nations; for these offscourings of the boiling sea are valued at the price which fashion sets on coveted luxuries.

The character of the people is here, as elsewhere, formed by the position of their country and its climate. They cover their persons down to the feet with fine muslin, are shod with sandals, and coil round their heads cloths of linen (cotton). They hang precious stones as pendants from their ears, and persons of high social rank, or of great wealth, deck their wrist and upper arm with bracelets of gold. They frequently comb, but seldom cut, the hair of their head. The beard of the chin they never cut at all, but they shave off the hair from the rest of the face, so that it looks polished. The luxury of their kings, or as they call it, their magnificence, is carried to a vicious excess without a parallel in the world.

When the king condescends to show himself in public his attendants carry in their hands silver censers, and perfume with incense all the road by which it is his pleasure to be conveyed. He lolls in a golden palanquin, garnished with pearls, which dangle all round it, and he is robed in fine muslin embroidered with purple and gold. Behind his palanquin follow men-at-arms and his bodyguards, of whom some carry boughs of trees, on which birds are perched trained to interrupt business with their cries. The palace is adorned with gilded pillars clasped all round by a vine embossed in gold, while silver images of those birds which most charm the eye diversify the workmanship. The palace is open to all comers even when the king is having his hair combed and dressed. It is then that he gives audience to ambassadors and administers justice to his subjects. His slippers being after this taken off, his feet are rubbed with scented ointments.

His principal exercise is hunting; amid the vows and songs of his courtesans he shoots the game enclosed within the royal park. The arrows, which are two cubits long, are discharged with more effort than effect, for though the force of these missiles depends on their lightness they are loaded with an obnoxious weight. He rides on horseback when making short journeys, but when bound on a distant expedition he rides in a chariot (howdah) mounted on elephants, and, huge as these animals are, their bodies are covered completely over with trappings of gold. That no form of shameless profligacy may be wanting, he is accompanied by a long train of courtesans carried in golden palanquins, and this troop holds a separate place in the procession from the queen's retinue, and is as sumptuously appointed.

His food is prepared by women, who also serve him with wine, which is much used by all the Indians. When the king falls into a drunken sleep his courtesans carry him away to his bedchamber, invoking the gods of the night in their native hymns.

Amid this corruption of morals who would expect to find the culture of philosophy? Notwithstanding, they have men whom they call philosophers, of whom one class lives in the woods and fields, and is extremely uncouth. These think it glorious to anticipate the hour of destiny, and arrange to have themselves burned alive when age has destroyed their activity, or the failure of health has made life burdensome. They regard death if waited for as a disgrace to their life, and when dissolution is simply the effect of old age funeral honours are denied to the dead body. They think that the fire is polluted unless the pyre receives the body before the breath has yet left it. Those philosophers again who lead a civilized life in cities are said to observe the motions of the heavenly bodies, and to predict future events on scientific principles. These believe that no one accelerates the day of his death who can without fear await its coming.

They regard as gods whatever objects they value, especially trees, to violate which is a capital offence. Their months they make to consist each of fifteen days, but they nevertheless assign to the year its full duration. They mark the divisions of time by the course of the moon, not like most nations when that planet shows a full face, but when she begins to appear horned, and hence, by fixing the duration of a month to correspond with this phase of the moon, they have their months one half shorter than the months of other people. Many other things have been related of them, but to interrupt with them the progress of the narrative I consider quite out of place.

Campaign in the Regions West of the Indus

Alexander had no sooner entered India than the chiefs of various tribes came to meet him with proffers of service. He was, they said, the third descendant of Jupiter who had visited their country, and that while Father Bacchus and Hercules were known to them merely by tradition, him they saw present before their eyes. To these he accorded a gracious reception, and intending to employ them as his guides, he bade them to accompany him. But when no more chiefs came to surrender, he dispatched Hephaestion and Perdiccas in advance with a part of his army to reduce whatever tribes declined his authority. He ordered them to proceed to the Indus and build boats for transporting the army to the other side of that river. Since many rivers would have to be crossed, they so constructed the vessels that, after being taken to pieces, the sections could be conveyed in wagons, and be again pieced together. He himself, leaving Craterus to follow with the infantry, pressed forward with the cavalry and light troops, and falling in with the enemy easily routed them, and chased them into the nearest city. Craterus had now rejoined him, and the king, wishing to strike terror into this people, who had not yet proved the Macedonian arms, gave previous orders that when the fortifications of the city under siege had been burned, not a soul was to be left alive. Now, in riding up to the walls he was wounded by an arrow, but he captured the place, and having massacred all the inhabitants, vented his rage even upon the buildings.

Having conquered this obscure tribe, he moved thence towards the city of Nysa. The camp, it so happened, was pitched under the walls on woody ground, and as the cold at night was more piercing than had ever before been felt, it made the soldiers shiver. But they were fortunate enough to have at hand the means of making a fire, for felling the copses they kindled a flame, and fed it with faggots, so that it seized the tombs of the citizens, which, being made of old cedar wood, spread the fire they had caught in all directions till every tomb was burned down. The barking of dogs was now heard from the town, followed by the clamour of human voices from the camp. Thus the citizens discovered that the enemy had arrived, and the Macedonians that they were close to the city.

The king had now drawn out his forces and was assaulting the walls, when some of the defenders risked an engagement. These were, however, overpowered with darts, so that dissensions broke out among the Nysaeans, some advising submission, but others the trial of a battle. Alexander, on discovering that their opinions were divided, instituted a close blockade, but forbade further bloodshed.

Alexander Captures Nysa

After a while they surrendered, unable to endure longer the miseries of a blockade. Their city, so they asserted, was founded by Father Bacchus, and this was in fact its origin. It was situated at the foot of a mountain which the inhabitants call Meros, whence the Greeks took the license of coining the fable that Father Bacchus had been concealed in the thigh of Jupiter. The king learned from the inhabitants where the mountain lay, and sending provisions on before, climbed to its summit with his whole army. There they saw the ivy plant and the vine growing in great luxuriance all over the mountain, and perennial waters gushing from its slopes. The juices of the fruits were various and wholesome since the soil favoured the growth of chance-sown seeds, and even the crags were frequently overhung with thickets of laurel and spikenard. I attribute it not to any divine impulse, but to wanton folly, that they wreathed their brows with chaplets of gathered ivy and vine leaves, and roved at large through the woods like bacchanals; so that, when the folly initiated by a few had, as usually happens, suddenly infected the whole multitude, the slopes and peaks of the mountain rang with the shouts of thousands paying their homage to the guardian divinity of the grove. Nay, they even flung themselves down full length on the greensward, or on heaps of leaves as if peace reigned all around.

The king himself, so far from looking askance at this extemporaneous revel, supplied with a liberal hand all kinds of viands for feasting, and kept the army engaged for ten days in celebrating the orgies of Father Bacchus. Who then can deny that even distinguished glory is a boon for which mortals are oftener indebted to fortune than to merit, seeing that when they had abandoned themselves to feasting and were drowsed with wine the enemy had not even the courage to fall upon them, being terrified no less by the uproar and howling made by the revellers than if the shouts of warriors rushing to battle had rung in their ears. The like good fortune afterwards protected them in the presence of their enemies when on returning from the ocean they gave themselves up to drunken festivity.

From Nysa they came to a region called Daedala. The inhabitants had deserted their habitations and fled for safety to the trackless recesses of their mountain forests. He therefore passed on to Acadira, which he found burned, and like Daedala deserted by the flight of the inhabitants. Necessity made him therefore change his plan of operations. For having divided his forces he showed his arms at many points at once, and the inhabitants taken by surprise were overwhelmed with calamities of every kind. Ptolemy took a greater number of cities, and Alexander himself those that were more important. This done, he again drew together his scattered forces. Having next crossed the river Choaspes, he left Coenus to besiege an opulent city – the inhabitants called it Beira – while he himself went on to Mazaga.

Siege of Mazaga and Its Surrender

Assacanus, its previous sovereign, had lately died, and his mother Cleophis now ruled the city and the realm. An army of 38,000 infantry defended the city which was strongly fortified both by nature and art. For on the east, an impetuous mountain stream with steep banks on both sides barred approach to the city, while to south and west nature, as if designing to form a rampart, had piled up gigantic rocks, at the base of which lay sloughs and yawning chasms hollowed in the course of ages to vast depths, while a ditch of mighty labour drawn from their extremity continued the line of defence. The city was besides surrounded with a wall 35 stadia in circumference which had a basis of stonework supporting a super structure of unburnt, sun-dried bricks. The brickwork was bound into a solid fabric by means of stones so interposed that the more brittle material rested upon the harder, while moist clay had been used for mortar. Lest, however, the structure should all at once sink, strong beams had been laid upon these, supporting wooden floors which covered the walls and afforded a passage along them.

Alexander while reconnoitering the fortifications, and unable to fix on a plan of attack, since nothing less than a vast mole, necessary for bringing up his engines to the walls, would suffice to fill up the chasms, was wounded from the ramparts by an arrow which chanced to hit him in the calf of the leg. When the barb was extracted, he called for his horse, and without having his wound so much as bandaged, continued with unabated energy to prosecute the work on hand. But when the injured limb was hanging without support, and the gradual cooling, as the blood dried, aggravated the pain, he is reported to have said that though he was called, as all knew, the son of Jupiter, he felt notwithstanding all the defects of the weak body. He did not, however, return to the camp till he had viewed everything and ordered what he wanted to be done.

Accordingly, some of the soldiers began, as directed, to destroy the houses outside the city and to take from the ruins much material for raising a mole, while others cast into the hollows large trunks of trees, branches and all, together with great masses of rock. When the mole had now been raised to a level with the surface of the ground, they proceeded to erect towers; and so zealously did the soldiers prosecute the works, that they finished them completely within nine days. These the king, before his wound had as yet closed, proceeded to inspect. He commended the troops, and then from the engines which he had ordered to be propelled a great storm of missiles was discharged against the defenders on the ramparts. What had most effect in intimidating the barbarians was the spectacle of the movable towers, for to works of that description they were utter strangers. Those vast fabrics moving without visible aid, they believed to be propelled by the agency of the gods. It was impossible, they said, that those javelins for attacking walls – those ponderous darts hurled from engines could be within the compass of mortal power.

Giving up therefore the defence as hopeless, they withdrew into the citadel, whence, as nothing but to surrender was open to the besieged, they sent down envoys to the king to sue for pardon. This being granted, the queen came with a great train of noble ladies who poured out libations of wine from golden bowls. The queen herself, having placed her son, still a child, at Alexander's knees, obtained not only pardon, but permission to retain her former dignity, for she was styled queen, and some have believed that this indulgent treatment was accorded rather to the charms of her person than to pity for her misfortunes. At all events she afterwards gave birth to a son who received the name of Alexander, whoever his father may have been.

Siege and Capture of the Rock Aornis

Polypercon being despatched hence with an army to the city of Nora, defeated the undisciplined multitude which he encountered, and pursuing them within their fortifications compelled them to surrender the place. Into the king's own hands there fell many inconsiderable towns, deserted by their inhabitants who had escaped in time with their arms and seized a rock called Aornis. A report was current that this stronghold had been in vain assaulted by Hercules, who had been compelled by an earthquake to raise the siege. The rock being on all sides steep and rugged, Alexander was at a loss how to proceed, when there came to him an elderly man familiar with the locality accompanied by two sons, offering, if Alexander would make it worth his while, to show him a way of access to the summit. Alexander agreed to give him eighty talents, and, keeping one of his sons as a hostage, sent him to make good his offer. Mullinus (Eumenes?), the king's secretary, was put in command of the light-armed men, for these, as had been decided, were to climb to the summit by a detour, to prevent their being seen by the enemy.

This rock does not, like most eminences, grow up to its towering top by gradual and easy acclivities, but rises up straight just like the *meta*, which from a wide base tapers off in ascending till it terminates in a sharp pinnacle. The river Indus, here very deep and enclosed between rugged banks, washes its roots. In another quarter are swamps and craggy ravines; and only by filling up these could an assault upon the stronghold be rendered practicable. A wood which was contiguous the king directed to be cut down. The trees where they fell were stripped of their leaves and branches which would otherwise have proved an impediment to their transport. He himself threw in the first trunk, whereupon followed a loud cheer from the army, a token of its alacrity, no one refusing a labour to which the king was the first to put his hand. Within the seventh day they had filled up the hollows, and then the king directed the archers and the Agrianians to struggle up the steep ascent. He selected besides from his personal staff thirty of the most active among the young men, whom he placed under the command of Charus and Alexander. The latter he reminded of the name which he bore in common with himself.

And at first, because the peril was so palpable, a resolution was passed that the king should not hazard his safety by taking part in the assault. But when the trumpet sounded the signal, the audacious prince at once turned to his bodyguards, and bidding them to follow was the first to assail the rock. None of the Macedonians then held back, but all spontaneously left their posts and followed the king. Many perished by a dismal fate, for they fell from the shelving crags and were engulfed in the river which flowed underneath-a piteous sight even for those who were not themselves in danger. But when reminded by the destruction of their comrades what they had to dread for themselves, their pity changed to fear, and they began to lament not for the dead but for themselves.

And now they had attained a point whence they could not return without disaster unless victorious, for as the barbarians rolled down massive stones upon them while they climbed, such as were struck fell headlong from their insecure and slippery positions. Alexander and Charus, however, whom the king had sent in advance with the thirty chosen men, reached the summit, and had by this time engaged in a hand-to-hand fight; but since the barbarians discharged their darts from higher ground, the assailants received more wounds than they inflicted. So then Alexander, mindful alike of his name and his promise, in fighting with more spirit than judgment, fell pierced with many darts. Charus, seeing him lying dead, made a rush upon the enemy, caring for nothing but revenge. Many received their death from his spear and others from his sword. But as he was single-handed against overwhelming odds, he sank lifeless on the body of his friend.

The king, duly affected by the death of these heroic youths and the other soldiers, gave the signal for retiring. It conduced to the safety of the troops that they retreated leisurely, preserving their coolness, and that the barbarians, satisfied with having driven them downhill, did not close on them when they withdrew. But, though Alexander had resolved to abandon the enterprise, deeming the capture of the rock hopeless, he still made demonstrations of persevering with the siege, for by his orders the avenues were blocked, the towers advanced, and the working parties relieved when tired. The Indians, on seeing his pertinacity, by way of demonstrating not only their confidence but their triumph, devoted two days and nights to festivity and beating their national music out of their drums. But on the third night the rattle of the drums ceased to be heard. Torches, however, which, as the night was dark, the barbarians had to make their flight safer down the precipitous crags, shed their glare over every part of the rocks.

The king learned from Balacrus, who had been sent forward to reconnoitre, that the Indians had fled and abandoned the rock. He thereupon gave a signal that his men should raise a general shout, and he thus struck terror into the fugitives as they were making off in disorder. Then many, as if the enemy were already upon them, flung themselves headlong over the slippery rocks and precipices and perished, while a still greater number, who were hurt, were left to their fate by those who had descended without accident. Although it was the position rather than the enemy he had conquered, the king gave to this success the appearance of a great victory by offering sacrifices and worship to the gods. Upon the rock he erected altars dedicated to Minerva and Victory. To the guides who had shown the way to the light-armed detachment which had been sent to scale the rock he honourably paid the stipulated recompense, even although their performance had fallen short of their promises. The defence of the rock and the country surrounding was entrusted to Sisocostus.

Alexander Crosses the Indus – Received by Omphis, King of Taxila

Thence he marched towards Embolima, but on learning that the pass which led thereto was occupied by 20,000 men in arms under Erix, he hurried forward himself with the archers and slingers, leaving the heavy armed troops under the command of Coenus to advance leisurely. Having dislodged those men who beset the defile, he cleared the passage for the army which followed. The Indians, either from disaffection to their chief or to court the favour of the conqueror, set upon Erix during his flight and killed him. They brought his head and his armour to Alexander, who did not punish them for their crime, but to condemn their example gave them no reward. Having left this pass, he arrived after the sixteenth encampment at the river Indus, where he found that Hephaestion, agreeably to his orders, had made all the necessary preparations for the passage across it.

The sovereign of the territories on the other side was Omphis, who had urged his father to surrender his kingdom to Alexander, and had moreover at his father's death sent envoys to enquire whether it was Alexander's pleasure that he should meanwhile exercise authority or remain in a private capacity till his arrival. He was permitted to assume the sovereignty, but modestly forbore to exercise its functions. He had extended to Hephaestion marks of civility, and given corn gratuitously to his soldiers, but he had not gone to join him, from a reluctance to make trial of the good faith of any but Alexander. Accordingly, on Alexander's approach, he went to meet him at the head of an army equipped for the field. He had even brought his elephants with him, which, posted at short intervals amidst the ranks of the soldiery, appeared to the distant spectator like towers.

Alexander at first thought it was not a friendly but a hostile army that approached, and had already ordered the soldiers to arm themselves, and the cavalry to divide to the wings, and was ready for action. But the Indian prince, on seeing the mistake of the Macedonians, put his horse to the gallop, leaving orders that no one else was to stir from his place. Alexander likewise galloped forward, not knowing whether it was an enemy or a friend he had to encounter, but trusting for safety perhaps to his valour, perhaps to the other's good faith. They met in a friendly spirit, as far as could be gathered from the expression of each one's face, but from the want of an interpreter to converse was impossible. An interpreter was therefore procured, and then the barbarian prince explained that he had come with his army to meet Alexander that he might at once place at his disposal all the forces of his empire, without waiting to tender his allegiance through deputies. He surrendered, he said, his person and his kingdom to a man who, as he knew, was fighting not more for fame than fearing to incur the reproach of perfidy.

The king, pleased with the simple honesty of the barbarian, gave him his right hand as a pledge of his own good faith, and confirmed him in his sovereignty. The prince had brought with him six-and-fifty elephants, and these he gave to Alexander, with a great many sheep of an extraordinary size, and 3,000 bulls of a valuable breed, highly prized by the rulers of the country. When Alexander asked him whether he had more husbandmen or soldiers, he replied that as he was at war with two kings he required more soldiers than field labourers. These kings were Abisares and Porus, but Porus was superior in power and influence. Both of them held sway beyond the river Hydaspes, and had resolved to try the fortune of war whatever invader might come.

Omphis, under Alexander's permission, and according to the usage of the realm, assumed the ensigns of royalty along with the name which his father had borne. His people called him Taxiles, for such was the name which accompanied the sovereignty, on whomsoever it devolved. When, therefore, he had entertained Alexander for three days with lavish hospitality, he showed him on the fourth day what quantity of corn he had supplied to Hephaestion's troops, and then presented him and all his friends with golden crowns, and eighty talents besides of coined silver. Alexander was so exceedingly gratified with this profuse generosity that he not only sent back to Omphis the presents he had given, but added 1,000 talents from the spoils which he carried, along with many banqueting vessels of gold and silver, a vast quantity of Persian drapery, and thirty chargers from his own stalls, caparisoned as when ridden by himself.

This liberality, while it bound the barbarian to his interests, gave at the same time the deepest offence to his own friends. One of them, Meleager, who had taken too much wine at supper, said that he congratulated Alexander on having found in India, if nowhere else, someone worthy of 1,000 talents. The king, who had not forgotten what remorse he had suffered when he killed Clitus for audacity of speech, controlled his temper, but remarked that envious persons were nothing but their own tormentors.

Alexander and Porus Confront Each Other on Opposite Banks of the Hydaspes

On the following day envoys from Abisares reached the king, and, as they had been instructed, surrendered to him all that their master possessed. After pledges of good faith had been interchanged, they were sent back to their sovereign. Alexander, thinking that by the mere prestige of his name Porus also would be induced to surrender, sent Cleochares to tell him in peremptory terms that he must pay tribute and come to meet his sovereign at the very frontiers of his own dominions. Porus answered that he would comply with the second of these demands, and when Alexander entered his realm he would meet him, but come armed for battle. Alexander had now resolved to cross the Hydaspes, when Barzaentes, who had instigated the Arachosians to revolt, was brought to him in chains, along with thirty captured elephants, an opportune reinforcement against the Indians, since these huge beasts more than the soldiery constituted the hope and main strength of an Indian army.

Samaxus was also brought in chains, the king of a small Indian state, who had espoused the cause of Barzaentes. Alexander having then put the traitor and his accomplice under custody, and consigned the elephants to the care of Taxiles, advanced till he reached the river Hydaspes, where on the further bank Porus had encamped to prevent the enemy from landing. In the van of his army he had posted eighty-five elephants of the greatest size and strength, and behind these 300 chariots and somewhere about 30,000 infantry, among whom were the archers, whose arrows, as already stated, were too ponderous to be readily discharged. He was himself mounted on an elephant which towered above all its fellows, while his armour, embellished with gold and silver, set off his supremely majestic person to great advantage. His courage matched his bodily vigour, and his wisdom was the utmost attainable in a rude community.

The Macedonians were intimidated not only by the appearance of the enemy, but by the magnitude of the river to be crossed, which, spreading out to a width of no less than four stadia in a deep channel which nowhere opened a passage by fords, presented the aspect of a vast sea. Yet its rapidity did not diminish in proportion to its wider diffusion, but it rushed impetuously like a seething torrent compressed into a narrow bed by the closing in of its banks. Besides, at many points the presence of sunken rocks was revealed where the waves were driven back in eddies. The bank presented a still more formidable aspect, for, as far as the eye could see, it was covered with cavalry and infantry, in the midst of which, like so many massive structures, stood the huge elephants, which, being of set purpose provoked by their drivers, distressed the ear with their frightful roars.

The enemy and the river both in their front, struck with sudden dismay the hearts of the Macedonians, disposed though they were to entertain good hopes, and knowing from experience against what fearful odds they had ere now contended. They could not believe that boats so unhandy could be steered to the bank or gain it in safety. In the middle of the river were numerous islands to which both the Indians and Macedonians began to swim over, holding their weapons above their heads. Here they would engage in skirmishes, while each king endeavoured from the result of these minor conflicts to gauge the issue of the final struggle. In the Macedonian army were Symmachus and Nicanor, both young men of noble lineage, distinguished for their hardihood and enterprise, and from the uniform success of their side in whatever they assayed, inspired with a contempt for every kind of danger. Led by these, a party of the boldest youths, equipped with nothing but lances, swam over to the island when it was occupied by crowds of the enemy.

Armed with audacious courage, the best of all weapons, they slew many of the Indians, and might have retired with glory if temerity when successful could ever keep within bounds. But while with contempt and pride they waited till succours reached the enemy, they were surrounded by men who had unperceived swum over to the island, and were overthrown by discharges of missiles. Such as escaped the enemy were either swept away by the force of the current or swallowed up in its eddies. This fight exalted the confidence of Porus, who had witnessed from the bank all its vicissitudes.

Alexander, perplexed how to cross the river, at last devised a plan for duping the enemy. In the river lay an island larger than the rest, wooded and suitable for concealing an ambuscade. A deep hollow, moreover, which lay not far from the bank in his own occupation, was capable of hiding not only foot-soldiers but mounted cavalry. To divert, therefore, the attention of the enemy from a place possessing such advantages, he ordered Ptolemy with all his squadrons of horse to ride up and down at a distance from the island in view of the enemy, and now and then to alarm the Indians by shouting, as if he meant to make the passage of the river. For several days Ptolemy repeated this feint, and thus obliged Porus to concentrate his troops at the point which he pretended to threaten.

The island was now beyond view of the enemy. Alexander then gave orders that his own tent should be pitched on a part of the bank looking the other way, that the guard of honour which usually attended him should be posted before it, and that all the pageantry of royal state should be paraded before the eyes of the enemy on purpose to deceive them. He besides requested Attalus, who was about his own age, and not unlike him in form and feature, especially when seen from a distance, to wear the royal mantle, and so make it appear as if the king in person was guarding that part of the bank without any intention of crossing the river.

The state of the weather at first hindered, but afterwards favoured, the execution of this design, fortune making even untoward circumstances turn out to his ultimate advantage. For when the enemy was busy watching the troops under Ptolemy which occupied the bank lower down, and Alexander with the rest of his forces was making ready to cross the river and reach the land over against the island already mentioned, a storm poured down torrents of rain, against which even those under cover could scarcely protect themselves. The soldiers, overcome by the fury of the elements, deserted the boats and ships, and fled back for safety to land, but the din occasioned by their hurry and confusion could not be heard by the enemy amid the roar of the tempest. All of a sudden the rain then ceased, but clouds so dense overspread the sky that they hid the light, and made it scarcely possible for men conversing together to see each other's faces.

Any other leader but Alexander would have been appalled by the darkness drawn over the face of heaven just when he was starting on a voyage across an unknown river, with the enemy perhaps guarding the very bank to which his men were blindly and imprudently directing their course. But the king deriving glory from danger and regarding the darkness which terrified others as his opportunity, gave the signal that all should embark in silence, and ordered that the galley which carried himself should be the first to be run aground on the other side. The bank, however, towards which they steered was not occupied by the enemy, for Porus was in fact still intently watching Ptolemy only. Hence all the ships made the passage in safety except just one, which stuck on a rock whither it had been driven by the wind. Alexander then ordered the soldiers to take their arms and to fall into their ranks.

Battle with Porus on the Left Bank of the Hydaspes

He was already in full march at the head of his army, which he had divided into two columns, when the tidings reached Porus that the bank was occupied by a military force, and that the crisis of his fortunes was now imminent. In keeping with the infirmity of our nature, which makes us ever hope the best, he at first indulged the belief that this was his ally Abisares come to help him in the war as had been agreed upon. But soon after, when the sky had become clearer, and showed the ranks to be those of the enemy, he sent 100 chariots and 4,000 horse to obstruct their advance. The command of this detachment he gave to his brother Hages. Its main strength lay in the chariots, each of which was drawn by four horses and carried six men, of whom two were shield bearers, two [were] archers posted on each side of the chariot, and the other two, charioteers, as well as men-at-arms, for when the fighting was at close quarters they dropped the reins and hurled dart after dart against the enemy.

But on this particular day these chariots proved to be scarcely of any service, for the storm of rain, which, as already said, was of extraordinary violence, had made the ground slippery, and unfit for horses to ride over, while the chariots kept sticking in the muddy sloughs formed by the rain, and proved almost immovable from their great weight. Alexander, on the other hand, charged with the utmost vigour, because his troops were lightly armed and unencumbered. The Scythians and Dahae first of all attacked the Indians, and then the king launched Perdiccas with his horse upon their right wing. The fighting had now become hot everywhere, when the drivers of the chariots rode at full speed into the midst of the battle, thinking they could thus most effectively succour their friends. It would be hard to say which side suffered most from this charge, for the Macedonian foot soldiers, who were exposed to the first shock of the onset, were trampled down, while the charioteers were hurled from their seats, when the chariots in rushing into action jolted over broken and slippery ground. Some again of the horses took fright and precipitated the carriages not only into the sloughs and pools of water, but even into the river itself.

A few which were driven off the field by the darts of the enemy made their way to Porus, who was making most energetic preparations for the contest. As soon as he saw his chariots scattered amid his ranks, and wandering about without their drivers, he distributed his elephants to his friends who were nearest him. Behind them he had posted the infantry and the archers and the men who beat the drums, the instruments which the Indians use instead of trumpets to produce their war music. The rattle of these instruments does not in the least alarm the elephants, their ears, through long familiarity, being deadened to the sound. An image of Hercules was borne in front of the line of infantry, and this acted as the strongest of all incentives to make the soldiers fight well. To desert the bearers of this image was reckoned a disgraceful military offence, and they had even ordained death as a penalty for those who failed to bring it back from the battlefield, for the dread which the Indians had conceived for the god when he was their enemy had been toned down to a feeling of religious awe and veneration.

The sight not only of the huge beasts, but even of Porus himself, made the Macedonians pause for a time, for the beasts, which had been placed at intervals between the armed ranks, presented, when seen from a distance, the appearance of towers, and Porus himself not only sur passed the standard of height to which we conceive the human figure to be limited, but, besides this, the elephant on which he was mounted seemed to add to his proportions, for it towered over all the other elephants even as Porus himself stood taller than other men. Hence Alexander, after attentively viewing the king and the army of the Indians, remarked to those near him, 'I see at last a danger that matches my courage. It is at once with wild beasts and men of uncommon mettle that the contest now lies.' Then turning to Coenus, 'When I,' he said, 'along with Ptolemy, Perdiccas, and Hephaestion, have fallen upon the enemy's left wing, and you see me in the heat of the conflict, do you then advance the right wing, and charge the enemy when their ranks begin to waver. And you, sirs,' he added, turning to Antigenes, Leonnatus, and Tauron, 'must bear down upon their centre, and press them hard in front. The formidable length and strength of our pikes will never be so useful as when they are directed against these huge beasts and their drivers. Hurl, then, their riders to the ground, and stab the beasts themselves. Their assistance is not of a kind to be depended on, and they may do their own side more damage than ours, for they are driven against the enemy by constraint, while terror turns them against their own ranks.'

Having spoken thus he was the first to put spurs to his horse. And now, as had been arranged, Coenus, upon seeing that Alexander was at close quarters with the enemy, threw his cavalry with great fury upon their left wing. The phalanx besides, at the first onset, broke through the centre of the Indians. But Porus ordered his elephants to be driven into action where he had seen cavalry charging his ranks. The slow-footed unwieldy animals, however, were unfitted to cope with the rapid movements of horses, and the barbarians were besides unable to use even their arrows. These weapons were really so long and heavy that the archers could not readily adjust them on the string unless by first resting their bow upon the ground. Then, as the ground was slippery and hindered their efforts, the enemy had time to charge them before they could deliver their blows.

The king's authority was in these circumstances unheeded, and, as usually happens when the ranks are broken, and fear begins to dictate orders more peremptorily than the general himself, as many took the command upon themselves as there were scattered bodies of troops. Some proposed that these bodies should unite, others that they should form separate detachments, some that they should wait to be attacked, others that they should wheel round and charge the enemy in the rear. No common plan of action was after all concerted. Porus, however, with a few friends in whom the sense of honour was stronger than fear, rallied his scattered forces, and marching in front of his line advanced against the enemy with the elephants. These animals inspired great terror, and their strange dissonant cries frightened not only the horses, which shy at everything, but the men also, and disordered the ranks, so that those who just before were victorious began now to look round them for a place to which they could flee. Alexander thereupon despatched against the elephants the lightly-armed Agrianians and the Thracians, troops more serviceable in skirmishing than in close combat. They assailed the elephants and their drivers with a furious storm of missiles, and the phalanx, on seeing the resulting terror and confusion, steadily pressed forward.

Some, however, by pursuing too eagerly, so irritated the animals with wounds that they turned their rage upon them, and they were in consequence trampled to death under their feet, thus warning others to attack them with greater caution. The most dismal of all sights was when the elephants would, with their trunks, grasp the men, arms and all, and hoisting them above their heads, deliver them over into the hands of their drivers. Thus the battle was doubtful, the Macedonians sometimes pursuing and sometimes fleeing from the elephants, so that the struggle was prolonged till the day was far spent. Then they began to hack the feet of the beasts with axes which they had prepared for the purpose, having besides a kind of sword somewhat curved like a scythe, and called a chopper, wherewith they aimed at their trunks. In fact, their fear of the animals led them not only to leave no means untried for killing them, but even for killing them with unheard-of forms of cruelty.

Hence the elephants, being at last spent with wounds, spread havoc among their own ranks, and threw their drivers to the ground, who were then trampled to death by their own beasts. They were therefore driven from the field of battle like a flock of sheep, as they were maddened with terror rather than vicious. Porus, meanwhile, being left in the lurch by the majority of his men, began to hurl from his elephant the darts with which he had beforehand provided himself, and while many were wounded from afar by his shot he was himself exposed as a butt for blows from every quarter. He had already received nine wounds before and behind, and became so faint from the great loss of blood that the darts were dropped rather than flung from his feeble hands. But his elephant, waxing furious though not yet wounded, kept charging the ranks of the enemy until the driver, perceiving the king's condition – his limbs failing him, his weapons dropping from his grasp, and his consciousness almost gone – turned the beast round and fled.

Alexander pursued, but his horse being pierced with many wounds fainted under him, and sank to the ground, laying the king down gently rather than throwing him from his seat. The necessity of changing his horse retarded of course his pursuit. In the meantime the brother of Taxiles, the Indian king whom Alexander had sent on before, advised Porus not to persist in holding out to the last extremity, but to surrender himself to the conqueror. Porus, however, though his strength was exhausted, and his blood nearly spent, yet roused himself at the well-known voice, and said, 'I recognize the brother of Taxiles, who gave up his throne and kingdom.' Therewith he flung at him the one dart that had not slipped from his grasp, and flung it too with such force that it pierced right through his back to his chest. Having roused himself to this last effort of valour, he began to flee faster than before, but his elephant, which had by this time received many wounds, was now, like himself, quite exhausted, so that he stopped the flight, and made head against the pursuers with his remaining infantry.

Alexander had now come up, and knowing how obstinate Porus was, forbade quarter to be given to those who resisted. The infantry therefore, and Porus himself, were assailed with darts from all points, and as he could no longer bear up against them he began to slip from his elephant. The Indian driver, thinking the king wished to alight, made the elephant kneel down in the usual manner. On seeing this the other elephants also knelt down, for they had been trained to lower themselves when the royal elephant did so. Porus and his men were thus placed entirely at the mercy of the conqueror. Alexander, supposing that he was dead, ordered his body to be stripped, and men then ran forward to take off his breastplate and robes, when the elephant turned upon them in defence of its master, and lifting him up placed him once more on its back.

Porus Surrenders

Upon this the animal was on all sides overwhelmed with darts, and when it was stabbed to death, Porus was placed upon a wagon. But the king perceiving him to lift up his eyes, forgot all animosity, and being deeply moved with pity, said to him, 'What the plague! what madness induced you to try the fortune of war with me, of whose exploits you have heard the fame, especially when in Taxiles you had a near example of my clemency to those who submit to me?' He answered thus: 'Since you propose a question, I shall answer with the freedom which you grant by asking it. I used to think there was no one braver than myself, for I knew my own strength, but had not yet experienced thine. The result of the war has taught me that you are the braver man, but even in ranking next to you, I consider myself to be highly fortunate.' Being asked again how he thought the victor should treat him, 'in accordance,' he replied, 'with the lesson which this day teaches a day in which you have witnessed how readily prosperity can be blasted.'

By giving this admonition he gained more than if he had resorted to entreaty, for Alexander, in consideration of the greatness of his courage which scorned all fear, and which adversity could not break down, extended pity to his misfortunes and honour to his merits. He ordered his wounds to be as carefully attended to as if he had fought in his service, and when he had recovered strength, he admitted him into the number of his friends, and soon after presented him with a larger kingdom than that which he had. And in truth his nature had no more essential or more permanent quality than a high respect for true merit and renown; but he estimated more candidly and impartially glory in an enemy than in a subject. In fact, he thought that the fabric of his fame might be pulled down by his own people, while it could but receive enhanced lustre the greater those were whom he vanquished.

Alexander's Speech After the Victory

Alexander rejoicing in a victory so memorable, which led him to believe that the East to its utmost limits had been opened up to his arms, sacrificed to the sun, and having also summoned the soldiers to a general meeting, he praised them for their services, that they might with the greater alacrity undertake the wars that yet remained. He pointed out to them that all power of opposition on the part of the Indians had been quite overthrown in the battle just fought. What now remained for them was a noble spoil. The much-rumoured riches of the East abounded in those very regions, to which their steps were now bent. The spoils accordingly which they had taken from the Persians had now become cheap and common. They were going to fill with pearls, precious stones, gold, and ivory, not only their private abodes, but all Macedonia and Greece. The soldiers who coveted money as well as glory, and who had never known his promises to fail, on hearing all this, readily placed their services at his command. He sent them away full of good hope, and ordered ships to be built in order that when he had overrun all Asia, he might be able to visit the sea which formed the boundary of the world.

Abisares Sends Him an Embassy

In the neighbouring mountains was abundance of timber fit for building ships, and the men in hewing down the trees came upon serpents of most extraordinary size. There they also found the rhinoceros, an animal rarely met with elsewhere. This is not the name it bears among the Indians, but one given it by the Greeks, who were ignorant of the speech of the country. The king having built two cities, one on each side of the river which he had lately crossed, presented each of the generals with a crown, in addition to 1,000 pieces of gold. Others also received rewards in accordance either with the place which they held in his friendship, or the value of the services which they had rendered. Abisares, who had sent envoys to Alexander before the battle with Porus had come off, now sent others to assure him that he was ready to do whatever he commanded, provided only he was not obliged to surrender his person; for he could neither live, he said, without having the power of a king, nor have that power if he were to be kept in captivity. Alexander bade them tell their master that if he grudged to come to Alexander, Alexander would go to him.

Alexander Captures Sangala

After crossing a river some distance farther on, he advanced into the interior parts of India. The forests there extended over an almost boundless tract of country, and abounded with umbrageous trees of stateliest growth, that rose to an extraordinary height. Numerous branches, which for size equalled the trunk of ordinary trees, would bend down to the earth, and then shoot straight up again at the point where they bent upward, so that they had more the appearance of a tree growing from its own root than of a bough branching out from its stem. The climate is salubrious, for the dense shade mitigates the violence of the heat, and copious springs supply the land with abundance of water. But here, also, were multitudes of serpents, the scales of which glittered like gold. The poison of these is deadlier than any other, since their bite was wont to prove instantly fatal, until a proper antidote was pointed out by the natives. From thence they passed through deserts to the river Hyarotis, the banks of which were covered with a dense forest, abounding with trees not elsewhere seen, and filled with wild peacocks. Decamping hence, he came to a town that lay not far off. This he captured by a general attack all round the walls, and having received hostages, imposed a tribute upon the inhabitants. He came next to a great city – great at least for that region – and found it not only encompassed with a wall, but further defended by a morass.

The barbarians nevertheless sallied out to give battle, taking their wagons with them, which they fastened together each to each. For weapons of offence some had pikes and others axes, and they were in the habit of leaping nimbly from wagon to wagon if they saw their friends hard pressed and wished to help them. This mode of fighting being quite new to the Macedonians, at first alarmed them, since they were wounded by enemies beyond their reach, but coming afterwards to look with contempt upon a force so undisciplined, they completely surrounded the wagons and began stabbing all the men that offered resistance. The king then commanded the cords which fastened the wagons together to be cut that it might be easier for the soldiers to beset each wagon separately. The enemy after a loss of 8,000 men withdrew into the town. Next day the walls were escaladed all round and captured. A few were indebted for their safety to their swiftness of foot. Those who swam across the sheet of water when they saw the city was sacked, carried great consternation to the neighbouring towns, where they reported that an invincible army, one of gods assuredly, had arrived in the country.

Alexander having sent Perdiccas with a body of light troops to ravage the country, and given another detachment to Eumenes to be employed in bringing the barbarians to submission, marched himself with the rest of the army against a strong city within which the inhabitants of some other cities had taken refuge. The citizens sent deputies to appease the king's anger, but continued all the same to make warlike preparations. A dissension, it seems, had arisen among them and divided their counsels, some preferring to submit to the last extremities rather than surrender, others thinking that resistance on their part would be altogether futile. But as no consultation was held in common, those who were bent on surrendering threw open the gates and admitted the enemy. Alexander would have been justified in making the advocates of resistance feel his displeasure, but he nevertheless pardoned them all without exception, and after taking hostages marched forward to the next city. As the hostages were led in the van of the army, the defenders on the wall recognized them to be their own countrymen, and invited them to a conference. Here they were prevailed on to surrender, when they were informed of the king's clemency to the submissive, and his severity if opposed. In a similar way he gained over other towns, and placed them under his protection.

Enters the Kingdom of Sopithes

They entered next the dominions of King Sopithes, whose nation in the opinion of the barbarians excels in wisdom, and lives under good laws and customs. Here they do not acknowledge and rear children according to the will of the parents, but as the officers entrusted with the medical inspection of infants may direct, for if they have remarked anything deformed or defective in the limbs of a child they order it to be killed. In contracting marriages they do not seek an alliance with high birth, but make their choice by the looks, for beauty in the children is a quality highly appreciated.

Alexander had brought up his army before the capital of this nation where Sopithes was himself resident. The gates were shut, but as no men-at-arms showed themselves either on the walls or towers, the Macedonians were in doubt whether the inhabitants had deserted the city, or were hiding themselves to fall upon the enemy by surprise. The gate, however, was on a sudden thrown open, and the Indian king with two grown-up sons issued from it to meet Alexander. He was distinguished above all the other barbarians by his tall and handsome figure. His royal robe, which flowed down to his very feet, was all inwrought with gold and purple. His sandals were of gold and studded with precious stones, and even his arms and wrists were curiously adorned with pearls. At his ears he wore pendants of precious stones which from their lustre and magnitude were of an inestimable value. His sceptre too was made of gold and set with beryls, and this he delivered up to Alexander with an expression of his wish that it might bring him good luck, and be accepted as a token that he surrendered into his hands his children and his kingdom.

His country possesses a noble breed of dogs, used for hunting, and said to refrain from barking when they sight their game which is chiefly the lion. Sopithes wishing to show Alexander the strength and mettle of these dogs, caused a very large lion to be placed within an enclosure where four dogs in all were let loose upon him. The dogs at once fastened upon the wild beast, when one of the huntsmen who was accustomed to work of this kind tried to pull away by the leg one of the dogs which with the others had seized the lion, and when the limb would not come away, cut it off with a knife. The dog could not even by this means be forced to let go his hold, and so the man proceeded to cut him in another place, and finding him still clutching the lion as tenaciously as before, he continued cutting away with his knife one part of him after another. The brave dog, however, even in dying kept his fangs fixed in the lion's flesh; so great is the eagerness for hunting which nature has implanted in these animals, as testified by the accounts transmitted to us.

I must observe, however, that I copy from preceding writers more than I myself believe, for I neither wish to guarantee statements of the truth of which I am doubtful, nor yet to suppress what I find recorded. Alexander therefore leaving Sopithes in possession of his kingdom, advanced to the river Hyphasis, where he was rejoined by Hephaestion who had subdued a district situated in a different direction. Phegeus, who was king of the nearest nation, having beforehand ordered his subjects to attend to the cultivation of their fields according to their wont, went forth to meet Alexander with presents and assurances that whatever he commanded he would not fail to perform.

Alexander Obtains Information About the Ganges

The king made a halt of two days with this prince, designing on the third day to cross the river, the passage of which was difficult, not only from its great breadth, but also because its channel was obstructed with rocks. Having therefore requested Phegeus to tell him what he wanted to know, he learned the following particulars: Beyond the river lay extensive deserts which it would take eleven days to traverse. Next came the Ganges, the largest river in all India, the farther bank of which was inhabited by two nations, the Gangaridae and the Prasii, whose king Agrammes kept in the field for guarding the approaches to his country 20,000 cavalry and 200,000 infantry, besides 2,000 four-horsed chariots, and, what was the most formidable force of all, a troop of elephants which he said ran up to the number of 3,000.

All this seemed to the king to be incredible, and he therefore asked Porus, who happened to be in attendance, whether the account was true. He assured Alexander in reply that, as far as the strength of the nation and kingdom was concerned, there was no exaggeration in the reports, but that the present king was not merely a man originally of no distinction, but even of the very meanest condition. His father was in fact a barber, scarcely staving off hunger by his daily earnings, but who, from his being not uncomely in person, had gained the affections of the queen, and was by her influence advanced to too near a place in the confidence of the reigning monarch. Afterwards, however, he treacherously murdered his sovereign; and then, under the pretence of acting as guardian to the royal children, usurped the supreme authority, and having put the young princes to death begot the present king, who was detested and held cheap by his subjects, as he rather took after his father than conducted himself as the occupant of a throne.

The attestation of Porus to the truth of what he had heard made the king anxious on manifold grounds; for while he thought contemptuously of the men and elephants that would oppose him, he dreaded the difficult nature of the country that lay before him, and in particular, the impetuous rapidity of the rivers. The task seemed hard indeed, to follow up and unearth men removed almost to the uttermost bounds of the world. On the other hand, his avidity of glory and his insatiable ambition forbade him to think that any place was so far distant or inaccessible as to be beyond his reach. He did indeed sometimes doubt whether the Macedonians who had traversed all those broad lands and grown old in battlefields and camps, would be willing to follow him through obstructing rivers and the many other difficulties which nature would oppose to their advance. Overflowing and laden with booty, they would rather, he judged, enjoy what they had won than wear themselves out in getting more. They could not of course be of the same mind as himself, for while he had grasped the conception of a worldwide empire, and stood as yet but on the threshold of his labours, they were now worn out with toil, and longed for the time when, all their dangers being at length ended, they might enjoy their latest winnings. In the end ambition carried the day against reason; and, having summoned a meeting of the soldiers, he addressed them very much to this effect:

His Speech to the Soldiers

'I am not ignorant, soldiers, that during these last days the natives of this country have been spreading all sorts of rumours designed expressly to work upon your fears; but the falsehood of those who invent such lies is nothing new in your experience. The Persians in this sort of way sought to terrify you with the gates of Cilicia, with the plains of Mesopotamia, with the Tigris and Euphrates, and yet this river you crossed by a ford, and that by means of a bridge. Fame is never brought to a clearness in which facts can be seen as they are. They are all magnified when she transmits them. Even our own glory, though resting on a solid basis, is more indebted for its greatness to rumour than to reality. Who but till the other day believed that it was possible for us to bear the shock of those monstrous beasts that looked like so many ramparts, or that we could have passed the Hydaspes, or conquered other difficulties which after all were more formidable to hear of than they proved to be in actual experience. By my troth we had long ago fled from Asia could fables have been able to scare us.

'Can you suppose that the herds of elephants are greater than of other cattle when the animal is known to be rare, hard to be caught, and harder still to tame? It is the same spirit of falsehood which magnifies the number of horse and foot possessed by the enemy; and with respect to the river, why, the wider it spreads the liker it becomes to a placid pool. Rivers, as you know, that are confined between narrow banks and choked by narrow channels flow with torrent speed, while on the other hand the current slackens as the channel widens out. Besides, all the danger is at the bank where the enemy waits to receive us as we disembark; so that, be the breadth of the river what it may, the danger is all the same when we are in the act of landing. But let us suppose that these stories are all true, is it then, I ask, the monstrous size of the elephants or the number of the enemy that you dread? As for the elephants, we had an example of them before our eyes in the late battle when they charged more furiously upon their own ranks than upon ours, and when their vast bodies were cut and mangled by our bills and axes. What matters it then whether they be the same number as Porus had, or be 3,000, when we see that if one or two of them be wounded, the rest swerve aside and take to flight. Then again, if it be no easy task to manage but a few of them, surely when so many thousands of them are crowded together, they cannot but hamper each other when their huge unwieldy bodies want room either to stand or run. For myself, I have such a poor opinion of the animals that, though I had them, I did not bring them into the field, being fully convinced they occasion more danger to their own side than to the enemy.

'But it is the number, perhaps, of the horse and foot that excites your fears! for you have been wont, you know, to fight only against small numbers, and will now for the first time have to withstand undisciplined multitudes! The river Granicus is a witness of the courage of the Macedonians unconquered in fighting against odds; so too is Cilicia deluged with the blood of the Persians, and Arbela, where the plains are strewn with the bones of your vanquished foes. It is too late, now that you have depopulated Asia by your victories, to begin counting the enemy's legions. When we were crossing the Hellespont, it was then we should have thought about the smallness of our numbers, for now Scythians follow us, Bactrian troops are here to assist us, Dahans and Sogdians are serving in our ranks. But it is not in such a throng I put my trust. It is to your hands, Macedonians, I look. It is your valour I take as the gage and surety of the deeds I mean to perform.

'As long as it is with you I shall stand in battle, I count not the number either of my own or the enemy's army. Do ye only, I entreat, keep your minds full of alacrity and confidence. We are not standing on the threshold of our enterprise and our labours, but at their very close. We have already reached the sunrise and the ocean, and unless your sloth and cowardice prevent, we shall thence return in triumph to our native land, having conquered the earth to its remotest bounds. Act not then like foolish husbandmen who, when their crops are ripe, loose them out of hand from sheer indolence to gather them. The prizes before you are greater than the risks, for the country to be invaded not only teems with wealth, but is at the same time feebly defended. So then I lead you not so much to glory as to plunder. You have earned the right to carry back to your own country the riches which that sea casts upon its shores; and it would ill become you if through fear you should leave anything unattempted or unperformed. I conjure you then by that glory of yours whereby ye soar above the topmost pinnacle of human greatness – I beseech you by my services unto you, and yours unto me (a strife in which we still contend unconquered), that ye desert not your foster son, your fellow soldier, not to say your king, just at the moment when he is approaching the limits of the inhabited world.

'All things else you have done at my orders – for this one thing I shall hold myself to be your debtor. I, who never ordered you upon any service in which I did not place myself in the forefront of the danger, I who have often with mine own buckler covered you in battle, now entreat you not to shatter the palm which is already in my grasp, and by which, if I may so speak without incurring the ill will of heaven, I shall become the equal of Hercules and Father Bacchus. Grant this to my entreaties, and break at last your obstinate silence. Where is that familiar shout, the wonted token of your alacrity? Where are the cheerful looks of my Macedonians? I do not recognize you, soldiers, and, methinks, I seem not to be recognized by you. I have all along been knocking at deaf ears, I am trying to rouse hearts that are disloyal and crushed with craven fears.'

When the soldiers, with their heads bent earthwards, still suppressed what they felt, 'I must,' he said, 'have inadvertently given you some offence that you will not even look at me. Methinks I am in a solitude. No one answers me; no one so much as says me nay. Is it to strangers I am speaking? Am I claiming anything unreasonable? Why, it is your glory and your greatness we are asserting. Where are those whom but the other day I saw eagerly striving which should have the prerogative of receiving the person of their wounded king? I am deserted, forsaken, surrendered into the hands of the enemy. But I shall still persist in going forward, even though I should march alone.

'Expose me then to the dangers of rivers, to the rage of elephants, and to those nations whose very names fill you with terror. I shall find men that will follow me though I be deserted by you. The Scythians and Bactrians, once our foemen, but now our soldiers – these will still be with me. Let me tell you, I had die rather than be a commander on sufferance. Begone then to your homes, and go triumphing because ye have forsaken your king! For my part, I shall here find a place, either for the victory of which you despair, or for an honourable death.'

Speech of Coenus on Behalf of the Army

But not even by this appeal could a single word be elicited from any of the soldiers. They waited for the generals and chief captains to report to the king that the men, exhausted with their wounds and incessant labours in the field, did not refuse the duties of war, but were simply unable to discharge them. The officers, however, paralyzed with terror, kept their eyes steadfastly fixed on the ground, and remained silent. Then there arose, no one knew how, first a sighing and then a sobbing, until, little by little, their grief began to vent itself more freely in streaming tears, so that even the king, whose anger had been turned into pity, could not himself refrain from tears, anxious though he was to suppress them. At last, when the whole assembly had abandoned itself to an unrestrained passion of weeping, Coenus, on finding that the others were reluctant to open their lips, made bold to step forward to the tribunal where the king stood, and signified that he had somewhat to say. When the soldiers saw him removing his helmet from his head – a custom observed in addressing the king – they earnestly besought him that he would plead the cause of the army.

'May the gods,' he then said, 'defend us from all disloyal thoughts; and assuredly they do thus defend us. Your soldiers are now of the same mind towards you as they ever were in times past, being ready to go wherever you order them, ready to fight your battles, to risk their lives, and to give your name in keeping to after ages. So then, if you still persist in your purpose, all unarmed, naked and bloodless though we be, we either follow you, or go on before you, according to your pleasure. But if you desire to hear the complaints of your soldiers, which are not feigned, but wrung from them by the sorest necessity, vouchsafe, I entreat you, a favourable hearing to men who have most devotedly followed your authority and your fortunes, and are ready to follow you wherever you may go. Oh, sir! you have conquered, by the greatness of your deeds, not your enemies alone, but your own soldiers as well.

'We again have done and suffered up to the full measure of the capacity of mortal nature. We have traversed seas and lands, and know them better than do the inhabitants themselves. We are standing now almost on the earth's utmost verge, and yet you are preparing to go to a sphere altogether new – to go in quest of an India unknown even to the Indians themselves. You would fain root out from their hidden recesses and dens a race of men that herd with snakes and wild beasts, so that you may traverse as a conqueror more regions than the sun surveys. The thought is altogether worthy of a soul so lofty as thine, but it is above ours; for while thy courage will be ever growing, our vigour is fast waning to its end.

'See how bloodless be our bodies, pierced with how many wounds, and gashed with how many scars! Our weapons are now blunt, our armour quite worn out. We have been driven to assume the Persian garb since that of our own country cannot be brought up to supply us. We have degenerated so far as to adopt a foreign costume. Among how many of us is there to be found a single coat of mail? Which of us has a horse? Cause it to be inquired how many have servants to follow them, how much of his booty each one has now left. We have conquered all the world, but are ourselves destitute of all things. Can you think of exposing such a noble army as this, all naked and defenceless, to the mercy of savage beasts, whose numbers, though purposely exaggerated by the barbarians, must yet, as I can gather from the lying report itself, be very considerable.

'If, however, you are bent on penetrating still farther into India, that part of it which lies towards the south is not so vast, and were this subdued you could then quickly find your way to that sea which nature has ordained to be the boundary of the inhabited world. Why do you make a long circuit in pursuit of glory when it is placed immediately within your reach, for even here the ocean is to be found. Unless, then, you wish to go wandering about, we have already reached the goal unto which your fortune leads you. I have preferred to speak on these matters in your presence, O King! rather than to discuss them with the soldiers in your absence, not that I have in view to gain thereby for myself the good graces of the army here assembled, but that you might learn their sentiments from my lips rather than be obliged to hear their murmurs and their groans.'

Alexander's Displeasure at the Refusal of the Soldiers to Advance

When Coenus had made an end of speaking there arose from all parts of the audience assenting shouts, mingled with lamentations and confused voices, calling Alexander king, father, lord, and master. And now also the other officers, especially the seniors, who from their age possessed all the greater authority, and could with a better grace beg to be excused from any more service, united in making the same request. Alexander therefore found himself unable either to rebuke them for their stubbornness or to appease their angry mood. Being thus quite at a loss what to do, he leaped down from the tribunal and shut himself up in the royal pavilion, into which he forbade anyone to be admitted except his ordinary attendants.

For two days he indulged his anger, but on the third day he emerged from his seclusion, and ordered twelve altars of square stone to be erected as a monument of his expedition. He ordered also the fortifications around the camp to be drawn out wide, and couches of a larger size than was required for men of ordinary stature to be left, so that by making things appear in magnificent proportions he might astonish posterity by deceptive wonders. From this place he marched back the way he had come, and encamped near the river Acesines. There Coenus caught an illness, which carried him off.

The king was doubtless deeply grieved by his death, but yet he could not forbear remarking that it was but for the sake of a few days he had opened a long-winded speech as though he alone were destined to see Macedonia again. The fleet which he had ordered to be built was now riding in the stream ready for service. Memnon also had meanwhile brought from Thrace a reinforcement of 5,000 cavalry, together with 7,000 infantry sent by Harpalus. He also brought 25,000 suits of armour inlaid with silver and gold, and these Alexander distributed to the troops, commanding the old suits to be burned.

Designing now to make for the ocean with 1,000 ships, he left Porus and Taxiles, the Indian kings who had been disagreeing and raking up old feuds, in friendly relations with each other, strengthened by a marriage alliance; and as they had done their utmost to help him forward with the building of his fleet, he confirmed each in his sovereignty. He built also two towns, one of which he called Nicaea, and the other Bucephala, dedicating the latter to the memory of the horse which he had lost. Then leaving orders for the elephants and baggage to follow him by land, he sailed down the river, proceeding every day about 40 stadia, to allow the troops to land from time to time where they could conveniently be put ashore.

Alexander Subdues Various Tribes on His Way to the Indus

Thus he came at length into the country where the river Hydaspes falls into the Acesines, and thence flows down to the territories of the Sibi. These people allege that their ancestors belonged to the army of Hercules, and that being left behind on account of sickness had possessed themselves of the seats which their posterity now occupied. They dressed themselves with the skins of wild beasts, and had clubs for their weapons. They showed besides many other traces of their origin, though in the course of time Greek manners and institutions had grown obsolete. He landed among them, and marching a distance of 250 stadia into the country beyond their borders, laid it waste, and took its capital town by an assault made against the walls all round. The nation, consisting of 40,000 foot soldiers, had been drawn up along the bank of the river to oppose his landing, but he nevertheless crossed the stream, put the enemy to flight, and, having stormed the town, compelled all who were shut up within its walls to surrender. Those who were of military age were put to the sword, and the rest were sold as slaves.

He then laid siege to another town, but the defenders made so gallant a resistance that he was repulsed with the loss of many of his Macedonians. He persevered, however, with the siege till the inhabitants, despairing of their safety, set fire to their houses, and cast themselves along with their wives and children into the flames. War then showed itself in a new form, for while the inhabitants were destroying their city by spreading the flames, the enemy were striving to save it by quenching them, so completely does war invert natural relations. The citadel of the town had escaped damage, and Alexander accordingly left a garrison behind in it. He was himself conveyed by means of boats around the fortress, for the three largest rivers in India (if we except the Ganges) washed the line of its fortifications. The Indus on the north flows close up to it, and on the south the Acesines unites with the Hydaspes.

Disasters to His Fleet at the Meeting of the Rivers

But the meeting of the rivers makes the waters swell in great billows like those of the ocean, and the navigable way is compressed into a narrow channel by extensive mud banks kept continually shifting by the force of the confluent waters. When the waves, therefore, in thick succession dashed against the vessels, beating both on their prows and sides, the sailors were obliged to take in sail; but partly from their own flurry, and partly from the force of the currents, they were unable to execute their orders in time, and before the eyes of all, two of the large ships were engulphed in the stream. The smaller craft, however, though they also were unmanageable, were driven on shore without sustaining injury. The ship which had the king himself on board was caught in eddies of the greatest violence, and by their force was irresistibly driven athwart and whirled onward without answering the helm.

He had already stripped off his clothes preparatory to throwing himself into the river, while his friends were swimming about not far off ready to pick him up, but as it was evident that the danger was about equal whether he threw himself into the water or remained on board, the boatmen vied with each other in stretching to their oars, and made every exertion possible for human beings to force their vessel through the raging surges. It then seemed as though the waves were being cloven asunder, and as though the whirling eddies were retreating, and the ship was thus at length rescued from their grasp. It did not, however, gain the shore in safety, but was stranded on the nearest shallows. One would suppose that a war had been waged against the river. Alexander there erected as many altars as there were rivers, and having offered sacrifices upon them marched onward, accomplishing a distance of thirty stadia.

His Campaign Against the Sudracae and Malli

Thence he came into the dominions of the Sudracae and the Malli, who hitherto had usually been at war with each other, but now drew together in presence of the common danger. Their army consisted of 90,000 foot soldiers, all fit for active service, together with 10,000 cavalry and 900 war chariots. But when the Macedonians, who believed that they had by this time got past all their dangers, found that they had still on hand a fresh war, in which the most warlike nations in all India would be their antagonists, they were struck with an unexpected terror, and began again to upbraid the king in the language of sedition. Though he had been driven,' they said, 'to give up the river Ganges and regions beyond it, he had not ended the war, but only shifted it. They were now exposed to fierce nations that with their blood they might open for him a way to the ocean. They were dragged onward outside the range of the constellations and the sun of their own zone, and forced to go to places which nature meant to be hidden from mortal eyes. New enemies were forever springing up with arms ever new, and though they put them all to rout and flight, what reward awaited them? What but mists and darkness and unbroken night hovering over the abyss of ocean? What but a sea teeming with multitudes of frightful monsters – stagnating waters in which expiring nature has given way in despair?'

The king, troubled not by any fears for himself, but by the anxiety of the soldiers about their safety, called them together, and pointed out to them that those of whom they were afraid were weak and unwarlike; that after the conquest of these tribes there was nothing in their way, once they had traversed the distance now between them and the ocean, to prevent their coming to the end of the world, which would be also the end of their labours; that he had given way to their fears of the Ganges and of the numerous tribes beyond that river, and turned his arms to a quarter where the glory would be equal but the hazard less; that they were already in sight of the ocean, and were already fanned by breezes from the sea. They should not then grudge him the glory to which he aspired. They would overpass the limits reached by Hercules and Father Bacchus, and thus at a small cost bestow upon their king an immortality of fame. They should permit him to return from India with honour, and not to escape from it like a fugitive.

Every assemblage, and especially one of soldiers, is readily carried away by any chance impulse, and hence the measures for quelling a mutiny are less important than the circumstances in which it originates. Never before did so eager and joyous a shout ring out as was now sent forth by the army asking him to lead them forward, and expressing the hope that the gods would prosper his arms and make him equal in glory to those whom he was emulating. Alexander, elated by these acclamations, at once broke up his camp and advanced against the enemy, which was the strongest in point of numbers of all the Indian tribes. They were making active preparations for war, and had selected as their head a brave warrior of the nation of the Sudracae. This experienced general had encamped at the foot of a mountain, and had ordered fires to be kindled over a wide circuit to make his army appear so much the more numerous. He endeavoured also at times, but in vain, to alarm the Macedonians when at rest by making his men shout and howl in their own barbarous manner.

As soon as day dawned, the king, full of hope and confidence, ordered his soldiers, who were eager for action, to take their arms and march to battle. The barbarians, however, fled all of a sudden, but whether through fear or dissensions that had arisen among them, there is no record to show. At any rate, they escaped timeously to their mountain recesses, which were difficult of approach. The king pursued the fugitives, but to no purpose; however, he took their baggage.

Assails Their Chief Stronghold and is Left Standing Alone on the Wall

Thence he came into the city of the Sudracae, into which most of the enemy had fled, trusting for safety as much to their arms as to the strength of the fortifications. The king was now advancing to attack the place, when a soothsayer warned him not to undertake the siege, or at all events to postpone it, since the omens indicated that his life would be in danger. The king fixing his eyes upon Demophon (for this was the name of the soothsayer), said: 'If anyone should in this manner interrupt thyself, while busied with thine art and inspecting entrails, wouldst thou not regard him as impertinent and troublesome?' 'I certainly would so regard him,' said Demophon. Then rejoined Alexander, 'Dost thou not think then that when I am occupied with such important matters, and not with the inspection of the entrails of cattle, there can be any interruption more unseasonable to me than a soothsayer enslaved by superstition?' Without more loss of time than was required for returning the answer, he ordered the scaling ladders to be applied to the wall, and while the others were hesitating to mount them, he himself scaled the ramparts.

The parapet which ran round the rampart was narrow, and was not marked out along the coping with battlements and embrasures, but was built in an unbroken line of breastwork, which obstructed assailants in attempting to get over. The king then was clinging to the edge of the parapet, rather than standing upon it, warding off with his shield the darts that fell upon him from every side, for he was assailed by missiles from all the surrounding towers. Nor were the soldiers able to mount the wall under the storm of arrows discharged against them from above. Still at last a sense of shame overcame their fear of the greatness of the danger, for they saw that by their hesitation the king would fall into the hands of his enemies. But their help was delayed by their hurry, for while everyone strove to get soonest to the top of the wall, they were precipitated from the ladders which they overloaded till they broke, thus balking the king of his only hope. He was in consequence left standing in sight of his numerous army, like a man in a solitude, whom all the world has forsaken.

Alexander is Severely Wounded by an Arrow

By this time his left hand, with which he was shifting his buckler about, became tired with parrying the blows directed against him from all round, and his friends cried out to him that he should leap down, and were standing ready to catch him when he fell. But instead of taking this course, he did an act of daring past all belief and unheard of an act notable as adding far more to his reputation for rashness than to his true glory. For with a headlong spring he flung himself into the city filled with his enemies, even though he could scarcely expect to die fighting, since before he could rise from the ground he was likely to be overpowered and taken prisoner. But, as luck would have it, he had flung his body with such nice poise that he alighted on his feet, which gave him the advantage of an erect attitude when he began fighting. Fortune had also so provided that he could not possibly be surrounded, for an aged tree which grew not far from the wall, had thrown out branches thickly covered with leaves, as if for the very purpose of sheltering the king. Against the huge bole of this tree he so planted himself that he could not be surrounded, and as he was thus protected in rear, he received on his buckler the darts with which he was assailed in front; for single handed though he was, not one of the many who set upon him ventured to come to close-quarters with him, and their missiles lodged more frequently in the branches of the tree than in his buckler.

What served him well at this juncture was the far spread renown of his name, and next to that despair, which above everything nerves men to die gloriously. But as the numbers of the enemy were constantly increasing, his buckler was by this time loaded with darts, and his helmet shattered by stones, while his knees sank under him from the fatigue of his protracted exertions. On seeing this, they who stood nearest incautiously rushed upon him in contempt of the danger. Two of these he smote with his sword, and laid them dead at his feet, and after that no one could muster up courage enough to go near him. They only plied him with darts and arrows from a distance off.

But though thus exposed as a mark for every shot, he had no great difficulty in protecting himself while crouching on his knees, until an Indian let fly an arrow two cubits long (for the Indians, as remarked already, use arrows of this length), and pierced him through his armour a little above his right side. Struck down by this wound, from which the blood spirted in great jets, he let his weapon drop as if he were dying without strength enough left to let his right hand extract the arrow. The archer, accordingly, who had wounded him, exulting in his success, ran forward with eager haste to strip his body.

But Alexander no sooner felt him lay hands on his person, than he became so exasperated by the supreme indignity, I imagine, of the outrage, that he recalled his swooning spirit, and with an upward thrust of his sword pierced the exposed side of his antagonist. Thus there lay dead around the king three of his assailants, while the others stood off like men stupefied.

Meanwhile he endeavoured to raise himself up with his buckler, that he might die sword in hand, before his last breath left him, but finding he had not strength enough for the effort, he grasped with his right hand some of the defending boughs, and tried to rise with their help. His strength was, however, inadequate even to support his body, and he fell down again upon his knees, waving his hand as a challenge to the enemy to meet him in close combat if any of them dared. At length Peucestas in a different quarter of the town beat off the men who were defending the wall, and following the king's traces came to where he was. Alexander on seeing him thought that he had come not to succour him in life, but to comfort him in his death, and giving way through sheer exhaustion, fell over on his shield.

Then came up Timaeus, and a little afterwards Leonnatus followed by Aristonus. The Indians, on discovering that the king was within their walls, abandoned all other places and ran in crowds to where he was, and pressed hard upon those who defended him. Timaeus, one of such, after receiving many wounds and making a gallant struggle, fell. Peucestas again, though pierced with three javelin wounds, held up his buckler not for his own, but the king's protection. Leonnatus, while endeavouring to drive back the barbarians who were eagerly pressing forward, was severely wounded in the neck, and fell down in a swoon at the king's feet. Peucestas was also now quite exhausted with the loss of blood from his wounds and could no longer hold up his buckler. Thus all the hope now lay in Aristonus, but he also was desperately wounded, and could no longer sustain the onset of so many assailants. In the meantime, the rumour that the king had fallen reached the Macedonians.

What would have terrified others only served to stimulate their ardour, for, heedless of every danger, they broke down the wall with their pickaxes, and where they had made an entrance burst into the city and massacred great numbers of the Indians, chiefly in the pursuit, no resistance being offered except by a mere handful. They spared neither old men, women, nor children, but held whomsoever they met to have been the person by whom the king had been wounded, and in this way they at length satiated their righteous indignation.

Clitarchus and Timagenes state that Ptolemy, who afterwards became a king, was present at this fighting, but Ptolemy himself, who would not of course gainsay his own glory, has recorded in his memoirs that he was away at the time, as the king had sent him on an expedition elsewhere. This instance shows how great was the carelessness of the authors who composed these old books of history, or, it may be, their credulity, which is just as great a dereliction of their duty. The king was carried into a tent, where the surgeons cut off the wooden shaft of the arrow which had pierced him, taking care not to stir its point. When his armour was taken off they discovered that the weapon was barbed, and that it could not be extracted without danger except by making an incision to open the wound. But here again they were afraid lest in operating they should be unable to staunch the flow of blood, for the weapon was large and had been driven home with such force that it had evidently pierced to the inwards.

The Arrow is Extracted by Critobulus

Critobulus, who was famous for his surgical skill, was nevertheless swayed by fear in a case so precarious, and dreaded to put his hand to the work lest his failure to effect a cure should recoil on his own head. The king observing him to weep, and to be showing signs of fear, and looking ghastly pale, said to him: 'For what and how long are you waiting that you do not set to work as quickly as possible? If die I must, free me at least from the pain I suffer. Are you afraid lest you should be held to account because I have received an incurable wound?' Then Critobulus, at last overcoming, or perhaps dissembling his fear, begged Alexander to suffer himself to be held while he was extracting the point, since even a slight motion of his body would be of dangerous consequence. To this the king replied that there was no need of men to hold him, and then, agreeably to what had been enjoined him, he did not wince the least during the operation.

When the wound had then been laid wide open and the point extracted, there followed such a copious discharge of blood that the king began to swoon, while a dark mist came over his eyes, and he lay extended as if he were dying. Every remedy was applied to staunch the blood, but all to no purpose, so that the king's friends, believing him to be dead, broke out into cries and lamentations. The bleeding did, however, at last stop, and the patient gradually recovered consciousness and began to recognize those who stood around him. All that day and the night which followed the army lay under arms around the royal tent. All of them confessed that their life depended on his single breath, and they could not be prevailed on to withdraw until they had ascertained that he had fallen into a quiet sleep. Thereupon they returned to the camp entertaining more assured hopes of his recovery.

Alexander Recovers – His Officers Remonstrate for His Recklessness

The king, who had now been kept for the space of seven days under treatment for his wound without its being as yet cicatrized, on hearing that a report of his death had gained a wide currency among the barbarians, caused two ships to be lashed together and his tent to be set up in the centre where it would be conspicuous to everyone, so that he might therefrom show himself to those who believed him to be dead. By thus exposing himself to the view of the inhabitants he crushed the hope with which the false report had inspired his enemies. He then sailed down the river,' starting a good while before the rest of the fleet, lest the repose which his weak bodily condition still required should be disturbed by the noise of rowing. On the fourth day after he had embarked he reached a country deserted by its inhabitants, but fruitful in corn and well stocked with cattle. Here along with his soldiers he enjoyed a welcome season of rest.

Now it was a custom among the Macedonians that the king's especial friends and those who had the guard of his person watched before his tent during any occasional illness. This custom being now observed as usual, they all entered his chamber in a body. Alexander fearing they might be the bearers of some bad news, since they had all come together, enquired whether they had come to inform him that the enemy had that moment arrived. Then Craterus, who had been chosen by the others as their medium to let the king know the entreaties of his friends, addressed him in these terms: 'Can you imagine,' he began, 'that we could be more alarmed by the enemy's approach, even if they were already within our lines, than we are concerned for your personal safety, by which, it seems, you set but little store? Were the united powers of the whole world to conspire against us, were they to cover the land all over with arms and men, to cover the seas with fleets, and lead ferocious wild beasts against us, we shall prove invincible to every foe when we have you to lead us. But which of the gods can ensure that this the stay and star of Macedonia will be long preserved to us when you are so forward to expose your person to manifest dangers, forgetting that you draw into peril the lives of so many of your countrymen? For which of us wishes to survive you, or even has it within his power? Under your conduct and command we have advanced so far that there is no one but yourself who can lead us back to our hearths and homes.

'No doubt while you were still contending with Darius for the sovereignty of Persia, one could not even think it strange (though no one wished it) that you were ever ready and eager to rush boldly into danger, for where the risk and the reward are fairly balanced, the gain is not only more ample in case of success, but the solace is greater in case of defeat. But that your very life should be paid as the price of an obscure village, which your soldiers, nay, what inhabitant of any barbarous country that has heard of your greatness can tolerate such an idea? My soul is struck with horror when I think of the scene which was lately presented to our eyes.

'I cannot but tremble to relate that the hands of the greatest dastards would have polluted the spoils stripped from the invincible Alexander, had not fortune, looking with pity on us, interfered for your deliverance. We are no better than traitors, no better than deserters, all of us who were unable to keep up with you when you ran into danger; and should you therefore brand us all with dishonour, none of us will refuse to give satisfaction for that from the guilt of which he could not secure himself. Show us, we beseech you then, in some other way, how cheap you hold us. We are ready to go wherever you order. We solicit that for us you reserve obscure dangers and inglorious battles, while you save yourself for those occasions which give scope for your greatness. Glory won in a contest with inferior opponents soon becomes stale, and nothing can be more absurd than to let your valour be wasted where it cannot be displayed to view.'

Ptolemy and others who were present addressed him in the same or similar terms, and all of them, as one man, besought him with tears that, sated as he was with glory, he would at last set some limits to that passion and have more regard for his own safety, on which that of the public depended. The affection and loyalty of his friends were so gratifying to the king that he embraced them one by one with more than his usual warmth, and requested them all to be seated.

His Reply to Their Appeal

Then, in addressing them, he went far back in a review of his career and said: 'I return you, most faithful and most dutiful subjects and friends, my most heartfelt thanks, not only because you at this time prefer my safety to your own, but also because from the very outset of the war you have lost no opportunity of showing by every pledge and token your kindly feelings towards myself, so that I must confess my life has never been so dear to me as it is at present, and chiefly so, that I may long enjoy your companionship. At the same time, I must point out that those who are willing to lay down their lives for me do not look at the matter from my point of view, inasmuch as I judge myself to have deserved by my bravery your favourable inclinations towards me, for you may possibly be coveting to reap the fruit of my favour for a great length of time, perhaps even in perpetuity, but I measure myself not by the span of age, but by that of glory.

'Had I been contented with my paternal heritage, I might have spent my days within the bounds of Macedonia, in slothful ease, to an obscure and inglorious old age; although even those who remain indolently at home are not masters of their own destiny, for while they consider a long life to be the supreme good, an untimely death often takes them by surprise. I, however, who do not count my years but by my victories, have already had a long career of life, if I reckon aright the gifts of fortune. Having begun to reign in Macedonia, I now hold the supremacy of Greece. I have subdued Thrace and the people of Illyria; I give laws to the Triballi and the Maedi, and am master of Asia from the shores of Hellespont as far south as the shores of the Indian Ocean. And now I am not far from the very ends of the earth, which when I have passed I purpose to open up to myself a new realm of nature a new world. In the turning-point of a single hour I crossed over from Asia into the borders of Europe. Having conquered both these continents in the ninth year of my reign, and in my twenty-eighth year, do you think I can pause in the task of completing my glory, to which, and to which only, I have entirely devoted myself? No, I shall not fail in my duty to her, and wheresoever I shall be fighting I shall imagine myself on the world's theatre, with all mankind for spectators. I shall give celebrity to places before unnoted. I shall open up for all nations a way to regions which nature has hitherto kept far distant.

'If fortune shall so direct that in the midst of these enterprises my life be cut short, that would only add to my renown. I am sprung from such a stock that I am bound to prefer living much to living long. Reflect, I pray you, that we have come to lands in the eyes of which the name of a woman is the most famed for valour. What cities did Semiramis build! What nations did she bring to subjection! What mighty works did she plan! We have not yet equalled the glorious achievements of a woman, and have we already had our fill of glory? No, I say. Let the gods, however, but favour us, and things still greater remain for us yet to do. But the countries we have not yet reached shall only become ours on condition that we consider nothing little in which there is room for great glory to be won. Do you but defend me against domestic treason and the plots of my own household, and I will fearlessly face the dangers of battle and war.

'Philip was safer in the field of fight than in the theatre. He often escaped the hands of his enemies – he could not elude those of his subjects. And if you examine how other kings also came by their end, you can count more that were slain by their own people than by their enemies. But now lastly, since an opportunity has presented itself to me of disclosing a matter which I have for a long time been turning over and over in my mind, I give you to understand that to me the greatest rewards of all my toils and achievements will be this, that my mother Olympias shall be deified as soon as she departs this life. If I be spared, I shall myself discharge that duty, but if death anticipate me, bear in memory that I have entrusted this office to you.' With these words he dismissed his friends; but for a good many days he remained in the same encampment.

The Affair of Biton and Boxus at Baktra

While these things were doing in India, the Greek soldiers who had been recently drafted by the king into settlements around Bactra disagreed among themselves and revolted, for the stronger faction, having killed some of their countrymen who remained loyal, had recourse to arms, and making themselves masters of the citadel of Bactra, which happened to be carelessly guarded, forced even the barbarians to join their party. Their leader was Athenodorus, who had also assumed the title of king, not so much from an ambition to reign as from a wish to return to his native country along with those who acknowledged his authority. Against his life one Biton, a citizen of the same Greek state as himself, but who hated him from envy, laid a plot, and having invited him to a banquet, had him assassinated during the festivities by the hands of a native of Margiana called Boxus. The day following Biton, in a general meeting which had been convoked, persuaded the majority that Athenodorus had without any provocation formed a plot to take away his life. Others, however, suspected there had been foul play on Biton's part, and by degrees this suspicion spread itself about among the rest. The Greek soldiers, therefore, took up arms to put Biton to death should an opportunity present itself.

But the leading men appeased the anger of the multitude, and Biton being thus freed from his imminent danger, contrary to what he had anticipated, soon after wards conspired against the very man to whom he owed his safety. But when his treachery came to their knowledge they seized both Biton himself and Boxus. The latter they ordered to be at once put to death, but Biton not till after he had undergone torture. The instruments for this purpose were already being applied to his limbs when the soldiers, it is not known why, ran to their arms like so many madmen. On hearing the uproar they made, the men who had orders to torture Biton desisted from their office, thinking that the object of the rioters, whom they had heard shouting, was to prevent them going on with their work. Biton, stripped as he was, ran for protection to the Greeks, and the sight of the wretched man sentenced to death caused such a revulsion of their feelings that they ordered him to be set at liberty. Having twice escaped punishment, he returned to his native country with the rest of those who left the colonies which the king had assigned to them. These things were done about Bactra and the borders of Scythia.

Embassy from the Sudracae and Malli

In the meantime, 100 ambassadors came to the king from the two nations we have before mentioned. They all rode in chariots and were men of uncommon stature and of a very dignified bearing. Their robes were of linen and embroidered with inwrought gold and purple. They informed him that they surrendered into his hands themselves, their cities, and their territories, and that he was the first to whose authority and protection they had entrusted their liberty which for so many ages they had preserved inviolate. The gods, they said, were the authors of their submission and not fear, seeing that they had submitted to his yoke while their strength was quite unbroken.

The king at a meeting of his council accepted their proffer of submission and allegiance, and imposed on them the tribute which the two nations paid in instalments to the Arachosians. He further ordered them to furnish him with 2,500 horsemen, all which commands were faithfully carried out by the barbarians. After this he gave orders for the preparation of a splendid banquet to which he invited the ambassadors and the petty kings of the neighbouring tribes. Here 100 couches of gold had been placed at a small distance from each other, and these were hung round with tapestry curtains which glittered with gold and purple. In a word he displayed at this entertainment all that was corrupt in the ancient luxury of the Persians as well as in the new-fangled fashions which had been adopted by the Macedonians, thus intermixing the vices of both nations.

At this banquet there was present Dioxippus the Athenian, a famous boxer, who on account of his surprising strength was already well known to the king, and one even of his favourites. Some there were who from envy and malice used to carp at him between jest and earnest, remarking they had a full-fed good-for-nothing beast in their company, who when others went forth to fight would rub himself with oil and take exercise to get up his appetite. Now at the banquet a Macedonian called Horratus, who was by this time 'flown with wine', began to taunt him in the usual style, and challenged him, if he were a man, to fight him next day with his sword, after which the king would judge of his temerity or of the cowardice of Dioxippus. The terms of the challenge were accepted by Dioxippus, who treated with contempt the bravado of the insolent soldier. The king finding next day that the two men were more than ever bent on fighting, and that he could not dissuade them, allowed them to do as they pleased. The soldiers came in crowds to witness the affair, and among others Greeks who backed up Dioxippus.

Single Combat Between a Macedonian and an Athenian Champion

The Macedonian came with the proper arms, carrying in his left hand a brazen shield and the long spear called the *sarissa*, and in his right a javelin. He wore also a sword by his side as if he meant to fight with several opponents at once. Dioxippus again entered the ring shining with oil, wearing a garland about his brows, having a scarlet cloak wrapped about his left arm, and carrying in his right hand a stout knotty club. This singular mode of equipment kept all the spectators for a time in suspense, because it seemed not temerity but downright madness for a naked man to engage with one armed to the teeth. The Macedonian accordingly, not doubting for a moment but that he could kill his adversary from a distance, cast his javelin at him, but this Dioxippus avoided by a slight bending of his body, and before the other could shift the long pike to his right hand, sprang upon him and broke the weapon in two by a stroke of his club. The Macedonian, having thus lost two of his weapons, prepared to draw his sword, but Dioxippus closed with him before he was ready to wield it, and suddenly tripping up his heels, knocked him down as with a blow from a battering-ram. He then wrested his sword from his grasp, planted his foot on his neck as he lay prostrate, and brandishing his club would have brained him with it, had he not been prevented by the king.

The result of the match was mortifying not only to the Macedonians, but even to Alexander himself, for he saw with vexation that the vaunted bravery of the Macedonians had fallen into contempt with the barbarians who attended the spectacle. This made the king lend his ear all too readily to the accusations of those who owed Dioxippus a grudge. So at a feast which he attended a few days afterwards a golden bowl was by a private arrangement secretly taken off the table, and the attendants went to the king to complain of the loss of the article which they themselves had hidden. It often enough happens that one who blushes at a false insinuation has less control of his countenance than one who is really guilty. Dioxippus could not bear the glances which were turned upon him as if he were the thief, and so when he had left the banquet he wrote a letter which he addressed to the king, and then killed himself with his sword. The king took his death much to heart, judging that the man had killed himself from sheer indignation, and not from remorse of conscience, especially since the intemperate joy of his enemies made it clear that he had been falsely accused.

Alexander Receives Submission of the Malli

The Indian ambassadors were dismissed to their several homes, but in a few days they returned with presents for Alexander which consisted of 300 horsemen, 1,030 chariots each drawn by four horses, 1,000 Indian bucklers, a great quantity of linen cloth, 100 talents of steel, some tame lions and tigers of extraordinary size, the skins also of very large lizards, and a quantity of tortoise shells. The king commanding Craterus to move forward in advance with his troops and to keep always near the river, down which he intended himself to sail, took ship along with his usual retinue, and dropping down stream came to the territories of the Malli. Thence he marched towards the Sabarcae, a powerful Indian tribe where the form of government was democratic and not regal. Their army consisted of 60,000 foot and 6000 cavalry attended by 500 chariots.

They had elected three generals renowned for their valour and military skill; but when those who lived near the river, the banks of which were most thickly studded with their villages, saw the whole river as far as the eye could reach covered with ships, and saw besides the many thousands of men and their gleaming arms, they took fright at the strange spectacle and imagined that an army of the gods and a second Father Bacchus, a name famous in that country, were coming into their midst. The shouts of the soldiers and the noise of the oars, together with the confused voices of the sailors encouraging each other, so filled their alarmed ears that they all ran off to the army and cried out to the soldiers that they would be mad to offer battle to the gods, that the number of ships carrying these invincible warriors was past all counting. By these reports they created such a terror in the ranks of their own army that they sent ambassadors commissioned to surrender their whole nation to Alexander.

Invades the Musicani and the Praesti

Having received their submission, he came on the fourth day after to other tribes which had as little inclination for fighting as their neighbours. Here therefore he built a town, which by his orders was called Alexandrea, and then he entered the country of the people known as the Musicani. While he was here he held an enquiry into the complaints advanced by the Parapamisadae against Terioltes, whom he had made their satrap, and, finding many charges of extortion and tyranny proved against him, he sentenced him to death. On the other hand, Oxyartes, the governor of the Bactriani, was not only acquitted, but, as he had claims upon Alexander's affections, was rewarded with an extension of the territory under his jurisdiction.

Having thereafter reduced the Musicani, Alexander put a garrison into their capital, and marched thence into the country of the Praesti, another Indian tribe. Their king was Porticanus, and he with a great body of his countrymen had shut himself up within a strongly fortified city. Alexander, however, took it after a three days' siege. Porticanus, who had taken refuge within the citadel after the capture of the city, sent deputies to the king to arrange about terms of capitulation. Before they reached him, however, two towers had fallen down with a dreadful crash, and the Macedonians having made their way through the ruins into the citadel, captured it and slew Porticanus, who with a few others had offered resistance.

Attacks King Sambus

Having demolished the citadel and sold all the prisoners, he marched into the territories of King Sambus, where he received the submission of numerous towns. The strongest, however, of all the cities which belonged to this people, he took by making a passage into it under ground. To the barbarians, who had no previous knowledge of this device for entering fortified places, it seemed as if a miracle had been wrought when they saw armed men rise out of the ground in the middle of their city almost without any trace of the mine by which they had entered being visible. Clitarchus says that 80,000 Indians were slain in that part of the country, and that numerous prisoners were sold as slaves. The Musicani again rebelled, and Pithon being sent to crush them, brought the chief of the tribe, who was also the author of the insurrection, to the king, who ordered him to be

crucified, and then returned to the river, where the fleet was waiting
for him.

The fourth day thereafter he sailed down the river to a town that
lay at the very extremity of the kingdom of Sambus. That prince
had but lately surrendered himself to Alexander, but the people of
the city refused to obey him, and had even closed their gates against
him. The king, however, despising the paucity of their numbers,
ordered 500 Agrianians to go close up to the walls and then to retire
by little, in order to entice the enemy from the town, who would in
that case certainly pursue under the belief that they were retreating.

Musicanus Captured and Executed

The Agrianians, after some skirmishing, suddenly showed their backs
to the enemy as they had been ordered, and were hotly pursued by the
barbarians, who fell in with other troops led by the king in person.
The fighting was therefore renewed, with the result that out of the
3000 barbarians who were in the action, 600 were killed, 1,000 taken
prisoners, and the rest driven back into the city. But this victory did
not end so happily as at first sight it promised to do, for the barbarians
had used poisoned swords, and the wounded soon afterwards died;
while the surgeons were at a loss to discover why a slight wound should
be incurable, and followed by so violent a death. The barbarians had
been in hopes that the king, who was known to be rash and reckless
of his safety, might be in this way cut off, and in fact it was only by
sheer good luck that he escaped untouched, fighting as he did among
the very foremost.

Ptolemy is Wounded, but Recovers

Ptolemy was wounded in the left shoulder, slightly indeed, but
yet dangerously on account of the poison, and his case caused

the king especial anxiety. He was his own kinsman; some even believed that Philip was his father, and it is at all events certain that he was the son of one of that king's mistresses. He was a member of the royal bodyguard, and the bravest of soldiers. At the same time, he was even greater and more illustrious in civil pursuits than in war itself. He lived in a plain style like men of common rank, was liberal in the extreme, easy too of access, and a man who gave himself none of the high airs so often assumed by courtiers. These qualities made it doubtful whether he was more loved by the king or by his countrymen. At all events, now that his life was in danger, he was for the first time made aware of the great affection entertained for him by the Macedonians, who by this time seem to have presaged the greatness to which he afterwards rose, for they showed as much solicitude for him as they did for Alexander himself. Alexander, again, though fatigued with fighting and anxiety, sat watching over Ptolemy, and when he wished to take some rest, did not leave the sick room, but had his bed brought into it.

He had no sooner laid himself down than he fell into a profound sleep, from which, when he awoke, he told his attendants that in a vision he had seen a creature in the form of a serpent carrying in its mouth a plant, which it offered him as an antidote to the poison. He gave besides such a description of the colour of the plant as he was sure would enable anyone falling in with it to recognize it. The plant was found soon afterwards, as many had gone to search for it, and was laid upon the wound by Alexander himself. The application at once removed the pain and speedily cicatrized the wound. The barbarians finding themselves disappointed of their first hopes, surrendered themselves and their city.

Alexander Reaches Patala and Sails Down the Indus

Alexander marched thence into the Patalian territory. Its king was Moeres, but he had abandoned the town and fled for safety to the mountains. Alexander then took possession of the place, and ravaged the surrounding country, from which he carried off a great booty of sheep and cattle, besides a great quantity of corn. After this, taking some natives acquainted with the river to pilot his way, he sailed down the stream to an island which had sprung up almost in the middle of the channel.

Perils Encountered on the Voyage

Here he was obliged to make a longer stay than he had anticipated, because the pilots, finding they were not strictly guarded, had absconded. He then sent out a party of his men to search for others. They returned without finding any, but his unquenchable ambition to see the ocean and reach the boundaries of the world, made him entrust his own life and the safety of so many gallant men to an unknown river without any guides possessed of the requisite local knowledge. They thus sailed on ignorant of everything on the way they had to pass. It was entirely left to haphazard and baseless conjecture how far off they were from the sea, what tribes dwelt along the banks, whether the river was placid at its mouth, and whether it was thereabouts of a depth sufficient for their warships. The only comfort in this rash adventure was a confident reliance on Alexander's uniform good fortune. The expedition had in this manner now proceeded a distance of 400 stadia, when the pilots brought to his notice that they began to feel sea-air, and that they believed the ocean was not now far off.

The king, elated by the news, exhorted the sailors to bend to their oars. The end of their labours, he said, for which they had always been hoping and praying, was close at hand; nothing was now wanting to complete their glory; nothing left to withstand their valour. They could now, without the hazard of fighting, without any bloodshed, make the whole world their own. Even nature herself could advance no farther, and within a short time they would see what was known to none but the immortal gods. He nevertheless sent a small party ashore in a boat in order to take some of the natives straggling about, from whom he hoped some correct information might be obtained. After all the huts near the shore had been searched, some natives at last were found hidden away in them. These, on being asked how far off the sea was, answered that they had never so much as heard of such a thing as the sea, but that on the third day they might come to water of a bitter taste which corrupted the fresh water. From this it was understood they meant the sea, whose nature they did not understand. The mariners therefore plied their oars with increased alacrity, and still more strenuously on the following day as they drew nearer to the fulfilment of their hopes.

On the third day they observed that the sea, coming up with a tide as yet gentle, began to mingle its brine with the fresh water of the river. Then they rowed out to another island that lay in the middle of the river, making, however, slower progress in rowing since the stream of the river was now beaten back by the force of the tide. They put into the shore of the island, and such as landed ran hither and thither in quest of provisions, never dreaming of the mishap which was to overtake them from their ignorance of tides. It was now about the third hour of the day when the ocean, undergoing its periodic change, rose in flood-tide, and began to burst upon them and force back the current of the river, which being at first retarded, and then more violently repelled, was driven upward contrary to its natural direction with more than the impetuosity of rivers in flood rushing down precipitous beds. The men in general were ignorant of the nature of the sea, and so, when they saw it continually swelling higher, and overflowing the beach which before was dry, they looked upon this as something supernatural by which the gods signified their wrath against their rash presumption.

When the vessels were now fairly floated, and the whole squadron scattered in different directions, the men who had gone on shore ran back in consternation to the ships, confounded beyond measure by a calamity of a nature so unexpected. But amid the tumult their haste served only to mar their speed. Some were to be seen pushing the vessels with poles; others had taken their seats to row, but in doing so had meanwhile been preventing the proper adjustment of the oars. Others again, in hastening to sail out into the clear channel, without waiting for the requisite number of sailors and pilots, worked the vessels to little effect, crippled as these were and otherwise difficult to handle. At the same time several other vessels drifted away with the stream before those who were pell-mell crowding into them could all get on board, and in this case the crowding caused as much delay in hurrying off as did the scarcity of hands in the other vessels. From one side were shouted orders to stay, from another to put off, so that amid this confusion of contradictory orders nothing that was of any service could be seen or even heard. In such an emergency the pilots themselves were useless, since their commands could neither be heard for the uproar, nor executed by men so distracted with terror.

The ships accordingly ran afoul of each other, broke away each other's oars, and bumped each other's sterns. A spectator could not have supposed that what he saw was the fleet of one and the same army, but rather two hostile fleets engaged in a sea fight. Prows were dashed against poops, and vessels that damaged other vessels in front of them were themselves damaged in turn by vessels at their stern.

The men, as was but natural, lost their temper, and from high words fell to blows.

By this time the tide had overflowed all the level lands near the river's edge, leaving only sandheaps visible above the water like so many islands. To these numbers of the men swam for safety, neglecting through fear the safety of the vessels they quitted, some of which were riding in very deep water where depressions existed in the ground, while others were stranded on shoals where the waves had covered the more or less elevated parts of the channel. But now they were suddenly surprised with a new danger, still greater than the first, for the sea, which had begun to ebb, was rushing back whence it came with a strong current, and was rendering back the lands which just before had been deeply submerged. This pitched some of the stranded vessels upon their sterns, and caused others to fall upon their sides, and that too with such violence that the fields around them were strewn with baggage, arms, broken oars, and wreckage.

The soldiers, meanwhile, neither dared to trust themselves to the land nor to leave their ships, as they dreaded that some calamity, worse than before, might at any moment befall them. They could scarcely indeed believe what they saw and experienced, these shipwrecks upon dry land, and the presence of the sea in the river. Nor did their misfortunes end here, for as they did not know that the tide would soon afterwards bring back the sea and float their ships, they anticipated that they would be reduced by famine to the most dismal extremities. To add to their terror monstrous creatures of frightful aspect, which the sea had left behind it, were seen wandering about.

As night drew on the hopelessness of the situation oppressed even the king himself with harassing anxieties. But no care could ever daunt his indomitable spirit, and great as was his anxiety it did not prevent him from remaining all night on the watch and giving out his orders. He even sent some horsemen to the mouth of the river with instructions that when they saw the tide returning they should go before it and announce its approach. Meanwhile he caused the shattered vessels to be repaired, and those that were overturned to be set upright, at the same time ordering the men to be ready and on the alert when the land would be inundated by the return of the tide.

Alexander Returns from the Mouth of the River to Patala

The whole of that night had been spent by the king in watching and addressing words of encouragement to his men, when the horsemen came back at full gallop, with the tide following at their heels. It came at first with a gentle current which sufficed to set the ships afloat, but it soon gathered strength enough to set the whole fleet in motion. Then the soldiers and sailors, giving vent to their irrepressible joy at their unexpected deliverance, made the shores and banks resound with their exulting cheers. They asked each other wonderingly wherefrom so vast a sea had suddenly returned, whereto it had retired the day before, what was the nature of this strange element, which at one time was out of harmony with the natural laws of space, but at another was obedient to some fixed laws in respect of time?

The king conjecturing from what had happened that the tide would return after sunrise, took advantage of it, and starting at midnight sailed down the river attended by a few ships, and having passed its mouth, advanced into the sea a distance of 400 stadia, and thus at last accomplished the object he had so much at heart. Having then sacrificed to the tutelary gods of the sea and of the places adjacent, he took the way back to his fleet.

Alexander Goes Homeward by Land

He sailed thence up the river, and next day reached a place of anchorage not far from a salt lake, the peculiar properties of which being unknown to his men, deceived those who thoughtlessly bathed in its waters. For scabs broke out over their bodies, and the disease being contagious, infected even others who had not bathed. The application of oil, however, cured the sores. Then as the country through which the army was to pass was dry and waterless, Alexander sent on Leonnatus in advance to dig wells, while he remained himself with the troops where he was, waiting for the arrival of spring. In the meantime he built a good many cities, and ordered Nearchus and Onesicritus, who were experienced navigators, to sail with the stoutest ships down to the ocean, and proceeding as far as they could with safety to make themselves acquainted with the nature of the sea. Having done this, they might return to join him by sailing up either the same river or the Euphrates.

Disastrous March Through Gedrosia

The winter being now wellnigh over, he burned the useless ships, and marched homeward with his army by land. In the course of nine encampments he reached the land of the Arabites, and in nine more the land of the Cedrosii – a free people, who agreed to surrender after holding a council to consider the subject. As they surrendered voluntarily, nothing was exacted from them except a supply of provisions. On the fifth day there after he came to a river, which the natives called the Arabus, and beyond it he found the country barren and waterless. This he traversed, and entered the dominions of the Oritae. Here he gave Hephaestion the great bulk of the army, and divided the rest of it, consisting of light-armed troops, between Ptolemy,

Leonnatus, and himself. These three divisions plundered the Indians simultaneously, and carried off a large booty. Ptolemy devastated the maritime country, while the king himself and Leonnatus between them ravaged all the interior. Here too he built a city, which he peopled with Arachosians. Thence he came to those Indians who inhabit the seacoast, possessing a great extent of country, and holding no manner of intercourse even with their next neighbours.

This isolation from the rest of the world has brutalized their character, which even by nature is far from humane. They have long claw-like nails and long shaggy hair, for they cut the growth of neither. They live in huts constructed of shells and other offscourings of the sea. Their clothing consists of the skins of wild beasts, and they feed on fish dried in the sun, and on the flesh of sea monsters cast on the shore during stormy weather. The Macedonians having by this time consumed all their provisions, suffered first from scarcity and at last from hunger, so that they were driven to search everywhere for the roots of the palm, which is the only tree that country produces. When even this kind of food failed them, they began to kill their beasts of burden, and did not spare even their horses. They were thus deprived of the means of carrying their baggage, and had to burn the rich spoils taken from their enemies, for the sake of which they had marched to the utmost extremities of the East.

A pestilence succeeded the famine, for the new juices of the unwholesome esculents on which they fed, superadded to the fatigue of marching and the strain of their mental anxiety, had spread various distempers among them, so that they were threatened with destruction whether they remained where they were or resumed their march. If they stayed famine would assail them, and if they advanced a still deadlier enemy, pestilence, would have them in its grasp. The plains were in consequence bestrewn with almost more bodies of the dying than of the dead. Even those who suffered least from the distemper could not keep pace with the main army, because everyone believed that the faster he travelled he advanced the more surely to health and safety. The men, therefore, whose strength failed craved help from all and sundry, whether known to them or unknown. But there were no beasts of burden now by which they could be taken on, and the soldiers had enough to do to carry their arms, whilst at the same time the dreadful figure of the calamity impending over themselves was ever before their eyes. Being thus repeatedly appealed to, they could not so much as bear to cast back a look at their comrades, their pity for others being lost in their fears for themselves.

Those, on the other hand, who were thus forsaken, implored the king, in the name of the gods and by the rites of their common religion, to help them in their sore need, and when they found that they vainly importuned deaf ears, their despair turned to frantic rage, so that they fell to imprecations, wishing for those who refused to help them a similar death and similar friends. The king, feeling himself to be the cause of so great a calamity, was oppressed with grief and shame, and sent orders to Phrataphernes, the satrap of the Parthyaeans, to forward him upon camels provisions ready cooked, and he also notified his wants to the governors of the adjacent provinces. In obedience to his orders the supplies were at once forwarded, and the army being thus rescued, from famine at least, reached eventually the frontiers of Cedrosia, a region which alone of all these parts produces everything in great abundance. Here, therefore, he halted for some time to refresh his harassed troops by an interval of repose.

Alexander Arrives in Carmania, Celebrates
His Conquests

Meanwhile he received a letter from Leonnatus reporting that he had defeated the Oritae, who had brought against him a force of 8,000 foot and 300 horse. Word came also from Craterus that he had crushed an incipient rebellion, instigated by two Persian nobles, Ozines and Zariaspes, whom he had seized and placed under custody. On leaving this place Alexander appointed Sibyrtius to be governor of that province in succession to Memnon, who had lately been cut off by some malady, and he then marched into Carmania, which was governed by the satrap Aspastes, whom he suspected of having designed to make himself independent while he was a great distance off in India. Aspastes came to meet Alexander, who, dissembling his resentment, received him graciously, and let him remain in office till he could inquire into the charges preferred against him. Then as the different governors, in compliance with his demands, had sent him a large supply of horses and draught cattle from their respective provinces, he accommodated all his men who wanted them with horses and wagons. He restored also their arms to their former splendour, for they were now not far from Persia, which was a rich country and in the enjoyment of profound peace.

So then Alexander, whose soul aspired to more than human greatness, since he had rivalled, as we said before, the glory which Father Bacchus had achieved by his conquest of India, resolved also to match his reputation by imitating the Bacchanalian procession which that divinity first invented, whether that was a triumph or merely some kind of frolic with which his Bacchanals amused themselves. To this end he ordered the streets through which he was to pass to be strewn with flowers and chaplets, and beakers and other capacious vessels brimming with wine to be placed at all the house doors. Then he ordered wagons to be made, each capable of holding many soldiers, and these to be decorated like tents, some with white canvas and others with costly tapestry.

The king headed the procession with his friends and the members of his select bodyguard, wearing on their heads chaplets made of a variety of flowers. The strains of music were to be heard in every part of the procession, here the breathings of the flute, and there the warblings of the lyre. All the army followed, feasting and carousing as they rode in the wagons, which they had decorated as gaily as they possibly could, and had hung round with their choicest and showiest weapons. The king himself and the companions of his revelry rode in a chariot, which groaned under the weight of goblets of gold and large drinking cups made of the same precious metal. The army for seven days advanced in this bacchanalian fashion, so that it might have fallen an easy prey to the vanquished if they had but had a spark of spirit to attack it when in this drunken condition. Why, 1,000 men only, if with some mettle in them and sober, could have captured the whole army in the midst of its triumph, besotted as it was with its seven days' drunken debauch.

But fortune, which assigns to everything its fame and value in the world's estimation, turned into glory this gross military scandal; and the contemporaries of Alexander, as well as those who came after his time, regarded it as a wonderful achievement, that his soldiers, though drunk, passed in safety through nations hardly as yet sufficiently subdued, the barbarians taking, what was in reality a piece of great temerity, to be a display of well-grounded confidence. All this grand exhibition, however, had the executioner in its wake, for the satrap Aspastes, of whom we before made mention, was ordered to be put to death. So true is it that cruelty is no obstacle to the indulgence of luxury, nor luxury to the indulgence of cruelty.

ANCIENT KINGS & LEADERS

Ancient cultures often traded with and influenced each other, while others grew independently. This section provides the key leaders from a number of regions, to offer comparative insights into developments across the ancient world.

SUMERIAN KING LIST

This list is based on the *Sumerian King List* or *Chronicle of the One Monarchy*. The lists were often originally carved into clay tablets and several versions have been found, mainly in southern Mesopotamia. Some of these are incomplete and others contradict one another. Dates are based on archaeological evidence as far as possible but are thus approximate. There may also be differences in name spellings between different sources. Nevertheless, the lists remain an invaluable source of information.

As with many civilizations, lists of leaders often begin with mythological and legendary figures before they merge into the more solidly historical, hence why you will see some reigns of seemingly impossible length.

After the kingship descended from heaven, the kingship was in Eridug.

Alulim	28,800 years (8 *sars**)
Alalngar	36,000 years (10 *sars*)

Then Eridug fell and the kingship was taken to Bad-tibira.

En-men-lu-ana	43,200 years (12 *sars*)
En-mel-gal-ana	28,800 years (8 *sars*
Dumuzid the Shepherd (or Tammuz)	36,000 years (10 *sars*)

Then Bad-tibira fell and the kingship was taken to Larag.

En-sipad-zid-ana   28,800 years (8 sars)

Then Larag fell and the kingship was taken to Zimbir.

En-men-dur-ana   21,000 years (5 sars and 5 ners)

Then Zimbir fell and the kingship was taken to Shuruppag.

Ubara-Tutu   18,600 years (5 sars and 1 ner*)

Then the flood swept over.

*A sar is a numerical unit of 3,600; a ner is a numerical unit of 600.

FIRST DYNASTY OF KISH

After the flood had swept over, and the kingship had descended from heaven, the kingship was in Kish.

Jushur	1,200 years	Zuqaqip	900 years
Kullassina-bel	960 years	Atab (or A-ba)	600 years
Nangishlisma	1,200 years	Mashda (son of Atab)	840 years
En-tarah-ana	420 years	Arwium (son of	
Babum	300 years	Mashda)	720 years
Puannum	840 years	Etana the Shepherd	1,500 years
Kalibum	960 years	Balih (son of Etana)	400 years
Kalumum	840 years	En-me-nuna	660 years

Melem-Kish (son of Enme-nuna)	900 years	Enmebaragesi (earliest proven ruler based on archaeological sources; Early Dynastic Period, 2900–2350 BCE)	900 years
Barsal-nuna (son of Enme-nuna)	1,200 years		
Zamug (son of Barsal-nuna)	140 years		
Tizqar (son of Zamug)	305 years	Aga of Kish (son of Enmebaragesi) (Early Dynastic Period, 2900–2350 BCE)	625 years
Ilku	900 years		
Iltasadum	1,200 years		

Then Kish was defeated and the kingship was taken to E-anna.

FIRST RULERS OF URUK

Mesh-ki-ang-gasher (son of Utu)	324 years	(Late Uruk Period, 4000–3100 BCE)
Enmerkar (son of Mesh-ki-ang-gasher)	420 years	(Late Uruk Period, 4000–3100 BCE)
Lugal-banda the shepherd	1200 years	(Late Uruk Period, 4000–3100 BCE)
Dumuzid the fisherman	100 years	(Jemdet Nasr Period, 3100–2900 BCE)
Gilgamesh	126 years	(Early Dynastic Period, 2900–2350 BCE)
Ur-Nungal (son of Gilgamesh)	30 years	
Udul-kalama (son of Ur-Nungal)	15 years	
La-ba'shum	9 years	
En-nun-tarah-ana	8 years	

Mesh-he	36 years
Melem-ana	6 years
Lugal-kitun	36 years

Then Unug was defeated and the kingship was taken to Urim (Ur).

FIRST DYNASTY OF UR

Mesh-Ane-pada	80 years
Mesh-ki-ang-Nuna (son of Mesh-Ane-pada)	36 years
Elulu	25 years
Balulu	36 years

Then Urim was defeated and the kingship was taken to Awan.

DYNASTY OF AWAN

| Three kings of Awan | 356 years |

Then Awan was defeated and the kingship was taken to Kish.

SECOND DYNASTY OF KISH

Susuda the fuller	201 years
Dadasig	81 years
Mamagal the boatman	360 years
Kalbum (son of Mamagal)	195 years

Tuge	360 years
Men-nuna (son of Tuge)	180 years
Enbi-Ishtar	290 years
Lugalngu	360 years

Then Kish was defeated and the kingship was taken to Hamazi.

DYNASTY OF HAMAZI

Hadanish	360 years

Then Hamazi was defeated and the kingship was taken to Unug (Uruk).

SECOND DYNASTY OF URUK

En-shag-kush-ana	60 years (*c.* 25th century BCE)
Lugal-kinishe-dudu	120 years
Argandea	7 years

Then Unug was defeated and the kingship was taken to Urim (Ur).

SECOND DYNASTY OF UR

Nanni	120 years
Mesh-ki-ang-Nanna II (son of Nanni)	48 years

Then Urim was defeated and the kingship was taken to Adab.

DYNASTY OF ADAB

Lugal-Ane-mundu   90 years (c. 25th century BCE)

Then Adab was defeated and the kingship was taken to Mari.

DYNASTY OF MARI

Anbu	30 years	Zizi of Mari, the fuller	20 years
Anba (son of Anbu)	17 years	Limer the 'gudug'	
Bazi the		priest	30 years
leatherworker	30 years	Sharrum-iter	9 years

Then Mari was defeated and the kingship was taken to Kish.

THIRD DYNASTY OF KISH

Kug-Bau (Kubaba)   100 years (c. 25th century BCE)

Then Kish was defeated and the kingship was taken to Akshak.

DYNASTY OF AKSHAK

Unzi	30 years	Ishu-Il	24 years
Undalulu	6 years	Shu-Suen (son of	
Urur	6 years	Ishu-Il)	7 years
Puzur-Nirah	20 years		

Then Akshak was defeated and the kingship was taken to Kish.

FOURTH DYNASTY OF KISH

Puzur-Suen (son of Kug-bau)	25 years (*c.* 2350 BCE)
Ur-Zababa (son of Puzur-Suen)	400 years (*c.* 2300 BCE)
Zimudar	30 years
Usi-watar (son of Zimudar)	7 years
Eshtar-muti	11 years
Ishme-Shamash	11 years
Shu-ilishu	15 years
Nanniya the jeweller	7 years

Then Kish was defeated and the kingship was taken to Unug (Uruk).

THIRD DYNASTY OF URUK

Lugal-zage-si	25 years (*c.* 2296–2271 BCE)

Then Unug was defeated and the kingship was taken to Agade (Akkad).

DYNASTY OF AKKAD

Sargon of Akkad	56 years (*c.* 2270–2215 BCE)
Rimush of Akkad (son of Sargon)	9 years (*c.* 2214–2206 BCE)
Manishtushu (son of Sargon)	15 years (*c.* 2205–2191 BCE)

Naram-Sin of Akkad (son of
Manishtushu)   56 years (*c.* 2190–2154 BCE)
Shar-kali-sharri (son of Naram-Sin)   24 years (*c.* 2153–2129 BCE)

Then who was king? Who was not the king?

Irgigi, Nanum, Imi and Ilulu   3 years (four rivals who fought
                                  to be king during a three-year
                                  period; *c.* 2128–2125 BCE)
Dudu of Akkad   21 years (*c.* 2125–2104 BCE)
Shu-Durul (son of Duu)   15 years (*c.* 2104–2083 BCE)

Then Agade was defeated and the kingship was taken to Unug (Uruk).

FOURTH DYNASTY OF URUK

Ur-ningin   7 years (*c.* 2091?–2061? BCE)
Ur-gigir (son of Ur-ningin)   6 years
Kuda   6 years
Puzur-ili   5 years
Ur-Utu (or Lugal-melem; son of Ur-gigir)   6 years

Unug was defeated and the kingship was taken to the army of Gutium.

GUTIAN RULE

Inkišuš   6 years (*c.* 2147–2050 BCE)
Sarlagab (or Zarlagab)   6 years

Shulme (or Yarlagash)	6 years
Elulmeš (or Silulumeš or Silulu)	6 years
Inimabakeš (or Duga)	5 years
Igešauš (or Ilu-An)	6 years
Yarlagab	3 years
Ibate of Gutium	3 years
Yarla (or Yarlangab)	3 years
Kurum	1 year
Apilkin	3 years
La-erabum	2 years
Irarum	2 years
Ibranum	1 year
Hablum	2 years
Puzur-Suen (son of Hablum)	7 years
Yarlaganda	7 years
Si'um (or Si-u)	7 years
Tirigan	40 days

Then the army of Gutium was defeated and the kingship taken to Unug (Uruk).

FIFTH DYNASTY OF URUK

Utu-hengal	427 years / 26 years / 7 years
	(conflicting dates; *c.* 2055–2048 BCE)

THIRD DYNASTY OF UR

Ur-Namma (or Ur-Nammu)	18 years	(c. 2047–2030 BCE)
Shulgi (son of Ur-Namma)	48 years	(c. 2029–1982 BCE)
Amar-Suena (son of Shulgi)	9 years	(c. 1981–1973 BCE)
Shu-Suen (son of Amar-Suena)	9 years	(c. 1972–1964 BCE)
Ibbi-Suen (son of Shu-Suen)	24 years	(c. 1963–1940 BCE)

Then Urim was defeated. The very foundation of Sumer was torn out. The kingship was taken to Isin.

DYNASTY OF ISIN

Ishbi-Erra	33 years	(c. 1953–1920 BCE)
Shu-Ilishu (son of Ishbi-Erra)	20 years	
Iddin-Dagan (son of Shu-Ilishu)	20 years	
Ishme-Dagan (son of Iddin-Dagan)	20 years	
Lipit-Eshtar (son of Ishme-Dagan or Iddin Dagan)	11 years	
Ur-Ninurta (son of Ishkur)	28 years	
Bur-Suen (son of Ur-Ninurta)	21 years	
Lipit-Enlil (son of Bur-Suen)	5 years	
Erra-imitti	8 years	
Enlil-bani	24 years	
Zambiya	3 years	
Iter-pisha	4 years	
Ur-du-kuga	4 years	
Suen-magir	11 years	
Damiq-ilishu (son of Suen-magir)	23 years	

ANCIENT EGYPTIAN PHARAOHS

There is dispute about the dates and position of pharaohs within dynasties due to several historical sources being incomplete or inconsistent. This list aims to provide an overview of the ancient Egyptian dynasties, but is not exhaustive and dates are approximate. There may also be differences in name spellings between different sources. Also please note that the throne name is given first, followed by the personal name – more commonly they are known by the latter.

ANCIENT EGYPTIAN DEITIES

Ancient Egyptian gods and goddesses were worshipped as deities. They were responsible for maat (divine order or stability), and different deities represented different natural forces, such as Ra the Sun God. After the Egyptian state was first founded in around 3100 BCE, pharaohs claimed to be divine representatives of these gods and were thought to be successors of the gods.

While there are many conflicting Egyptian myths, some of the significant gods and goddesses and their significant responsibilities are listed here.

Amun/Amen/Amen-Ra	Creation
Atem/Tem	Creation, the sun

Ra	The sun
Isis	The afterlife, fertility, magic
Osiris	Death and resurrection, agriculture
Hathor	The sky, the sun, motherhood
Horus	Kingship, the sky
Set	Storms, violence, deserts
Maat	Truth and justice, she personifies *maat*
Anubis	The dead, the underworld

PREDYNASTIC AND EARLY DYNASTIC PERIODS (c. 3000-2686 BCE)

First Dynasty (c. 3150-2890 BCE)

The first dynasty begins at the unification of Upper and Lower Egypt.

Narmer (Menes/M'na?)	c. 3150 BCE
Aha (Teti)	c. 3125 BCE
Djer (Itej)	54 years
Djet (Ita)	10 years
Merneith (possibly the first female Egyptian pharaoh)	c. 2950 BCE
Khasti (Den)	42 years
Merybiap (Adjib)	10 years
Semerkhet (Iry)	8.5 years
Qa'a (Qebeh)	34 years
Sneferka	c. 2900 BCE
Horus-Ba (Horus Bird)	c. 2900 BCE

Second Dynasty (c. 2890-2686 BCE)

Little is known about the second dynasty of Egypt.

Hetepsekhemwy (Nebtyhotep)	15 years
Nebra	14 years
Nynetjer (Banetjer)	43–45 years
Ba	unknown
Weneg-Nebty	c. 2740 BCE
Wadjenes (Wadj-sen)	c. 2740 BCE
Nubnefer	unknown
Senedj	c. 47 years
Peribsen (Seth-Peribsen)	unknown
Sekhemib (Sekhemib-Perenmaat)	c. 2720 BCE
Neferkara I	25 years
Neferkasokkar	8 years
Horus Sa	unknown
Hudejefa (real name missing)	11 years
Khasekhemwy (Bebty)	18 years

OLD KINGDOM (c. 2686–2181 BCE)

Third Dynasty (c. 2686–2613 BCE)

The third dynasty was the first dynasty of the Old Kingdom. Its capital was at Memphis.

Djoser (Netjerikhet)	c. 2650 BCE
Sekhemkhet (Djoser-Teti)	2649–2643 BCE
Nebka? (Sanakht)	c. 2650 BCE
Qahedjet (Huni?)	unknown
Khaba (Huni?)	2643–2637 BCE
Huni	2637–2613 BCE

Fourth Dynasty (c. 2613–2498 BCE)

The fourth dynasty is sometimes known as the 'golden age' of Egypt's Old Kingdom.

Snefru (Nebmaat)	2613–2589 BCE
Khufu, or Cheops (Medjedu)	2589–2566 BCE
Djedefre (Kheper)	2566–2558 BCE
Khafre (Userib)	2558–2532 BCE
Menkaure (Kakhet)	2532–2503 BCE
Shepseskaf (Shepeskhet)	2503–2498 BCE

Fifth Dynasty (c. 2498–2345 BCE)

There is some doubt over the succession of pharaohs in the fifth dynasty, especially Shepseskare.

Userkaf	2496/8–2491 BCE
Sahure	2490–2477 BCE
Neferirkare-Kakai	2477–2467 BCE
Neferefre (Izi)	2460–2458 BCE
Shepseskare (Netjeruser)	few months between 2458 and 2445 BCE
Niuserre (Ini)	2445–2422 BCE
Menkauhor (Kaiu)	2422–2414 BCE
Djedkare (Isesi)	2414–2375 BCE
Unis (Wenis)	2375–2345 BCE

Sixth Dynasty (c. 2345–2181 BCE)

Teti	2345–2333 BCE
Userkare	2333–2332 BCE
Meryre (Pepi I)	2332–2283 BCE

Merenre I (Nemtyemsaf I)	2283–2278 BCE
Neferkare (Pepi II)	2278–2183 BCE
Merenre II (Nemtyemsaf II)	2183 or 2184 BCE
Netjerkare (Siptah I) or Nitocris	2182–2179 BCE

FIRST INTERMEDIATE PERIOD (c. 2181–2040 BCE)

Seventh and Eighth Dynasties (c. 2181–2160 BCE)

There is little evidence on this period in ancient Egyptian history, which is why many of the periods of rule are unknown.

Menkare	c. 2181 BCE
Neferkare II	unknown
Neferkare III (Neby)	unknown
Djedkare (Shemai)	unknown
Neferkare IV (Khendu)	unknown
Merenhor	unknown
Sneferka (Neferkamin I)	unknown
Nikare	unknown
Neferkare V (Tereru)	unknown
Neferkahor	unknown
Neferkare VI (Peiseneb)	unknown to 2171 BCE
Neferkamin (Anu)	c. 2170 BCE
Qakare (Ibi)	2175–2171 BCE
Neferkaure	2167–2163 BCE
Neferkauhor (Khuwihapi)	2163–2161 BCE
Neferiirkkare (Pepi)	2161–2160 BCE

Ninth Dynasty (*c.* 2160–2130 BCE)

There is little evidence on this period in ancient Egyptian history which is why many of the periods of rule are unknown.

Maryibre (Khety I)	2160 BCE to unknown
Name unknown	unknown
Naferkare VII	unknown
Seneh (Setut)	unknown

The following pharaohs and their dates of rule are unknown or widely unconfirmed.

Tenth Dynasty (*c.* 2130–2040 BCE)

Rulers in the Tenth dynasty were based in Lower Egypt.

Meryhathor	2130 BCE to unknown
Neferkare VIII	2130–2040 BCE
Wahkare (Khety III)	unknown
Merykare	unknown to 2040 BCE
Name unknown	unknown

Eleventh Dynasty (*c.* 2134–1991 BCE)

Rulers in the eleventh dynasty were based in Upper Egypt.

Intef the Elder	unknown
Tepia (Mentuhotep I)	unknown to 2133 BCE
Sehertawy (Intef I)	2133–2117 BCE
Wahankh (Intef II)	2117–2068 BCE
Nakhtnebtepefer (Intef III)	2068–2060/40 BCE

MIDDLE KINGDOM (c. 2040-1802 BCE)

Eleventh Dynasty Continued (c. 2134–1991 BCE)

This period is usually known as the beginning of the Middle Kingdom.

Nebhepetre (Mentuhotep II)	2060–2040 BCE (Upper Egypt)
	2040–2009 BCE (Upper and Lower Egypt)
Sankhkare (Mentuhotep III)	2009–1997 BCE
Nebtawyre (Mentuhotep IV)	1997–1991 BCE

Twelfth Dynasty (c. 1991–1802 BCE)

The twelfth dynasty was one of the most stable prior to the New Kingdom, and is often thought to be the peak of the Middle Kingdom.

Sehetepibre (Amenemhat I)	1991–1962 BCE
Kheperkare (Senusret I / Sesostris I)	1971–1926 BCE
Nubkaure (Amenemhat II)	1929–1895 BCE
Khakheperre (Senusret II / Sesostris II)	1898–1878 BCE
Khakaure (Senusret III / Sesostris III)	1878–1839 BCE
Nimaatre (Amenemhat III)	1860–1815 BCE
Maakherure (Amenemhat IV)	1815–1807 BCE
Sobekkare (Sobekneferu/Nefrusobek)	1807–1802 BCE

SECOND INTERMEDIATE PERIOD (c. 1802-1550 BCE)

Thirteenth Dynasty (c. 1802–c. 1649 BCE)

There is some ambiguity on the periods of rule of the thirteenth dynasty, but it is marked by a period of several short rules. This dynasty is often combined with the eleventh, twelfth and fourteenth dynasties under the Middle Kingdom.

Sekhemre Khutawy (Sobekhotep I)	1802–1800 BCE
Mehibtawy Sekhemkare (Amenemhat Sonbef)	1800–1796 BCE
Nerikare (Sobek)	1796 BCE
Sekhemkare (Amenemhat V)	1796–1793 BCE
Ameny Qemau	1795–1792 BCE
Hotepibre (Qemau Siharnedjheritef)	1792–1790 BCE
Lufni	1790–1788 BCE
Seankhibre (Amenemhat VI)	1788–1785 BCE
Semenkare (Nebnuni)	1785–1783 BCE
Sehetepibre (Sewesekhtawy)	1783–1781 BCE
Sewadijkare I	1781 BCE
Nedjemibre (Amenemhat V)	1780 BCE
Khaankhre (Sobekhotep)	1780–1777 BCE
Renseneb	1777 BCE
Awybre (Hor)	1777–1775 BCE
Sekhemrekhutawy Khabaw	1775–1772 BCE
Djedkheperew	1772–1770 BCE
Sebkay	unknown
Sedjefakare (Kay Amenemhat)	1769–1766 BCE
Khutawyre (Wegaf)	c. 1767 BCE
Userkare (Khendjer)	c. 1765 BCE
Smenkhkare (Imyremeshaw)	started in 1759 BCE
Sehetepkare (Intef IV)	c. 10 years
Meribre (Seth)	ended in 1749 BCE
Sekhemresewadjtawy (Sobekhotep III)	1755–1751 BCE
Khasekhemre (Neferhotep I)	1751–1740 BCE

Menwadjre (Sihathor)	1739 BCE
Khaneferre (Sobekhotep IV)	1740–1730 BCE
Merhotepre (Sobekhotep V)	1730 BCE
Knahotepre (Sobekhotep VI)	c. 1725 BCE
Wahibre (Ibiau)	1725–1714 BCE
Merneferre (Ay I)	1714–1691 BCE
Merhotepre (Ini)	1691–1689 BCE
Sankhenre (Sewadjtu)	1675–1672 BCE
Mersekhemre (Ined)	1672–1669 BCE
Sewadjkare II (Hori)	c. 5 years
Merkawre (Sobekhotep VII)	1664–1663 BCE
Seven kings (names unknown)	1663–? BCE

Note: the remaining pharaohs of the thirteenth dynasty are not listed here as they are either unknown or there is a lot of ambiguity about when they ruled.

Fourteenth Dynasty (c. 1805/1710–1650 BCE)

Rulers in the fourteenth dynasty were based at Avaris, the capital of this dynasty.

Sekhaenre (Yakbim)	1805–1780 BCE
Nubwoserre (Ya'ammu)	1780–1770 BCE
Khawoserre (Qareh)	1770–1745 BCE
Aahotepre ('Ammu)	1760–1745 BCE
Maaibre (Sheshi)	1745–1705 BCE
Aasehre (Nehesy)	c. 1705 BCE
Khakherewre	unknown
Nebefawre	c. 1704 BCE
Sehebre	1704–1699 BCE

Merdjefare   c. 1699 BCE

Note: the remaining pharaohs of the fourteenth dynasty are not listed here as they are either unknown or there is a lot of ambiguity about when they ruled.

Fifteenth Dynasty (c. 1650–1544 BCE)

The fifteenth dynasty was founded by Salitas and covered a large part of the Nile region.

Salitas	c. 1650 BCE
Semqen	1649 BCE to unknown
'Aper-'Anat	unknown
Sakir-Har	unknown
Seuserenre (Khyan)	c. 30 to 35 years
Nebkhepeshre (Apepi)	1590 BCE?
Nakhtyre (Khamudi)	1555–1544 BCE

Sixteenth Dynasty (c. 1650–1580 BCE)

Rulers in the sixteenth dynasty were based at Thebes, the capital of this dynasty. The name and date of rule of the first pharaoh is unknown.

Sekhemresementawy (Djehuti)	3 years
Sekhemresemeusertawy (Sobekhotep VIII)	16 years
Sekhemresankhtawy (Neferhotep III)	1 year
Seankhenre (Mentuhotepi)	less than a year
Sewadjenre (Nebiryraw)	26 years
Neferkare (?) (Nebiryraw II)	c. 1600 BCE
Semenre	c. 1600 BCE

Seuserenre (Bebiankh)	12 years
Djedhotepre (Dedumose I)	c. 1588–1582 BCE
Djedneferre (Dedumose II)	c. 1588–1582 BCE
Djedankhre (Montensaf)	c. 1590 BCE
Merankhre (Mentuhotep VI)	c. 1585 BCE
Seneferibre (Senusret IV)	unknown
Sekhemre (Shedwast)	unknown

Seventeenth Dynasty (c. 1650–1550 BCE)

Rulers in the seventeenth dynasty ruled Upper Egypt.

Sekhemrewahkhaw (Rahotep)	c. 1620 BCE
Sekhemre Wadjkhaw (Sobekemsaf I)	c. 7 years
Sekhemre Shedtawy (Sobekemsaf II)	unknown to c. 1573 BCE
Sekhemre-Wepmaat (Intef V)	c. 1573–1571 BCE
Nubkheperre (Intef VI)	c. 1571–1565 BCE
Sekhemre-Heruhirmaat (Intef VII)	late 1560s BCE
Senakhtenre (Ahmose)	c. 1558 BCE
Seqenenre (Tao I)	1558–1554 BCE
Wadkheperre (Kamose)	1554–1549 BCE

NEW KINGDOM (c. 1550–1077 BCE)

Eighteenth Dynasty (c. 1550–1292 BCE)

The first dynasty of Egypt's New Kingdom marked the beginning of Ancient Egypt's highest power and expansion.

Nebpehtire (Ahmose I)	c. 1550–1525 BCE
Djeserkare (Amenhotep I)	1541–1520 BCE

Aakheperkare (Thutmose I)	1520–1492 BCE
Aakheperenre (Thutmose II)	1492–1479 BCE
Maatkare (Hatshepsut)	1479–1458 BCE
Menkheperre (Thutmose III)	1458–1425 BCE
Aakheperrure (Amenhotep II)	1425–1400 BCE
Menkheperure (Thutmose IV)	1400–1390 BCE
Nebmaatre 'the Magnificent' (Amehotep III)	1390–1352 BCE
Neferkheperure Waenre (Amenhotep IV)	1352–1336 BCE
Ankhkheperure (Smenkhkare)	1335–1334 BCE
Ankhkheperure mery Neferkheperure (Neferneferuaten III)	1334–1332 BCE
Nebkheperure (Tutankhamun)	1332–1324 BCE
Kheperkheperure (Aya II)	1324–1320 BCE
Djeserkheperure Setpenre (Haremheb)	1320–1292 BCE

Nineteenth Dynasty (c. 1550–1292 BCE)

The nineteenth dynasty is also known as the Ramessid dynasty as it includes Ramesses II, one of the most famous and influential Egyptian pharaohs.

Menpehtire (Ramesses I)	1292–1290 BCE
Menmaatre (Seti I)	1290–1279 BCE
Usermaatre Setpenre 'the Great', 'Ozymandias' (Ramesses II)	1279–1213 BCE
Banenre (Merneptah)	1213–1203 BCE
Menmire Setpenre (Amenmesse)	1203–1200 BCE
Userkheperure (Seti II)	1203–1197 BCE
Sekhaenre (Merenptah Siptah)	1197–1191 BCE
Satre Merenamun (Tawosret)	1191–1190 BCE

Twentieth Dynasty (c. 1190–1077 BCE)
This, the third dynasty of the New Kingdom, is generally thought to mark the start of the decline of Ancient Egypt.

Userkhaure (Setnakht)	1190–1186 BCE
Usermaatre Meryamun (Ramesses III)	1186–1155 BCE
Heqamaatre Setpenamun (Ramesses IV)	1155–1149 BCE
Heqamaatre Setpenamun (Ramesses IV)	1155–1149 BCE
Usermaatre Sekheperenre (Ramesses V)	1149–1145 BCE
Nebmaatre Meryamun (Ramesses VI)	1145–1137 BCE
Usermaatre Setpenre Meryamun (Ramesses VII)	1137–1130 BCE
Usermaatre Akhenamun (Ramesses VIII)	1130–1129 BCE
Neferkare Setpenre (Ramesses IX)	1128–1111 BCE
Khepermaatre Setpenptah (Ramesses X)	1111–1107 BCE
Menmaatre Setpenptah (Ramesses XI)	1107–1077 BCE

Twenty-first Dynasty (c. 1077–943 BCE)
Rulers in the twenty-first dynasty were based at Tanis and mainly governed Lower Egypt.

Hedjkheperre-Setpenre (Nesbanadjed I)	1077–1051 BCE
Neferkare (Amenemnisu)	1051–1047 BCE
Aakkheperre (Pasebakhenniut I)	1047–1001 BCE
Usermaatre (Amenemope)	1001–992 BCE
Aakheperre Setepenre (Osorkon the Elder)	992–986 BCE
Netjerikheperre-Setpenamun (Siamun)	986–967 BCE
Titkheperure (Pasebakhenniut II)	967–943 BCE

Twenty-second Dynasty (c. 943–728 BCE)
Sometimes called the Bubastite dynasty. Its pharaohs came from Libya.

Hedjkheneperre Setpenre (Sheshonq I)	943–922 BCE
Sekhemkheperre Setepenre (Osorkon I)	922–887 BCE
Heqakheperre Setepenre (Sheshonq II)	887–885 BCE
Tutkheperre (Sheshonq Llb)	c. the 880s BCE
Hedjkheperre Setepenre (Takelot I Meriamun)	885–872 BCE
Usermaatre Setpenre (Sheshonq III)	837–798 BCE
Hedjkheperre Setepenre (Sheshonq IV)	798–785 BCE
Usermaatre Setpenre (Pami Meriamun)	785–778 BCE
Aakheperre (Sheshonq V)	778–740 BCE
Usermaatre (Osorkon IV)	740–720 BCE

Twenty-third and Twenty-fourth Dynasties (c. 837–720 BCE)

These dynasties were led mainly by Libyans and mainly ruled Upper Egypt.

Hedjkheperre Setpenre (Takelot II)	837–813 BCE
Usermaatre Setpenamun (Meriamun Pedubaste I)	826–801 BCE
Usermaatre Meryamun (Sheshonq VI)	801–795 BCE
Usermaatre Setpenamun (Osorkon III)	795–767 BCE
Usermaatre-Setpenamun (Takelot III)	773–765 BCE
Usermaatre-Setpenamun (Meriamun Rudamun)	765–762 BCE
Shepsesre (Tefnakhte)	732–725 BCE
Wahkare (Bakenrenef)	725–720 BCE

Twenty-fifth Dynasty (c. 744–656 BCE)

Also known as the Kushite period, the twenty-fifth dynasty follows the Nubian invasions.

Piankhy (Piye)	744–714 BCE
Djedkaure (Shebitkku)	714–705 BCE
Neferkare (Shabaka)	705–690 BCE
Khuinefertemre (Taharqa)	690–664 BCE

LATE PERIOD (c. 664–332 BCE)

Twenty-sixth Dynasty (c. 664 – 525 BCE)

Also known as the Saite period, the twenty-sixth dynasty was the last native period before the Persian invasion in 525 BCE.

Wahibre (Psamtik I)	664–610 BCE
Wehemibre (Necho II)	610–595 BCE
Neferibre (Psamtik II)	595–589 BCE
Haaibre (Apreis)	589–570 BCE
Khemibre (Amasis II)	570–526 BCE
Ankhkaenre (Psamtik III)	526–525 BCE

Twenty-seventh Dynasty (c. 525–404 BCE)

The twenty-seventh dynasty is also known as the First Egyptian Satrapy and was ruled by the Persian Achaemenids.

Mesutre (Cambyses II)	525–1 July 522 BCE
Seteture (Darius I)	522–November 486 BCE
Kheshayarusha (Xerxes I)	November 486–December 465 BCE
Artabanus of Persia	465–464 BCE
Arutakhshashas (Artaxerxes I)	464–424 BCE
Ochus (Darius II)	July 423–March 404 BCE

Twenty-eighth Dynasty (c. 404–398 BCE)
The twenty-eighth dynasty consisted of a single pharaoh.

Amunirdisu (Amyrtaeus)   404–398 BCE

Twenty-ninth Dynasty (c. 398–380 BCE)
The twenty-ninth dynasty was founded following the overthrow of Amyrtaeus.

Baenre Merynatjeru (Nepherites I)   398–393 BCE
Khnemmaatre Setepenkhnemu (Hakor)   c. 392–391 BCE
Userre Setepenptah (Psammuthis)   c. 391 BCE
Khnemmaatre Setepenkhnemu (Hakor)   c. 390–379 BCE
Nepherites II   c. 379 BCE

Thirtieth Dynasty (c.379–340 BCE)
The thirtieth dynasty is thought to be the final native dynasty of Ancient Egypt.

Kheperkare (Nectanebo I)   c. 379–361 BCE
Irimaatenre (Teos)   c. 361–359 BCE
Snedjemibre Setepenanhur (Nectanebo II)   c. 359–340 BCE

Thirty-first Dynasty (c. 340–332 BCE)
The thirty-first dynasty is also known as the Second Egyptian Satrapy and was ruled by the Persian Achaemenids.

Ochus (Artaxerxes III)   c. 340–338 BCE
Arses (Artaxerxes IV)   338–336 BCE
Darius III   336–332 BCE

MACEDONIAN/ARGEAD DYNASTY (c. 332–309 BCE)

Alexander the Great conquered Persia and Egypt in 332 BCE.

Setpenre Meryamun (Alexander III of Macedon 'the Great')	332–323 BCE
Setpenre Meryamun (Philip Arrhidaeus)	323–317 BCE
Khaibre Setepenamun (Alexander IV)	317–309 BCE

PTOLEMAIC DYNASTY (c. 305–30 BCE)

The Ptolemaic dynasty in Egypt was the last dynasty of Ancient Egypt before it became a province of Rome.

Ptolemy I Soter	305–282 BCE
Ptolemy II Philadelphos	284–246 BCE
Arsinoe II	c. 277–270 BCE
Ptolemy III Euergetes	246–222 BCE
Berenice II	244/243–222 BCE
Ptolemy IV Philopater	222–204 BCE
Arsinoe III	220–204 BCE
Ptolemy V Epiphanes	204–180 BCE
Cleopatra I	193–176 BCE
Ptolemy VI Philometor	180–164, 163–145 BCE
Cleopatra II	175–164 BCE, 163–127 BCE and 124–116 BCE
Ptolemy VIII Physcon	171–163 BCE, 144–131 BCE and 127–116 BCE
Ptolemy VII Neos Philopator	145–144 BCE

Cleopatra III	142–131 BCE, 127–107 BCE
Ptolemy Memphites	113 BCE
Ptolemy IX Soter	116–110 BCE
Cleopatra IV	116–115 BCE
Ptolemy X Alexander	110–109 BCE
Berenice III	81–80 BCE
Ptolemy XI Alexander	80 BCE
Ptolemy XII Auletes	80–58 BCE, 55–51 BCE
Cleopatra V Tryphaena	79–68 BCE
Cleopatra VI	58–57 BCE
Berenice IV	58–55 BCE
Cleopatra VII	52–30 BCE
Ptolemy XIII Theos Philopator	51–47 BCE
Arsinoe IV	48–47 BCE
Ptolemy XIV Philopator	47–44 BCE
Ptolemy XV Caesar	44–30 BCE

In 30 BCE, Egypt became a province of the Roman Empire.

ANCIENT GREEK MONARCHS

This list is not exhaustive and dates are approximate. Where dates of rule overlap, emperors either ruled jointly or ruled in opposition to one another. There may also be differences in name spellings between different sources.

Because of the fragmented nature of Greece prior to its unification by Philip II of Macedon, this list includes mythological and existing rulers of Thebes, Athens and Sparta as some of the leading ancient Greek city-states. These different city-states had some common belief in the mythological gods and goddesses of ancient Greece, although their accounts may differ.

KINGS OF THEBES (c. 753–509 bce)

These rulers are mythological. There is much diversity over who the kings actually were, and the dates they ruled.

Calydnus (son of Uranus)
Ogyges (son of Poseidon, thought to be king of Boeotia or Attica)
Cadmus (Greek mythological hero known as the founder of Thebes, known as Cadmeia until the reign of Amphion and Zethus)
Pentheus (son of Echion, one of the mythological Spartoi, and Agave, daughter of Cadmus)

Polydorus (son of Cadmus and Harmonia, goddess of harmony)

Nycteus (like his brother Lycus, thought to be the son of a Spartoi and a nymph, or a son of Poseidon)

Lycus (brother of Nyceteus)

Labdacus (grandson of Cadmus)

Lycus (second reign as regent for Laius)

Amphion and Zethus (joint rulers and twin sons of Zeus, constructed the city walls of Thebes)

Laius (son of Labdacus, married to Jocasta)

Oedipus (son of Laius, killed his father and married his mother, Jocasta)

Creon (regent after the death of Laius)

Eteocles and Polynices (brothers/sons of Oedipus; killed each other in battle)

Creon (regent for Laodamas)

Laodamas (son of Eteocles)

Thersander (son of Polynices)

Peneleos (regent for Tisamenus)

Tisamenus (son of Thersander)

Autesion (son of Tisamenes)

Damasichthon (son of Peneleos)

Ptolemy (son of Damasichton, 12 century BCE)

Xanthos (son of Ptolemy)

KINGS OF ATHENS

Early legendary kings who ruled before the mythological flood caused by Zeus, which only Deucalion (son of Prometheus) and a few others survived (date unknown).

Periphas (king of Attica, turned into an eagle by Zeus)

Ogyges (son of Poseidon, thought to be king of either Boeotia or Attica)

Actaeus (king of Attica, father-in-law to Cecrops I)

Erechtheid Dynasty (1556–1127 BCE)

Cecrops I (founder and first king of Athens; half-man, half-serpent who married Actaeus' daughter)	1556–1506 BCE
Cranaus	1506–1497 BCE
Amphictyon (son of Deucalion)	1497–1487 BCE
Erichthonius (adopted by Athena)	1487–1437 BCE
Pandion I (son of Erichthonius)	1437–1397 BCE
Erechtheus (son of Pandion I)	1397–1347 BCE
Cecrops II (son of Erechtheus)	1347–1307 BCE
Pandion II (son of Cecrops II)	1307–1282 BCE
Aegeus (adopted by Pandion II, gave his name to the Aegean Sea)	1282–1234 BCE
Theseus (son of Aegeus, killed the minotaur)	1234–1205 BCE
Menestheus (made king by Castor and Pollux when Theseus was in the underworld)	1205–1183 BCE
Demophon (son of Theseus)	1183–1150 BCE
Oxyntes (son of Demophon)	1150–1136 BCE
Apheidas (son of Oxyntes)	1136–1135 BCE
Thymoetes (son of Oxyntes)	1135–1127 BCE

Melanthid Dynasty (1126–1068 BCE)

Melanthus (king of Messenia, fled to Athens when expelled)	1126–1089 BCE
Codrus (last of the semi-mythological Athenian kings)	1089–1068 BCE

LIFE ARCHONS OF ATHENS (1068-753 BCE)

These rulers held public office up until their deaths.

Medon	1068–1048 BCE	Pherecles	864–845 BCE
Acastus	1048–1012 BCE	Ariphon	845–825 BCE
Archippus	1012–993 BCE	Thespieus	824–797 BCE
Thersippus	993–952 BCE	Agamestor	796–778 BCE
Phorbas	952–922 BCE	Aeschylus	778–755 BCE
Megacles	922–892 BCE	Alcmaeon	755–753 BCE
Diognetus	892–864 BCE		

From this point, archons led for a period of ten years up to 683 BCE, then a period of one year up to 485 CE. Selected important leaders – including archons and tyrants – in this later period are as follows:

SELECTED LATER LEADERS OF ATHENS

Peisistratos 'the Tyrant of Athens'	561, 559–556, 546–527 BCE
Cleisthenes (archon)	525–524 BCE
Themistocles (archon)	493–492 BCE
Pericles	c. 461–429 BCE

KINGS OF SPARTA

These rulers are mythological and are thought to be descendants of the ancient tribe of Leleges. There is much diversity over who the kings actually were, and the dates they ruled.

Lelex (son of Poseidon or Helios, ruled Laconia)   c. 1600 BCE
Myles (son of Lelex, ruled Laconia)   c. 1575 BCE
Eurotas (son of Myles, father of Sparta)   c. 1550 BCE

From the Lelegids, rule passed to the Lacedaemonids when Lacedaemon married Sparta.
Lacedaemon (son of Zeus, husband of Sparta)
Amyklas (son of Lacedaemon)
Argalus (son of Amyklas)
Kynortas (son of Amyklas)
Perieres (son of Kynortas)
Oibalos (son of Kynortas)
Tyndareos (first reign; son of Oibalos, father of Helen of Troy)
Hippocoon (son of Oibalos)
Tyndareos (second reign; son of Oibaos, father of Helen of Troy)

From the Lacedaemons, rule passed to the Atreids when Menelaus married Helen of Troy.

Menelaus (son of Atreus, king of Mycenae,
    and husband of Helen)   c. 1250 BCE
Orestes (son of Agamemnon, Menelaus' brother)   c. 1150 BCE
Tisamenos (son of Orestes)
Dion   c. 1100 BCE

From the Atreids, rule passed to the Heraclids following war.

Aristodemos (son of Aristomachus, great-great-grandson of Heracles)

Theras (served as regent for Aristodemes' sons, Eurysthenes and Procles)

Eurysthenes   c. 930 BCE

From the Heraclids, rule passed to the Agiads, founded by Agis I. Only major kings during this period are listed here.

Agis I (conceivably the first historical Spartan king) c. 930–900 BCE
Alcamenes   c. 740–700 BCE,
                                      during First Messenian War
Cleomenes I (important leader in the
    Greek resistance against the Persians)   524 – 490 BCE
Leonidas I (died while leading the
    Greeks – the 300 Spartans – against
    the Persians in the Battle of
    Thermopylae, 480 BCE)   490–480 BCE
Cleomenes III (exiled following the
    Battle of Sellasia)   c. 235–222 BCE

KINGS OF MACEDON

Argead Dynasty (808–309 BCE)

Karanos	c. 808–778 BCE	Alcetas I	c. 576–547 BCE
Koinos	c. 778–750 BCE	Amyntas I	c. 547–498 BCE
Tyrimmas	c. 750–700 BCE	Alexander I	c. 498–454 BCE
Perdiccas I	c. 700–678 BCE	Alcetas II	c. 454–448 BCE
Argaeus I	c. 678–640 BCE	Perdiccas II	c. 448–413 BCE
Philip I	c. 640–602 BCE	Archelaus I	c. 413–339 BCE
Aeropus I	c. 602–576 BCE	Craterus	c. 399 BCE

Orestes	c. 399–396 BCE	Perdiccas III	c. 368–359 BCE
Aeropus II	c. 399–394/93 BCE	Amyntas IV	c. 359 BCE
Archelaus II	c. 394–393 BCE	Philip II	c. 359–336 BCE
Amyntas II	c. 393 BCE	Alexander III 'the Great'	
Pausanias	c. 393 BCE	(also King of Persia and	
Amyntas III	c. 393 BCE; first reign	Pharaoh of Egypt by end of reign)	c. 336–323 BCE
Argeus II	c. 393–392 BCE	Philip III	c. 323–317 BCE
Amyntas III	c. 392–370 BCE	Alexander IV	c. 323/ 317–309 BCE
Alexander II	c. 370–368 BCE		

Note: the Corinthian League or Hellenic League was created by Philip II and was the first time that the divided Greek city-states were unified under a single government.

Post-Argead Dynasty (309–168 BCE, 149–148 BCE)

Cassander	c. 305–297 BCE
Philip IV	c. 297 BCE
Antipater II	c. 297–294 BCE
Alexpander V	c. 297–294 BCE

Antigonid, Alkimachid and Aeacid Dynasties (294–281 BCE)

Demetrius	c. 294–288 BCE
Lysimachus	c. 288–281 BCE
Pyrrhus	c. 288–285 BCE; first reign

Ptolemaic Dynasty (281–279 BCE)

Ptolemy Ceraunus (son of Ptolemy I of Egypt)	c. 281–279 BCE
Meleager	279 BCE

Antipatrid, Antigonid, Aeacid Dynasties, Restored
(279–167 BCE)

Antipater	c. 279 BCE
Sosthenes	c. 279–277 BCE
Antigonus II	c. 277–274 BCE; first reign
Pyrrhus	c. 274–272 BCE; second reign
Antigonus II	c. 272–239 BCE; second reign
Demetrius II	c. 239–229 BCE
Antigonus III	c. 229–221 BCE
Philip V	c. 221–179 BCE
Perseus (deposed by Romans)	c. 179–168 BCE
Revolt by Philip VI (Andriskos)	c. 149–148 BCE

SELEUCID DYNASTY (c. 320 BCE–63 CE)

Seleucus I Nicator	c. 320–315, 312–305, 305–281 BCE
Antiochus I Soter	c. 291, 281–261 BCE
Antiochus II Theos	c. 261–246 BCE
Seleucus II Callinicus	c. 246–225 BCE
Seleucus III Ceraunus	c. 225–223 BCE
Antiochus III 'the Great'	c. 223–187 BCE
Seleucus IV Philopator	c. 187–175 BCE
Antiochus (son of Seleucus IV)	c. 175–170 BCE
Antiochus IV Epiphanes	c. 175–163 BCE
Antiochus V Eupater	c. 163–161 BCE
Demetrius I Soter	c. 161–150 BCE
Alexander I Balas	c. 150–145 BCE
Demetrius II Nicator	c. 145–138 BCE; first reign
Antiochus VI Dionysus	c. 145–140 BCE

Diodotus Tryphon	c. 140–138 BCE
Antiochus VII Sidetes	c. 138–129 BCE
Demetrius II Nicator	c. 129–126 BCE; second reign
Alexander II Zabinas	c. 129–123 BCE
Cleopatra Thea	c. 126–121 BCE
Seleucus V Philometor	c. 126/125 BCE
Antiochus VIII Grypus	c. 125–96 BCE
Antiochus IX Cyzicenus	c. 114–96 BCE
Seleucus VI Epiphanes	c. 96–95 BCE
Antiochus X Eusebes	c. 95–92/83 BCE
Demetrius III Eucaerus	c. 95–87 BCE
Antiochus XI Epiphanes	c. 95–92 BCE
Philip I Philadelphus	c. 95–84/83 BCE
Antiochus XII Dionysus	c. 87–84 BCE
Seleucus VII	c. 83–69 BCE
Antiochus XIII Asiaticus	c. 69–64 BCE
Philip II Philoromaeus	c. 65–63 BCE

Ptolemaic Dynasty (305–30 BCE)

The Ptolemaic dynasty in Greece was the last dynasty of Ancient Egypt before it became a province of Rome.

Ptolemy I Soter	305–282 BCE
Ptolemy II Philadelphos	284–246 BCE
Arsinoe II	c. 277–270 BCE
Ptolemy III Euergetes	246–222 BCE
Berenice II	244/243–222 BCE
Ptolemy IV Philopater	222–204 BCE
Arsinoe III	220–204 BCE
Ptolemy V Epiphanes	204–180 BCE

Cleopatra I	193–176 BCE
Ptolemy VI Philometor	180–164, 163–145 BCE
Cleopatra II	175–164 BCE, 163–127 BCE and 124–116 BCE
Ptolemy VIII Physcon	171–163 BCE, 144–131 BCE and 127–116 BCE
Ptolemy VII Neos Philopator	145–144 BCE
Cleopatra III	142–131 BCE, 127–107 BCE
Ptolemy Memphites	113 BCE
Ptolemy IX Soter	116–110 BCE
Cleopatra IV	116–115 BCE
Ptolemy X Alexander	110–109 BCE
Berenice III	81–80 BCE
Ptolemy XI Alexander	80 BCE
Ptolemy XII Auletes	80–58 BCE, 55–51 BCE
Cleopatra V Tryphaena	79–68 BCE
Cleopatra VI	58–57 BCE
Berenice IV	58–55 BCE

In 27 BCE, Caesar Augustus annexed Greece and it became integrated into the Roman Empire.

ANCIENT ROMAN LEADERS

This list is not exhaustive and some dates are approximate. The legitimacy of some rulers is also open to interpretation. Where dates of rule overlap, emperors either ruled jointly or ruled in opposition to one another. There may also be differences in name spellings between different sources.

KINGS OF ROME (753–509 BCE)

Romulus (mythological founder and first ruler of Rome)	753–716 BCE
Numa Pompilius (mythological)	715–672 BCE
Tullus Hostilius (mythological)	672–640 BCE
Ancus Marcius (mythological)	640–616 BCE
Lucius Tarquinius Priscus (mythological)	616–578 BCE
Servius Tullius (mythological)	578–534 BCE
Lucius Tarquinius Superbus (Tarquin the Proud; mythological)	534–509 BCE

ROMAN REPUBLIC (509-27 BCE)

During this period, two consuls were elected to serve a joint one-year term. Therefore, only a selection of significant consuls are included here.

Lucius Junius Brutus (semi-mythological)	509 BCE
Marcus Porcius Cato (Cato the Elder)	195 BCE
Scipio Africanus	194 BCE
Cnaeus Pompeius Magnus (Pompey the Great)	70, 55 and 52 BCE
Marcus Linius Crassus	70 and 55 BCE
Marcus Tullius Cicero	63 BCE
Caius Julius Caesar	59 BCE
Marcus Aemilius Lepidus	46 and 42 BCE
Marcus Antonius (Mark Anthony)	44 and 34 BCE
Marcus Agrippa	37 and 28 BCE

PRINCIPATE (27 BCE-284 CE)

Julio-Claudian Dynasty (27 BCE-68 CE)

Augustus (Caius Octavius Thurinus, Caius Julius Caesar, Imperator Caesar Divi filius)	27 BCE–14 CE
Tiberius (Tiberius Julius Caesar Augustus)	14–37 CE
Caligula (Caius Caesar Augustus Germanicus)	37–41 CE
Claudius (Tiberius Claudius Caesar Augustus Germanicus)	41–54 CE
Nero (Nero Claudius Caesar Augustus Germanicus)	54–68 CE

Year of the Four Emperors (68–69 CE)

Galba (Servius Sulpicius Galba Caesar Augustus)	68–69 CE
Otho (Marcus Salvio Otho Caesar Augustus)	Jan–Apr 69 CE
Vitellius (Aulus Vitellius Germanicus Augustus)	Apr–Dec 69 CE

Note: the fourth emperor, Vespasian, is listed below.

Flavian Dynasty (66–96 CE)

Vespasian (Caesar Vespasianus Augustus)	69–79 CE
Titus (Titus Caesar Vespasianus Augustus)	79–81 CE
Domitian (Caesar Domitianus Augustus)	81–96 CE

Nerva-Antonine Dynasty (69–192 CE)

Nerva (Nerva Caesar Augustus)	96–98 CE
Trajan (Caesar Nerva Traianus Augustus)	98–117 CE
Hadrian (Caesar Traianus Hadrianus Augustus)	138–161 CE
Antonius Pius (Caesar Titus Aelius Hadrianus Antoninus Augustus Pius)	138–161 CE
Marcus Aurelius (Caesar Marcus Aurelius Antoninus Augustus)	161–180 CE
Lucius Verus (Lucius Aurelius Verus Augustus)	161–169 CE
Commodus (Caesar Marcus Aurelius Commodus Antoninus Augustus)	180–192 CE

Year of the Five Emperors (193 CE)

Pertinax (Publius Helvius Pertinax)	Jan–Mar 193 CE
Didius Julianus (Marcus Didius Severus Julianus)	Mar–Jun 193 CE

Note: Pescennius Niger and Clodius Albinus are generally regarded as usurpers, while the fifth, Septimius Severus, is listed below

Severan Dynasty (193–235 CE)

Septimius Severus (Lucius Septimius Severus Pertinax)	193–211 CE
Caracalla (Marcus Aurelius Antonius)	211–217 CE
Geta (Publius Septimius Geta)	Feb–Dec 211 CE
Macrinus (Caesar Marcus Opellius Severus Macrinus Augustus)	217–218 CE
Diadumenian (Marcus Opellius Antonius Diadumenianus)	May–Jun 218 CE
Elagabalus (Caesar Marcus Aurelius Antoninus Augustus)	218–222 CE
Severus Alexander (Marcus Aurelius Severus Alexander)	222–235 CE

Crisis of the Third Century (235–285 CE)

Maximinus 'Thrax' (Caius Julius Verus Maximus)	235–238 CE
Gordian I (Marcus Antonius Gordianus Sempronianus Romanus)	Apr–May 238 CE
Gordian II (Marcus Antonius Gordianus Sempronianus Romanus)	Apr–May 238 CE
Pupienus Maximus (Marcus Clodius Pupienus Maximus)	May–Aug 238 CE
Balbinus (Decimus Caelius Calvinus Balbinus)	May–Aug 238 CE
Gordian III (Marcus Antonius Gordianus)	Aug 238–Feb 244 CE
Philip I 'the Arab' (Marcus Julius Philippus)	244–249 CE
Philip II 'the Younger' (Marcus Julius Severus Philippus)	247–249 CE
Decius (Caius Messius Quintus Traianus Decius)	249–251 CE
Herennius Etruscus (Quintus Herennius Etruscus Messius Decius)	May/Jun 251 CE

Trebonianus Gallus (Caius Vibius Trebonianus Gallus) 251–253 CE
Hostilian (Caius Valens Hostilianus Messius
   Quintus)   Jun–Jul 251 CE
Volusianus (Caius Vibius Afinius Gallus
   Veldumnianus Volusianus)   251–253 CE
Aemilian (Marcus Aemilius Aemilianus)   Jul–Sep 253 CE
Silbannacus (Marcus Silbannacus)   Sep/Oct 253 CE
Valerian (Publius Licinius Valerianus)   253–260 CE
Gallienus (Publius Licinius Egnatius Gallienus)   253–268 CE
Saloninus (Publius Licinius Cornelius
   Saloninus Valerianus)   Autumn 260 CE
Claudius II Gothicus (Marcus Aurelius Claudius)   268–270 CE
Quintilus (Marcus Aurelius Claudias
   Quintillus)   Apr–May/Jun 270 CE
Aurelian (Luciua Domitius Aurelianus)   270–275 CE
Tacitus (Marcus Claudius Tacitus)   275–276 CE
Florianus (Marcus Annius Florianus)   276–282 CE
Probus (Marcus Aurelius Probus Romanus;
   in opposition to Florianus)   276–282 CE
Carus (Marcus Aurelias Carus)   282–283 CE
Carinus (Marcus Aurelius Carinus)   283–285 CE
Numerian (Marcus Aurelius Numerianus)   283–284 CE

DOMINATE (284–610)

Tetrarchy (284–324)

Diocletian 'Iovius' (Caius Aurelius Valerius Diocletianus) 284–305
Maximian 'Herculius' (Marcus Aurelius Valerius
   Maximianus; ruled the western provinces) 286–305/late 306–308

Galerius (Caius Galerius Valerius Maximianus;
  ruled the eastern provinces)   305–311
Constantius I 'Chlorus' (Marcus Flavius Valerius
  Constantius; ruled the western provinces)   305–306
Severus II (Flavius Valerius Severus; ruled the
  western provinces)   306–307
Maxentius (Marcus Aurelius Valerius Maxentius)   306–312
Licinius (Valerius Licinanus Licinius; ruled the
  western, then the eastern provinces)   308–324
Maximinus II 'Daza' (Aurelius Valerius Valens;
  ruled the western provinces)   316–317
Martinian (Marcus Martinianus; ruled the
  western provinces)   Jul–Sep 324

Constantinian Dynasty (306–363)

Constantine I 'the Great' (Flavius Valerius
  Constantinus; ruled the western provinces
  then whole)   306–337
Constantine II (Flavius Claudius Constantinus)   337–340
Constans I (Flavius Julius Constans)   337–350
Constantius II (Flavius Julius Constantius)   337–361
Magnentius (Magnus Magnentius)   360–353
Nepotianus (Julius Nepotianus)   Jun 350
Vetranio   Mar–Dec 350
Julian 'the Apostate' (Flavius Claudius Julianus) 361–363
Jovian (Jovianus)   363–364

Valentinianic Dynasty (364–392)

Valentinian I 'the Great' (Valentinianus)   364–375
Valens (ruled the eastern provinces)   364–378

Procopius (revolted against Valens)	365–366
Gratian (Flavius Gratianus Augustus; ruled the western provinces then whole)	375–383
Magnus Maximus	383–388
Valentinian II (Flavius Valentinianus)	388–392
Eugenius	392–394

Theodosian Dynasty (379–457)

Theodosius I 'the Great' (Flavius Theodosius)	Jan 395
Arcadius	383–408
Honorius (Flavius Honorius)	395–432
Constantine III	407–411
Theodosius II	408–450
Priscus Attalus; usurper	409–410
Constantius III	Feb–Sep 421
Johannes	423–425
Valentinian III	425–455
Marcian	450–457

Last Emperors in the West (455–476)

Petronius Maximus	Mar–May 455
Avitus	455–456
Majorian	457–461
Libius Severus (Severus III)	461–465
Anthemius	467–472
Olybrius	Apr–Nov 472
Glycerius	473–474
Julius Nepos	474–475
Romulus Augustulus (Flavius Momyllus Romulus Augustulus)	475–476

Leonid Dynasty (East, 457–518)

Leo I (Leo Thrax Magnus)	457–474
Leo II	Jan–Nov 474
Zeno	474–475
Basiliscus	475–476
Zeno (second reign)	476–491
Anastasius I 'Dicorus'	491–518

Justinian Dynasty (East, 518–602)

Justin I	518–527
Justinian I 'the Great' (Flavius Justinianus, Petrus Sabbatius)	527–565
Justin II	565–578
Tiberius II Constantine	578–582
Maurice (Mauricius Flavius Tiberius)	582–602
Phocas	602–610

LATER EASTERN EMPERORS (610–1059)

Heraclian Dynasty (610–695)

Heraclius	610–641
Heraclius Constantine (Constantine III)	Feb–May 641
Heraclonas	Feb–Nov 641
Constans II Pogonatus ('the Bearded')	641–668
Constantine IV	668–685
Justinian II	685–695

Twenty Years' Anarchy (695–717)

Leontius	695–698
Tiberius III	698–705

Justinian II 'Rhinometus' (second reign)   705–711
Philippicus   711–713
Anastasius II   713–715
Theodosius III   715–717

Isaurian Dynasty (717–803)

Leo III 'the Isaurian'   717–741
Constantine V   741–775
Artabasdos   741/2–743
Leo V 'the Khazar'   775–780
Constantine VI   780–797
Irene   797–802

Nikephorian Dynasty (802–813)

Nikephoros I 'the Logothete'   802–811
Staurakios   July–Oct 811
Michael I Rangabé   813–820

Amorian Dynasty (820–867)

Michael II 'the Amorian'   820–829
Theophilos   829–842
Theodora   842–856
Michael III 'the Drunkard'   842–867

Macedonian Dynasty (867–1056)

Basil I 'the Macedonian'   867–886
Leo VI 'the Wise'   886–912
Alexander   912–913
Constantine VII Porphyrogenitus   913–959
Romanos I Lecapenus   920–944

Romanos II	959–963
Nikephoros II Phocas	963–969
John I Tzimiskes	969–976
Basil II 'the Bulgar-Slayer'	976–1025
Constantine VIII	1025–1028
Romanus III Argyros	1028–1034
Michael IV 'the Paphlagonian'	1034–1041
Michael V Kalaphates	1041–1042
Zoë Porphyrogenita	Apr–Jun 1042
Theodora Porphyrogenita	Apr–Jun 1042
Constantine IX Monomachos	1042–1055
Theodora Porphyrogenita (second reign)	1055–1056
Michael VI Bringas 'Stratioticus'	1056–1057
Isaab I Komnenos	1057–1059

ANCIENT CHINESE MONARCHS

This list concentrates on emperors with at least some proven legitimate claim and dates are approximate. Where dates of rule overlap, rulers either ruled jointly or ruled in opposition to one another. There may also be differences in name spellings between different sources.

THREE SOVEREIGNS OR PRIMEVAL EMPERORS, AND FIVE PREMIER EMPERORS (c. 2852–2070 BCE)

These are generally thought to be mythological figures. The history of China's rulers begins with a group of three *huáng* ('sovereigns') and a group of five *di* (emperors). There is much diversity over who the three sovereigns and five emperors actually were, and the dates they ruled.

Fuxi (Heavenly Sovereign)	18,000 years
NuWa (Earthly Sovereign)	11,000 years
Shennong (Human Sovereign)	45,600 years
Yellow Emperor (Xuanyuan)	100 years
Zhuanxu (Gaoyang)	78 years
Emperor Ku (Gaoxin)	70 years

Emperor Yao of Tang (Yiqi, Taotang or Fangxun)   100 years
Emperor Shun of Yu (Yao, Youyu or Chonghua)   42 years

XIA DYNASTY (c. 2070–1600 BCE)

This dynasty was thought to be established after the legendary Shun handed his throne to Yu the Great, also a legendary leader, whose historicity is debated.

Yu the Great	2150–2106 BCE
Qi of Xia	2106–2077 BCE
Tai Kang	2077–2048 BCE
Zhong Kang	2048–2036 BCE
Xiang of Xia	2036–2008 BCE
Shao Kang	1968–1946 BCE
Zhu of Xia	1946–1929 BCE
Huai of Xia	1929–1885 BCE
Mang of Xia	1885–1867 BCE
Xie of Xia	1867–1851 BCE
Bu Jiang	1851–1792 BCE
Jiong of Xia	1792–1771 BCE
Jin of Xia (Yin Jia)	1771–1750 BCE
Kong Jia	1750–1719 BCE
Gao of Xia	1719–1708 BCE
Fa of Xia (Hou Jin)	1708–1689 BCE
Jie of Xia (Lu Gui)	1689–1658 BCE

SHANG DYNASTY (c. 1600–1046 BCE)

Tang of Shang	1658–1629 BCE
Wai Bing	1629–1627 BCE
Zhong Ren	1627–1623 BCE
Tai Jia	1623–1611 BCE
Wo Ding	1611–1592 BCE
Tai Geng	1592–1567 BCE
Xiao Jia	1567–1550 BCE
Yong Ji	1550–1538 BCE
Tai Wu	1538–1463 BCE
Zhong Ding	1463–1452 BCE
Wai Ren	1452–1437 BCE
He Dan Jia	1437–1428 BCE
Zu Ji	1428–1409 BCE
Zu Xin	1409–1393 BCE
Wo Jia	1393–1368 BCE
Zu Ding	1368–1336 BCE
Nan Geng	1336–1307 BCE
Yang Jia	1307–1290 BCE
Pan Geng	1290–1262 BCE
Xiao Xin	1262–1259 BCE
Xiao Yi	1259–1250 BCE
Wu Ding	1250–1192 BCE
Zu Geng	1192–1185 BCE
Zu Jia	1185–1158 BCE
Lin Xin	1158–1152 BCE
Geng Ding	1152–1147 BCE
Wu Yi	1147–1112 BCE
Wen Wu Ding	1112–1102 BCE

Di Yi	1101–1076 BCE
King Zhou of Shang	1075–1046 BCE

ZHOU DYNASTY (c. 1046–256 BCE)

Western Zhou (1046–771 BCE)

King Wu of Zhou	1046–1043 BCE
King Cheng of Zhou	1042–1021 BCE
King Kang of Zhou	1020–996 BCE
King Zhao of Zhou	995–977 BCE
King Mu of Zhou	976–922 BCE
King Gong of Zhou	922–900 BCE
King Yi of Zhou (Jian)	899–892 BCE
King Xiao of Zhou	891–886 BCE
King Yi of Zhou (Xie)	885–878 BCE
King Li of Zhou	877–841 BCE

Gonghe Regency (827–827 BCE)

King Xuan of Zhou	827–782 BCE
King You of Zhou	781–771 BCE

Eastern Zhou (770–256 BCE)

Spring and Autumn Period (770–476 BCE)

King Ping of Zhou	770–720 BCE
King Huan of Zhou	719–697 BCE
King Zhuang of Zhou	696–682 BCE
King Xi of Zhou	681–677 BCE
King Hui of Zhou	676–652 BCE

King Xiang of Zhou	651–619 BCE
King Qing of Zhou	618–613 BCE
King Kuang of Zhou	612–607 BCE
King Ding of Zhou	606–586 BCE
King Jian of Zhou	585–572 BCE
King Ling of Zhou	571–545 BCE
King Jing of Zhou (Gui)	544–521 BCE
King Dao of Zhou	520 BCE
King Jing of Zhou (Gai)	519–476 BCE

Warring States Period (475–221 BCE)

King Yuan of Zhou	475–469 BCE
King Zhending of Zhou	468–442 BCE
King Ai of Zhou	441 BCE
King Si of Zhou	441 BCE
King Kao of Zhou	440–426 BCE
King Weilie of Zhou	425–402 BCE
King An of Zhou	401–376 BCE
King Lie of Zhou	375–369 BCE
King Xian of Zhou	368–321 BCE
King Shenjing of Zhou	320–315 BCE
King Nan of Zhou	314–256 BCE

QIN DYNASTY (c. 221–207 BCE)

Qin Shi Huang declared himself emperor rather than king, and this period is often thought to mark the beginning of Imperial China.

Qin Shi Huang   221–210 BCE
Qin Er Shi   209–207 BCE
Ziying   207 BCE

HAN DYNASTY (*c.* 202 BCE–9 CE, 25–220 CE)

Western Han (202 BCE–9 CE)

Emperor Gaozu of Han   202–195 BCE
Emperor Hui of Han   195–188 BCE
Emperor Qianshao of Han   188–184 BCE
Emperor Houshao of Han   184–180 BCE
Emperor Wen of Han   179–157 BCE
Emperor Jing of Han   156–141 BCE
Emperor Wu of Han   140–87 BCE
Emperor Zhao of Han   86–74 BCE
Marquis of Haihun   74 BCE
Emperor Xuan of Han   73–49 BCE
Emperor Yuan of Han   48–33 BCE
Emperor Cheng of Han   32–7 BCE
Emperor Ai of Han   6–1 BCE
Emperor Ping of Han   1 BCE–5 CE
Ruzi Ying   6–8 CE
Interregnum (9 CE–23 CE; see Xin dynasty below)
Gengshi Emperor   23–25 CE

XIN DYNASTY (*c.* 9–23 CE)

Wang Mang; possible usurper   9–23 CE

Eastern Han (25–220 CE)

Emperor Guangwu of Han	25–57 CE
Emperor Ming of Han	58–75 CE
Emperor Zhang of Han	76–88 CE
Emperor He of Han	89–105 CE
Emperor Shang of Han	106 CE
Emperor An of Han	106–125 CE
Emperor Shun of Han	125–144 CE
Emperor Chong of Han	144–145 CE
Emperor Zhi of Han	145–146 CE
Emperor Huan of Han	146–168 CE
Emperor Ling of Han	168–189 CE
Prince of Hongnong	189 CE
Emperor Xian of Han	189–220 CE

THREE KINGDOMS (c. 220–280 CE)

Cao Wei (220–266 CE)

Cao Pi	220–226 CE	Cao Mao	254–260 CE
Cao Rui	226–239 CE	Cao Huan	260–266 CE
Cao Fang	239–254 CE		

Shu Han (221–263 CE)

Liu Bei	221–223 CE
Liu Shan	223–263 CE

Eastern Wu (222–280 CE)

Sun Quan	222–252 CE	Sun Xiu	258–264 CE
Sun Liang	252–258 CE	Sun Hao	264–280 CE

JIN DYNASTY (c. 266-420 CE)

Western Jin (266-316 CE)

Emperor Wu of Jin	266–290 CE
Emperor Hui of Jin	290–306 CE
Emperor Huai of Jin	307–313 CE
Emperor Min of Jin	313–317 CE

Eastern Jin (317-420 CE)

Emperor Yuan of Jin	317–322 CE
Emperor Ming of Jin	322–325 CE
Emperor Cheng of Jin	325–342 CE
Emperor Kang of Jin	342–344 CE
Emperor Mu of Jin	345–361 CE
Emperor Ai of Jin	361–365 CE
Emperor Fei of Jin	365–371 CE
Emperor Jianwen of Jin	371–372 CE
Emperor Xiaowu of Jin	372–396 CE
Emperor An of Jin	396–418 CE
Emperor Gong of Jin	419–420 CE

SIXTEEN KINGDOMS (c. 304-439 CE)

Han Zhao (304-329 CE)
Northern Han (304-318 CE)

Liu Yuan	304–310 CE
Liu He	7 days in 310 CE
Liu Cong	310–318 CE
Liu Can	a month+ in 318 CE

Former Zhao (318–329 CE)

Liu Yao	318–329 CE

Cheng Han (304–347 CE)
Cheng (304–338 CE)

Li Te	303 CE
Li Lui	several months in 303 CE
Li Xiong	303–334 CE
Li Ban	7 months in 334 CE
Li Qi	334–338 CE

Han (338–347 CE)

Li Shou	338–343 CE
Li Shi	343–347 CE

Later Zhao (319–351 CE)

Shi Le	319–333 CE	Shi Zun	183 days in 349 CE
Shi Hong	333–334 CE	Shi Jian	73 days in 349–350 CE
Shi Hu	334–349 CE	Shi Zhi	350–351 CE
Shi Shi	73 days in 349 CE		

Former Liang (320–376 CE)

Zhang Mao	320–324 CE	Zhang Zuo	353–355 CE
Zhang Jun	324–346 CE	Zhang Xuanjing	355–363 CE
Zhang Chonghua	346–353 CE	Zhang Tianxi	364–376 CE
Zhang Yaoling	3 months in 353 CE		

Former Yan (337–370 CE)

Murong Huang	337–348 CE	Murong Wei	360–370 CE
Murong Jun	348–360 CE		

Former Qin (351–394 BCE)

Fu Jian	351–355 CE	Fu Pi	385–386 CE
Fu Sheng	355–357 CE	Fu Deng	386–394 CE
Fu Jian	357–385 CE	Fu Chong	394 CE

Later Yan (384–409 CE)

Murong Chui	384–396 CE	Murong Sheng	398–301 CE
Murong Bao	396–398 CE	Murong Xi	401–407 CE

Later Qin (384–417 CE)

Yao Chang	384–393 CE	Yao Hong	416–417 CE
Yao Xing	394–416 CE		

Western Qin (385–400 CE, 409–431 CE)

Qifu Guoren	385–388 CE	Qifu Chipan	412–428 CE
Qifu Qiangui	388–400 CE, 409–412 CE	Qifu Mumo	428–431 CE

Later Liang (386–403 CE)

Lü Guang	386–399 CE	Lü Zuan	399–401 CE
Lü Shao	399 CE	Lü Long	401–403 CE

Southern Liang (397–414 CE)

Tufa Wugu	397–399 CE	Tufa Rutan	402–414 CE
Tufa Lilugu	399–402 CE		

Northern Liang (397–439 CE)

Duan Ye	397–401 CE	Juqu Wuhui	442–444 CE
Juqu Mengxun	401–433 CE	Juqu Anzhou	444–460 CE
Juqu Mujian	433–439 CE		

Southern Yan (398–410 CE)

Murong De	398–405 CE	Murong Chao	405–410 CE

Western Liang (400–421 CE)

Li Gao	400–417 CE	Li Xun	420–421 CE
Li Xin	417–420 CE		

Hu Xia (407–431 CE)

Helian Bobo	407–425 CE	Helian Ding	428–431 CE
Helian Chang	425–428 CE		

Northern Yan (407–436 CE)

Gao Yun	407–409 CE	Feng Hong	430–436 CE
Feng Ba	409–430 CE		

NORTHERN AND SOUTHERN DYNASTIES (c. 386–589 CE)

Northern Dynasties (386–581 CE)

Northern Wei (386–535 CE)

Emperor Daowu of Northern Wei	386–409 CE
Emperor Mingyuan of Northern Wei	409–423 CE
Emperor Taiwu of Northern Wei	424–452 CE
Tuoba Yu	452 CE
Emperor Wencheng of Northern Wei	452–465 CE
Emperor Xianwen of Northern Wei	466–471 CE
Emperor Xiaowen of Northern Wei	471–499 CE
Emperor Xuanwu of Northern Wei	499–515 CE
Emperor Xiaoming of Northern Wei	516–528 CE

Yuan Zhao	528 CE
Emperor Xiaozhuang of Northern Wei	528–530 CE
Yuan Ye	530–531 CE
Emperor Jiemin of Northern Wei	531–532 CE
Yuan Lang	531–532 CE
Emperor Xiaowu of Northern Wei	532–535 CE

Eastern Wei (534–550 CE)

Emperor Xiaojing of Eastern Wei	534–550 CE

Western Wei (535–557 CE)

Emperor Wen of Western Wei	535–551 CE
Emperor Fei of Western Wei	552–554 CE
Emperor Gong of Western Wei	554–557 CE

Northern Qi (550–577 CE)

Emperor Wenxuan of Northern Qi	550–559 CE
Emperor Fei of Northern Qi	559–560 CE
Emperor Xiaozhao of Northern Qi	560–561 CE
Emperor Wucheng of Northern Qi	561–565 CE
Gao Wei	565–577 CE
Gao Heng	577 CE
Gao Shaoyi	577–579? CE

Northern Zhou (557–581 CE)

Emperor Xiaomin of Northern Zhou	557 CE
Emperor Ming of Northern Zhou	557–560 CE
Emperor Wu of Northern Zhou	561–578 CE
Emperor Xuan of Northern Zhou	578–579 CE
Emperor Jing of Northern Zhou	579–581 CE

Southern dynasties (420–589 CE)

Liu Song (420–497 CE)

Emperor Wu of Liu Song	420–422 CE
Emperor Shao of Liu Song	423–424 CE
Emperor Wen of Liu Song	424–453 CE
Emperor Xiaowu of Liu Song	454–464 CE
Emperor Ming of Liu Song	465–472 CE
Emperor Houfei of Liu Song	473–477 CE
Emperor Shun of Liu Song	477–479 CE

Southern Qi (479–502 CE)

Emperor Gao of Southern Qi	479–482 CE
Emperor Wu of Southern Qi	482–493 CE
Xiao Zhaoye	493–494 CE
Xiao Zhaowen	494 CE
Emperor Ming of Southern Qi	494–498 CE
Xiao Baojuan	499–501 CE
Emperor He of Southern Qi	501–502 CE

Liang Dynasty (502–557 CE)

Emperor Wu of Liang	502–549 CE
Emperor Jianwen of Liang	549–551 CE
Xiao Dong	551–552 CE
Emperor Yuan of Liang	552–555 CE
Xiao Yuanming	555 CE
Emperor Jing of Liang	555–557 CE

Western Liang (555–587 CE)

Emperor Xuan of Western Liang	555–562 CE

Emperor Ming of Western Liang	562–585 CE
Emperor Jing of Western Liang	585–587 CE

Chen Dynasty (557–589 CE)

Emperor Wu of Chen	557–559 CE
Emperor Wen of Chen	559–566 CE
Emperor Fei of Chen	566–568 CE
Emperor Xuan of Chen	569–582 CE
Chen Shubao	583–589 CE

SUI DYNASTY (c. 581–610 CE)

Emperor Wen of Sui	581–604 CE
Emperor Yang of Sui	605–617 CE
Yang You	617–618 CE
Yang Hao	618 CE
Yang Tong	618–619 CE

TANG DYNASTY (c. 618–690 CE, 705–907 CE)

Emperor Gaozu of Tang	618–626 CE
Emperor Taizong of Tang	627–649 CE
Emperor Gaozong of Tang	650–683 CE
Emperor Zhongzong of Tang	684 and 705–710 CE
Emperor Ruizong of Tang	684–690 and 710–712 CE
Emperor Shang of Tang	710 CE
Emperor Xuanzong of Tang	712–756 CE
Emperor Suzong of Tang	756–762 CE

Emperor Daizong of Tang	762–779 CE
Emperor Dezong of Tang	780–805 CE
Emperor Shunzong of Tang	805 CE
Emperor Xianzong of Tang	806–820 CE
Emperor Muzong of Tang	821–824 CE
Emperor Jingzong of Tang	824–826 CE
Emperor Wenzong of Tang	826–840 CE
Emperor Wuzong of Tang	840–846 CE
Emperor Xuanzong of Tang	846–859 CE
Emperor Yizong of Tang	859–873 CE
Emperor Xizong of Tang	873–888 CE
Emperor Zhaozong of Tang	888–904 CE
Emperor Ai of Tang	904–907 CE

Wu Zhou (690 – 705 CE)

Wu Zetian (only female considered legitimate)	690–705 CE

Huang Qi (881–884 CE)

Huang Chao	881–884 CE

FIVE DYNASTIES AND TEN KINGDOMS (c. 907–979 CE)

Five Dynasties (907–960 CE)
Later Liang (907–923 CE)

Zhu Wen	907–912 CE
Zhu Yougui	912–913 CE
Zhu Zhen	913–923 CE

Later Tang (923–937 CE)

Li Cunxu	923–926 CE
Li Siyuan (Li Dan)	923–926 CE
Li Conghou	933–934 CE
Li Congke	934–937 CE

Later Jin (936–947 CE)

Shi Jingtang	936–942 CE
Shi Chonggui	942–947 CE

Later Han (947–951 CE)

Liu Zhiyuan	947–948 CE
Liu Chengyou	948–951 CE

Later Zhou (951–960 CE)

Guo Wei	951–954 CE
Chai Rong	954–959 CE
Chai Zongxun	959–960 CE

Ten Kingdoms (907–979 CE)
Former Shu (907–925 CE)

Wang Jian	907–918 CE
Wang Zongyan	918–925 CE

Yang Wu (907–937 CE)

Yang Xingmi	904–905 CE
Yang Wo	905–908 CE
Yang Longyan	908–921 CE
Yang Pu	921–937 CE

Ma Chu (907–951 CE)

Ma Yin	897–930 CE
Ma Xisheng	930–932 CE
Ma Xifan	932–947 CE
Ma Xiguang	947–950 CE
Ma Xi'e	950 CE
Ma Xichong	950–951 CE

Wuyue (907–978 CE)

Qian Liu	904–932 CE
Qian Yuanguan	932–941 CE
Qian Hongzuo	941–947 CE
Qian Hongzong	947 CE
Qian Chu (Qian Hongchu)	947–978 CE

Min (909–945 CE) and Yin (943–945 CE)

Wang Shenzhi	909–925 CE
Wang Yanhan	925–926 CE
Wang Yanjun	926–935 CE
Wang Jipeng	935–939 CE
Wang Yanxi	939–944 CE
Wang Yanzheng	943–945 CE

Southern Han (917–971 CE)

Liu Yan	917–925 CE
Liu Bin	941–943 CE
Liu Sheng	943–958 CE
Liu Chang	958–971 CE

Jingnan (924–963 CE)

Gao Jixing	909–928 CE
Gao Conghui	928–948 CE
Gao Baorong	948–960 CE
Gao Baoxu	960–962 CE
Gao Jichong	962–963 CE

Later Shu (934–965 CE)

Meng Zhixiang	934 CE
Meng Chang	938–965 CE

Southern Tang (937–96 CE)

Li Bian	937–943 CE
Li Jing	943–961 CE
Li Yu	961–976 CE

Northern Han (951–979 CE)

Liu Min	951–954 CE
Liu Chengjun	954–968 CE
Liu Ji'en	970 CE
Liu Jiyuan	970–982 CE

ANCIENT INDIAN MONARCHS

This list takes up after the mythological Lunar dynasty (Chandravamsha), into which the Hindu god Krishna was born. Descendants include the god Budha (not to be confused with the Buddha). From his son, Pururavas, came several of the communities of India, including the Magadha dynasty founded by Brihadratha.

The list is not exhaustive and dates are approximate. Where dates of rule overlap, monarchs either ruled jointly or ruled in opposition to one another. There may also be differences in name spellings between different sources.

MAGADHA DYNASTIES (c. 1700–38 BCE)

The following kings and dates of their rule are uncertain.

Legendary: Brihadratha Dynasty (c. 1700–730 BCE)

Brihadratha (founded the Brihadratha dynasty, the earliest dynasty to rule Magadha) c. 1700 BCE	Somadhi	1661 BCE
	Srutasravas	1603 BCE
	Ayutayus	1539 BCE
	Niramitra	1503 BCE
Jarasandha (son of Brihadratha) ?	Sukshatra	1463 BCE
	Brihatkarman	1405 BCE
Sahadeva (son of Jarasandha) ?	Senajit	1382 BCE

Srutanjaya	1332 BCE	Dridhasena	970 BCE
Vipra	1292 BCE	Sumati	912 BCE
Suchi	1257 BCE	Subala	879 BCE
Kshemya	1199 BCE	Sunita	857 BCE
Subrata	1171 BCE	Satyajit	817 BCE
Dharma	1107 BCE	Viswajit	767 BCE
Susuma	1008 BCE	Ripunjaya	732 BCE

Pradyota Dynasty (c. 682–544 BCE)

This dynasty probably actually ruled in Avanti not Magadha.

Pradyota Mahasena		Visakhayupa	635 BCE
(dethr. Ripunjaya)	682 BCE	Ajaka	585 BCE
Palaka	659 BCE	Varttivarddhana	564 BCE

Haryanka Dynasty (c. 544–413 BCE)

Bimbisara (dethr.		Anirudha	428 BCE
Varttivarddhana)	544 BCE	Munda	419 BCE
Ajatashatru	491 BCE	Darshaka	417 BCE
Udayin	461 BCE	Nagadasaka	415 BCE

Shishunaga Dynasty (c. 413–345 BCE)

Shishunaga (dethr.		Kshatraujas	365 BCE
Nagadasaka)	413 BCE	Nandivardhana	355 BCE
Kalashhoka	395 BCE	Mahanandin	349 BCE
Kshemadharman	377 BCE		

Nanda Dynasty (c. 345–322 BCE)

Mahapadma Nanda (illegitimate son of Mahanandin) 345 BCE			
Pandhukananda	340 BCE	Bhutapalananda	338 BCE
Panghupatinanda	339 BCE	Rashtrapalananda	337 BCE

Govishanakananda	336 BCE	Karvinathanand	333 BCE
Dashasidkhakananda	335 BCE	Dana Nanda	330 BCE
Kaivartananda	334 BCE		

Note: this period was marked by Alexander the Great's invasion of parts of India, which was only halted after the Battle of the Hydaspes in 326 BCE when Alexander's troops revolted and refused to fight onwards.

Maurya Dynasty (*c.* 321–187 BCE)

Chandragupta Maurya		Samprati	224 BCE
(founder of first		Shalishuka	215 BCE
imperial dynasty)	321 BCE	Devavarman	202 BCE
Bindusara	297 BCE	Shatadhanvan	195 BCE
Ashoka	268 BCE	Brihadratha	187 BCE
Dasharatha Maurya	232 BCE		

Shunga Dynasty (*c.* 185–73 BCE)

Pushyamitra Shunga (dethr.		Pulindaka	122 BCE
Brihadratha)	185 BCE	Ghosha	119 BCE
Agnimitra	149 BCE	Vajremitra	108 BCE
Vasujyeshtha	141 BCE	Bhagabhadra	94 BCE
Vasumitra	131 BCE	Devabhuti	83 BCE
Bhadraka	124 BCE		

Kanva Dynasty (*c.* 73–28 BCE)

Vasudeva Kanva (dethr. Devabhuti)	73 BCE
Bhumimtra	64 BCE
Narayana	50 BCE
Susarman	38 BCE

SATAVAHANA DYNASTY (c. 228 BCE-217 CE)

This dynasty governed the Deccan region in southern India.

Simuka (dethr. Susarman)	228 BCE	Hala	61 CE
(Note: some sources give 30 BCE)		Mandalaka (Pulumavi II)	69 CE
Krishna	205 BCE	Purindrasena	71 CE
Sajakarni I	187 BCE	Sundara Satakarni	76 CE
Purnotsanga	177 BCE	Chakora Satakarni	77 CE
Skandhastambhi	159 BCE	Shivasvati	78 CE
Satakarni II	141 BCE	Gautamiputra Satkarni	106 CE
Lambodara	85 BCE	Vasisthiputra (Pulumavi III)	130 CE
Apilaka	67 BCE	Shiva Sri Satakarni	158 CE
Meghasvati	55 BCE	Shivaskanda Satakarni	165 CE
Svati	37 BCE		
Skandasvati	19 BCE		
Mrigendra Satakarni	12 BCE	Sir Yajna Satakarni	172 CE
Kunatala Satakarni	9 BCE	Bijaya Satakarni	201 CE
Satakarni III	1 BCE–1 CE	Chandra Sri Satakarni	207 CE
Pulumavi I	1 CE	Pulumavi IV	217 CE
Gaura Krishna	36 CE		

GUPTA DYNASTY (c. 240-750 CE)

Imperial Gupta Rulers (c. 240-540 CE)

Gupta (Srigupta)	240 CE	Chandragupta I (first emperor and founder of the Gupta empire)	320 CE
Ghatotkacha ('Maharaja')	300 CE		

Samudragupta	325/350 CE	Kumaragupta II	470/472 CE
Chandragupta II	376 CE	Budhagupta	475/479 CE
Kumaragupta I	415 CE	Narasimhagupta	496/515 CE
Skandagupta	455 CE	Kumaragupta III	530 CE
Purugupta	467 CE	Vishnagupta	540 CE

Later Gupta Rulers (*c.* 490–750 CE)

While the Later Guptas succeeded the Imperial Guptas, they seem to be descended from different families.

Krishna-Gupta	490–505 CE
Harsha-Gupta	505–525 CE
Jivita-Gupta I	525–550 CE
Kumara-Gupta	550–560 CE
Damodara-Gupta	560–562 CE
Mahasena-Gupta	562–601 CE
Madhava-Gupta	601–655 CE
Aditya-Sena	655–680 CE
Deva-Gupta	680–700 CE
Vishnu-Gupta	dates unknown
Jivita-Gupta II	dates unknown